About Island Press

Island Press is the only nonprofit organization in the United States whose principal purpose is the publication of books on environmental issues and natural resource management. We provide solutions-oriented information to professionals, public officials, business and community leaders, and concerned citizens who are shaping responses to environmental problems.

In 2004, Island Press celebrates its twentieth anniversary as the leading provider of timely and practical books that take a multidisciplinary approach to critical environmental concerns. Our growing list of titles reflects our commitment to bringing the best of an expanding body of literature to the environmental community throughout North America and the world.

Support for Island Press is provided by the Agua Fund, Brainerd Foundation, Geraldine R. Dodge Foundation, Doris Duke Charitable Foundation, Educational Foundation of America, The Ford Foundation, The George Gund Foundation, The William and Flora Hewlett Foundation, Henry Luce Foundation, The John D. and Catherine T. MacArthur Foundation, The Andrew W. Mellon Foundation, The Curtis and Edith Munson Foundation, National Environmental Trust, The New-Land Foundation, Oak Foundation, The Overbrook Foundation, The David and Lucile Packard Foundation, The Pew Charitable Trusts, The Rockefeller Foundation, The Winslow Foundation, and other generous donors.

The opinions expressed in this book are those of the author(s) and do not necessarily reflect the views of these foundations.

About the Lincoln Institute of Land Policy

The Lincoln Institute of Land Policy, based in Cambridge, Massachusetts, is a nonprofit and tax-exempt educational institution established in 1974 to study and teach land policy, including land economics and land taxation. The Institute is supported primarily by the Lincoln Foundation, which was established in 1947 by Cleveland industrialist John C. Lincoln.

The Institute's goals are to integrate theory and practice to better shape land policy decisions and to share understanding about the multidisciplinary forces that influence public policy in the United States and internationally.

The Lincoln Institute seeks to improve the quality of debate and disseminate knowledge of critical issues in land policy by bringing together scholars, policy makers, practitioners, and citizens with diverse backgrounds and experience. We study, exchange insights and work toward a broader understanding of complex land and tax policies. The Institute does not take a particular point of view, but rather serves as a catalyst to facilitate analysis and discussion of these issues—to make a difference today and to help policy makers plan for tomorrow. For more information: www. lincolninst.edu.

Practical Ecology

Dedicated to Richard T. T. Forman,
whose life's work has helped
humans live more harmoniously with nature

Practical Ecology

for Planners, Developers, and Citizens

Dan L. Perlman • Jeffrey C. Milder

Island Press

WASHINGTON. COVELO. LONDON

L LINCOLN INSTITUTE
OF LAND POLICY

Library of Congress Cataloging-in-Publication data.

Perlman, Dan L.
    Practical Ecology for Planners, Developers, and citizens / Dan L. Perlman,
Jeffrey C. Milder.
        p.   cm.
    Includes bibliographical references and index.
    ISBN 1-55963-634-3 (cloth : alk. paper) — ISBN 1-55963-716-1 (pbk. :
alk. paper)
1. Nature—Effect of human beings on.   2. Land use—Environmental
aspects.   3. City planning—Environmental aspects.   4. Regional planning—
Environmental aspects.   5. Urban ecology.   6. Conservation of natural
resources.   I. Milder, Jeffrey C.   II. Title.
    GF75.P47 2004
    304.2—dc22   2004012441

British Cataloguing-in-Publication data available.

♾ Printed on recycled, acid-free paper

Design by Teresa Bonner
Artwork by Lisa V. Leombruni
Photographs by Dan L. Perlman and Jeffrey C. Milder

Manufactured in the United States of America
10 9 8 7 6 5 4

Contents

List of Figures, Color Plates, and Tables

Figures

Color Plates

Tables

Acknowledgments

This book benefited tremendously from the input, support, and feedback of many people, and we greatly appreciate their time and efforts. Armando Carbonell of the Lincoln Institute of Land Policy suggested that we write the book, secured support from the Lincoln Institute, and was deeply helpful at every stage of the book's development. Ann LeRoyer and Lisa Cloutier of the Lincoln Institute provided thoughtful suggestions and were especially helpful in bringing the book to fruition. Heather Boyer, our editor at Island Press, was enthusiastic about the project and helped us get across the finish line during the final months. Our artist, Lisa Leombruni, put a great deal of effort, skill, and creativity into her work; we appreciate her talent, her contributions to the book, and especially her patience.

Early in the development of the book, an advisory committee consisting of Michael Binford, Peter Pollock, Frederick Steiner, and Jon Witten read a first draft of the book and helped shape the project's subsequent direction. We appreciate the time and energy that these advisors gave us, and we hope they recognize the value of their input.

We also owe our gratitude to those reviewers who read later drafts of the book and helped us think about how to improve the text: Jeanne Armstrong, Richard T. T. Forman, Eliza K. Jewett, Robert and Gail Milder, Robert Perlman, Christopher Ryan, Frederick Steiner, and David Tobias. Finally, we thank the following people who generously offered valuable information on real-life planning, design, and conservation issues: Steven Apfelbaum, Jae C. Choe, Dan

Cooper, Ed Dobb, Robert O. Lawton, Everose Schluter, Jon Sesso, Frederick Steiner, and David Tobias.

As anyone who has written a book or lived through the writing of a book knows, the people who live with the writers deserve the lion's share of credit for the book itself. Nora Abrahamer, Jeremy Abrahamer Perlman, and Nina Kohn gave us the precious gifts of time to write and support when things were most difficult. Without you, we would not have completed this book. It is your accomplishment as much as ours.

To all those who have helped us make this book a reality, thank you.

Introduction

Each year, the United States and Canada add more than 3.5 million people to their combined population. Each year, our appetite for land and resources grows as we demand more housing, more cars, more roads, more food, more forest products, and more leisure opportunities. As the human world expands, we leave less room and fewer resources for native species and ecosystems, and the natural world suffers. So, too, do we ourselves suffer when we fail to define a harmonious relationship with nature. Each year, natural disasters such as wildfires, floods, and devastating hurricanes cost lives and cause billions of dollars of damage to human communities; from 1995 to 1997, the United States alone suffered about $1 billion of natural hazard damages *each week*.[1] More insidiously, generations of children are growing up separated from nature and the wisdom, pleasure, and spiritual wealth that it offers.

Some environmentalists would address this crisis by setting aside large portions of the landscape as nature reserves that are off-limits to people. But while conservation areas are an important part of the solution, they fail to address the 80 or 90 percent of the land that humans do inhabit and use. For these areas, the challenge is to integrate humans and nature more beneficially by retaining ecological values in largely domesticated landscapes. Planners, designers, and developers must be at the forefront of this effort, for their activities transform the landscape in ways that are seldom environmentally neutral. If these professionals are not consciously working to bring forth an ecologically sounder world, they are often contributing, if only inadvertently, to the creation of a wasteful and potentially dangerous one.

For those who are inclined to write off ecological issues as tomorrow's problem, consider the tangible benefits of and strong mandate for addressing these problems now:

- Natural ecosystems annually provide humans with trillions of dollars of unpaid-for "services," such as flood control and water purification—services that would otherwise require engineered solutions and large public expenditures if these ecosystems became heavily degraded.
- When communities are designed without a careful understanding of natural ecological processes, humans expose themselves to health and safety risks from violent storms, wildfire, disease organisms, and other natural hazards.
- Retaining natural areas in cities and suburbs tends to increase real estate values, quality of life, and community desirability, thus increasing profitability for land developers and economic competitiveness for communities and regions.
- In national and local polls, citizens consistently rank environmental protection as a high priority. Elected and appointed public officials ignore these sentiments at their own peril.

This book is written for those who are ready to rise to the challenges of harmonizing human communities and nature in the United States and Canada, whether they are professional land use planners or members of a local planning commission, landscape architects or civil engineers who want to design more ecologically sound projects, developers or lenders who want to build or finance greener developments, or citizens interested in improving their towns or regions. Our focus is on the two central goals of ecologically based land use planning and landscape design: 1) to conduct human activities on the landscape in a way that conserves native species and healthy ecosystems, and 2) to promote livable communities that benefit from their surrounding ecosystems while protecting human health and safety. To help readers advance these goals, the book introduces key concepts of ecology and conservation biology that are valuable in creating communities and developments more respectful of their natural environment.

In presenting this material, we assume that readers are willing to engage themselves with a number of interesting and sometimes complex concepts essential to ecologically based planning and design, but we do not presuppose a great deal of background in these subjects. A major goal of the book is to synthesize and present relevant scientific information in a form that can help answer the questions that land use professionals and informed citizens face every day.

We also assume that readers are already interested in creating land use plans, designs, and decisions that are better informed by the scientific understanding that ecologists and conservationists have developed over the past few decades. This book, therefore, is not so much an exhortation to conserve nature as a practical explanation of how to do so in the context of land use planning and land development.

How to Use This Book

The three parts of this book lead the reader from concept to application, but these are closely intertwined throughout in recognition of the relevance of scientific information to planning and design practice. The first part introduces the paradigm of ecological thinking and the ways it differs from the planning paradigm. We then explore the fundamentals of the ecological world and humans' relationship to it: What is biodiversity and why is it important? What happens when human activities impinge on natural systems? How can people prepare meaningful plans in a natural world that is subject to chance and change?

The second part is a primer on ecology and conservation biology that emphasizes those aspects of the field most relevant to planners, designers, developers, and other interested in land use: How does nature change over time? How predictable are these changes, and what does this mean for planning? How do organisms and species interact in nature? What causes populations of plants and animals to thrive, falter, or go extinct? Finally, how does the arrangement of landscape elements, such as cities, farms, roads, and nature reserves, affect the form and function of ecological communities?

The book's final part discusses how ecological concepts can be applied to the two goals discussed above: improving the ecological integrity of human-influenced landscapes and ensuring that humans benefit from and are not endangered by local ecosystems. This part begins with large-scale applications, examining the factors that should inform the design of nature reserves and the ways in which human and ecological needs can be integrated across entire landscapes. We then move to the scale of communities and sites to discuss the design of smaller parks and nature areas as well as techniques for managing and restoring land. Next, we present a range of practical planning and design techniques from an ecological standpoint. The concluding chapter is a two-part planning exercise that lets readers practice applying the lessons of this book.

This book condenses into accessible form information that could easily fill several large volumes. For emphasis and convenient reference, important concepts are further distilled in gray boxes throughout the book. This format is tailored to the needs of busy land use professionals and citizens seeking a concise overview of ecology and its applications, but such brevity means that much about each topic has necessarily gone unsaid. We encourage readers to learn more about these topics in the sources referenced throughout the book.

We hope that this book will help planners, designers, developers, and citizens become more attuned to the workings of nature and more able to integrate ecological understanding into their work. By paying attention to the ecology of the places where they work, land use professionals can create a richer, healthier world for humans and for all living creatures.

Part One

HUMANS, NATURE, AND INTERACTIONS

All organisms live in ecological communities just as all people live in human communities. Often, however, we tend to forget that human communities also exist within an ecological context—that we cannot survive without the natural world around us. In this first part of the book, we consider some of the ties between humans and the ecological settings in which they live. We also begin to explore how humans can manipulate these ties for better and for worse.

Chapter 1 discusses what nature can do *for* us if we carefully plan interactions between human and ecological communities, as well as what nature can do *to* us if we are not careful. We also emphasize the importance of context and the need to think beyond the boundaries of official planning domains to create ecologically based plans and designs.

In Chapter 2, we introduce the Earth's living components, collectively known as *biodiversity*. Biodiversity is the focus of ecologists who try to understand how organisms interact with one another and their physical environment, and of conservationists as they determine how best to protect biodiversity. We explore different reasons why planners, designers, developers, and citizens may want to protect biodiversity as well as the reasons that the native biodiversity of a region is especially valuable.

Humans have significant impacts on the environments in which they live—impacts that, over time, can lead to the rise and fall of entire civilizations. Chapter 3 discusses different types of human impacts and lays the groundwork for thinking about how we can lessen these impacts, which is the focus of Part 3 of this book.

1

Humans Plan

"A man, a plan, a canal, Panama."

Palindrome describing the creation of the Panama Canal

"I returned, and saw under the sun, that the race is not to the swift, nor the battle to the strong, neither yet bread to the wise, nor yet riches to men of understanding, nor yet favor to men of skill; but time and chance happeneth to them all."

Ecclesiastes 9:11, *King James Bible*

Over the past few millennia, humans have spread to cover the globe. In the process, we have changed more of the earth, more profoundly, than any species before us. We have altered the face of the planet by building a canal between the Atlantic and Pacific oceans, reestablishing a connection that had not existed for more than 2 million years; by cutting vast forests at all latitudes; and by changing the global climate. As human communities grow, we shape nature. With our advanced technologies, however, we often forget that nature shapes us as well.

As we extend ourselves across the landscape, we plan. Sometimes our plans are explicit and carefully thought out documents, while other times they are implicit thoughts, such as, "If I create a farm here, it will be productive for several years," or "If we build a town here, it will be a safe place to live." Plans give us a secure feeling about the future and reinforce our sense that we can control the landscapes where we live. Drawings and carefully crafted words describe what a given site or region will look like if the plan goes into effect—but these plans can be misleading in two ways.

First, most plans focus primarily on the site or area for which they are planning. While they may consider roads and other aspects of human society outside the study area, they rarely consider ecological issues beyond the boundaries. A certain piece of terrain is either *in* the study area (and included in the plan) or *out* of the study area (and typically ignored). In fact, most plans show virtually nothing that is outside the planning area or site, as if it were an island floating in space (see Figure 1-1).

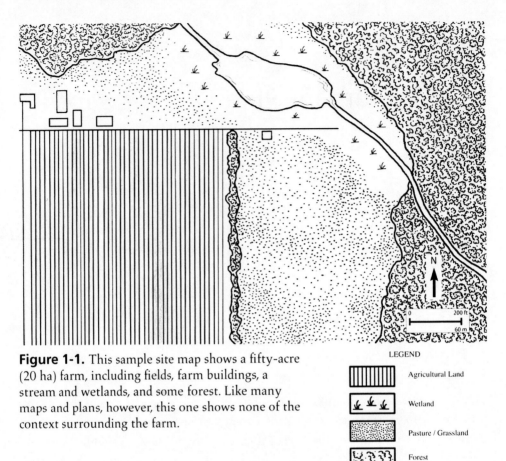

Figure 1-1. This sample site map shows a fifty-acre (20 ha) farm, including fields, farm buildings, a stream and wetlands, and some forest. Like many maps and plans, however, this one shows none of the context surrounding the farm.

LEGEND

Agricultural Land

Wetland

Pasture / Grassland

Forest

Second, the planning and design process is often built on the assumption that human beings fully control the future of the study area. A carefully produced plan is a prediction that verges on being a contract: the plan tells residents of an area what their subdivision or community will become if the plan is followed. As a result, plans typically depict only one or, at most, a handful of future states. The science of ecology, on the other hand, recognizes that "time and chance happeneth to them all." Yes, we can plan and predict, but despite the seeming solidity of our plans' words and images, we cannot guarantee what the future of a site holds. The world of nature is full of chance events, and the mere passage of time brings its own changes as well.

The following two case studies explore the relationship between planning—a wholly human enterprise—and the workings of nature. As these examples illustrate, planners, designers, and developers would do well to consider the effects of time, chance ecological events, and ecological processes occurring beyond their planning area. By taking these factors into account, we can develop plans that reap major benefits and avoid major problems. By ignoring these factors, we run the risk of costly or tragic consequences as nature runs its course.

New York City's Water

Beginning in the mid-nineteenth century, New York City developed one of the best municipal water supplies in the world in terms of quality, reliability, and innovative management.[1] Every day, the city's water system supplies 9 million people with 1.3 billion gallons of potable water.[2] The water comes from a system of nineteen reservoirs and lakes fed by a 1,969-square-mile (5,099 square km) *watershed* that extends more than 100 miles (160 km) north of the city. Perhaps most remarkable of all is that the foundations of this system were laid nearly two centuries ago, in 1835.[3] Today, almost all of New York's water still comes from upstate watersheds, and the main treatment that it receives is simply chlorination to kill the pathogens that are sometimes present at low levels.

In 1989, the U.S. Environmental Protection Agency (EPA) promulgated the Surface Water Treatment Rules, which grew out of the Safe Drinking Water Act of 1974.[4] Under these rules, New York City would have had to begin filtering its entire water supply for the first time. The filtration plants, according to the City, would have cost $6 to $8 billion to build and would have doubled the price of water for city residents. Instead, throughout the early and mid-1990s, the City and the EPA worked out an alternative to filtering the main water supply: the City would protect and improve water quality by helping towns in the watershed upgrade their sewage treatment facilities and by protecting thousands of acres of land in critical portions of the watershed. As of this writing, the City has purchased or obtained *conservation easements* on over 50,000 acres (20,000 ha) of land in the upstate watersheds.[5] The City alone has committed over $290 million for the land acquisition program, and city, state, and federal contributions to all facets of the watershed program total $1.4 billion.[6]

One of the most striking features of the agreement between the EPA and the city is the joint official recognition that nature can perform critical *ecosystem services* for humans. Instead of insisting on building giant filtration plants, the parties recognized that, through proper management, nature may be able to provide drinking water that is as safe as water provided by purely technological means. In addition to drinking water benefits, this watershed-based approach is helping protect rural landscapes just a couple of hours from New York City. Many farms will remain in business, and people are allowed to hike, fish, and hunt on much of the land that the city purchases.

In the early nineteenth century, the City of New York recognized that its water resources would become limiting, and the municipality looked beyond its borders to create a remarkable water supply system. At the end of the twentieth century, the city again looked beyond its borders—and beyond the confines of human technology—to envision a future in which humans protect natural areas in ways that help both humans and countless nonhuman organisms living across the landscape. This example offers the following lessons:

- Sometimes we are better served by letting nature provide necessary services than by using technology to fulfill our needs. When we protect and maintain healthy *ecosystems,* humans can reap significant health and economic benefits.
- By setting aside parcels of nature for one purpose—in this case, to provide safe drinking water—both human and ecological communities may benefit in other ways. The watershed lands protect the rural character of dozens of communities as well as high-quality habitat for the region's native species.

While looking beyond the boundaries of a site can help identify the benefits and services that nature provides, taking a broad view can also help one avoid some of the problems that nature can bring, as the next case study illustrates.

Fire in Colorado

Several years ago, some friends of ours purchased a house in Pine, Colorado. This small community, nestled beside and within the Pike National Forest, has become a bedroom community for Denver as the capacity of the highways into the city has expanded. The mountain ridges surrounding Pine are covered with maturing pine forests that are not only lovely to look at but also contain a surprisingly intact *ecological community* that includes black bear, elk, mule deer, coyotes, and even mountain lions—all less than an hour's drive from Denver. This ecosystem offers aesthetic and recreational amenities that have undoubtedly contributed to Pine's recent popularity among home buyers.

This ecosystem, however, is not entirely benign. Although the setting of our friends' house appears quite suburban, with several houses visible nearby, mountain lions are enough of a danger that many children do not play outside at dusk or dawn. But the single most notable species in this ecosystem is not one of the large mammal species but rather the Ponderosa pines (*Pinus ponderosa*) that dominate the landscape. And the single most notable process in the ecosystem is fire.

Left alone, Ponderosa pine forests typically burn lightly and frequently, with ground fires removing underbrush while leaving mature trees intact. However, in areas where fires have long been suppressed and underbrush has been allowed to accumulate, as is the case throughout much of the American West, fires burn heavily. As they engorge themselves on the dense growth left unpruned by the now-disrupted fire regime, they become massive, destructive crown fires capable of killing even the largest trees.

In June 2000, the Hi-Meadow Fire roared through the subdivisions and forests of Pine with impunity. The 10,800-acre (4,400 ha) fire destroyed fifty-eight structures, including several houses that could be seen from our friends' deck, but firefighters stopped the blaze thirty feet from their house (see Color Plate 1).[7] The fires around Pine offer several critical lessons:

- *Understand the ecological processes of the place you are planning or designing.* Developers creating new subdivisions in Ponderosa pine forests, and local planning commissions that approve these subdivisions, need to understand how the local ecosystems function. The same lesson applies to ecosystems across the continent.
- *Context is critically important.* What is outside the boundary of a site can add tremendous value—economic, ecological, recreational, or aesthetic—to the site, but it can also threaten health, safety, and property.
- *Always consider the array of possible futures for the land around a site.* This includes changes that may be brought about by humans, those that might occur naturally, and those that may occur through a combination of human and natural causes.
- *Plan with a measure of humility.* There are forces in nature that we may not be able to control.

The examples of New York City and Pine demonstrate that when we plan for the future, we need to look beyond the edges of our properties—which the planners of New York's water system certainly did, but which the designers of the subdivision in Pine did not do adequately.

Different Ways of Thinking about the Future

Planners, designers, ecologists, and conservationists all concern themselves with how specific landscapes will look and function in the future, and many of these professionals attempt to shape the future in different ways. But each profession approaches its work from a different background and with a different set of issues in mind, and each tends to view the world in a very different way (see Table 1-1). Developers who build houses in a wetland know that they may be penalized under the laws of humans and that some houses may end up with wet basements because of the laws of hydrology. Planners, in contrast, might be most concerned with how development in the wetland will affect the lives of humans, some of whom live far downstream from the wetland. Ecologists and conservationists would be more likely to focus on the effects of such development on nonhuman organisms, many of which spend only a small part of their lives in the wetland.

Land use planners, designers, and developers usually work within unambiguous geographic boundaries and over relatively short time periods. In considering the future of a site, designers and developers generally assume that they can alter only land that is part of the development site and not neighboring parcels. Similarly, planners have jurisdiction only within the municipality, county, district, state, or province where they work and not in adjacent jurisdictions. Of course, many land use professionals *do* make an effort to consider the larger context. For example, planner Randall Arendt, in his book *Growing Greener,* suggests that designers create site context maps that extend 1,000 to 2,000 feet (300 to 600 m) beyond the boundaries of their parcels.[8] But even this amount of context, which exceeds common practice, might not reveal important ecological processes that could affect the site under consideration—such as the Hayman Fire in Colorado, which ran seventeen linear miles (27 km) on June 9, 2002, needing only four minutes to spread half a mile (0.8 km) at one point.

By contrast, ecologists considering a piece of land would be aware of natural influences that exist *outside* the site's formal boundaries: physical processes, such as fire and wind, as well as biological impacts, such as pest outbreaks and *invasive species.* They would also consider how the landscape looked in the past and what it might look like in the future absent human intervention.

Another important difference among the professions is the certainty with which each anticipates future events. The planning and development processes involve several contractual and quasi-contractual relationships, unlike the practice of ecology, which involves none. A developer usually contracts with lenders and designers, and sometimes with landowners or future tenants, to create a specific building program on a site. In turn, the developer and the local government also have a quasi contract: developers can build within the community as long as they follow its zoning laws as well as building codes and other applicable regulations. These zoning laws are also the result of an implied contract between the community's residents and its planners and other officials to establish and maintain the community as a safe, healthy place to live.

Nature, in contrast, is not subject to contracts. In fact, ecologists hardly ever attempt to predict the future with certainty, and they are aware that the general rules they propose often hold true only in broad terms over long periods of time. Ecologists often say that the first law of ecology is "It depends." In thinking about the future, ecologists discuss what *might* happen or, at the strongest, what will *probably* happen. Ecological systems are too complex and contain too many interacting variables to allow us to be certain about the ecological future. Ecologists

Table 1-1.

Different Viewpoints among Professional Disciplines

Ways of Viewing the Land	Designers and Developers	Planners	Ecologists and Conservationists
Predictability of Events	Events are relatively predictable; the future will be shaped by today's actions. Human systems, such as laws, property rights, and financial markets, provide a large measure of predictability.	Future events can generally be predicted from current human policies and activities, but these can interact in complex ways resulting in unexpected outcomes.	The future may hold surprises, as unexpected ecological events (and historical patterns) shape the landscape. The first law of ecology is "It depends."
Role of History	Assuming a clear title and lack of contamination, a site's history is relatively unimportant in determining how it may be used.	We should learn from history (and, in some cases, try to preserve its legacy), but we are free to create our own future.	The ecological history of a site may constrain its future in important ways.
Boundaries	Sites have clear boundaries demarcated by property lines.	Jurisdictions and districts have clear boundaries, although those at different levels may overlap or coincide.	Boundaries are unclear; effects extend across human-drawn and natural boundaries; different organisms experience very different boundaries.

tell us that we need to know the history of a site *and* the natural patterns of ecological change for that landscape *and* the context of the site simply to understand the range of possibilities that might occur in the future. In this regard, ecological systems are much like the weather: at one level, they are deterministic and controlled by fundamental laws of physics and chemistry, yet they are too complex to allow humans to know every aspect of their workings. Instead, we infer and predict using a combination of observational and theoretical knowledge, improving our predictive power as time passes. With this level of ecological uncertainty, can a planner create an implied contract to keep members of the public safe within their ecological context?

Although it is impossible to capture all the nuances and complexities of these professions in such a brief space, the large differences in assumptions and approaches stand out clearly. There is nothing in the world of ecology and conservation—other than extinction—that is as clearly defined as a property boundary or a tax bill. But the certainty and finality of extinction drives much of the work of conservationists, for while a boundary or tax bill may be changed, extinction cannot.

Planning with Context in Mind

To appreciate the importance of considering a site's ecological context in space and time, let us return to Figure 1-1, in which we saw a hypothetical site as it exists today. The site contains fifty acres (20 ha), of which about thirty acres are currently farmland and fields, ten are forest, seven consist of a pond, stream, and wetland, and three are roads and buildings. Typically, developers and designers working on a site such as this will have considered the site's human context, such as the location of roads, schools, and nearby land uses, as well as such factors as zoning, property values, and the marketability of different development options. But what about the site's ecological context? Consider a series of three maps, each of which shows the site in a different ecological context (see Figure 1-2). These different contexts have profound implications for the site itself.

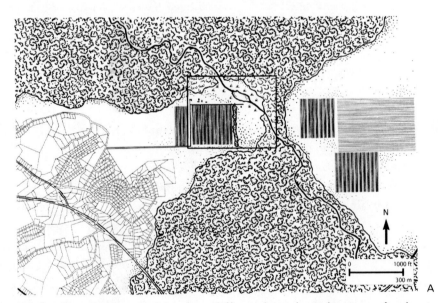

Figure 1-2. These three maps show three different hypothetical contexts for the site depicted in Figure 1-1. Each context might lead planners and developers to value the fifty-acre (20 ha) site in the middle very differently.

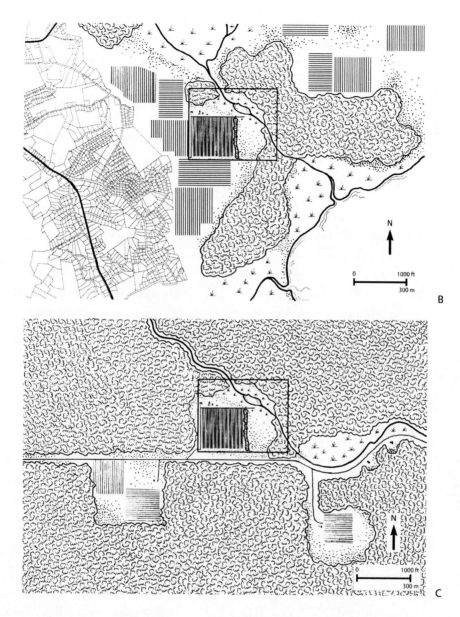

For example:

- *Are the forest patches on the eastern and northern sides of the site contiguous with additional forest, or are they isolated patches?* The forests are contiguous with larger forests in all three situations (Figures 1-2a, b, and c). In Figure 1-2a, the site's eastern forest plays a critical role in a habitat corridor connecting two large forested areas. In Figure 1-2b, the site's eastern forest is part of a buffer between agricultural lands and a lake/wetland system. The site's northern forest is part of a small forest patch that might be an important habitat "stepping stone" for birds crossing the landscape or that might be a relatively unimportant piece of habitat. In Figure 1-2c, the site's forests are just tiny parts of a large forest, although the eastern patch helps to buffer the stream that flows through the property. Cutting the northern patch of forest on the site would probably have little ecological effect.

- *What kind of forest does the site contain?* Is it a mature woodland or new growth on recently abandoned farmland? What tree species live there, and do threats exist to the health of any of the tree species (for example, are hemlocks being killed by insect pests, as in the eastern United States, or are tanoaks and other species dying off, as in California)? We cannot determine the age, condition, or ecological functioning of the forest from these maps alone, but an ecologist or forester would be able to answer these questions after examining the site.

- *What are the dominant processes in the forest—for example, fire, wind, or landslides?* This is an especially critical question, as the previously discussed example of Pine makes clear. In Figure 1-2c, the site is surrounded by forest; if this forest is fire-prone (as the Ponderosa pine forests of Colorado are), the site is at risk of fire approaching from any direction.

- *What role do the site's agricultural lands play in the larger landscape?* In Figure 1-2a, the site's fields are among the only ones near a growing suburban area. Farming may be an important part of the region's history, and this particular farm may function as an important reminder of that past. In Figure 1-2b, this farm is just one of several in the region, and there may be no special reason to preserve it as agricultural land.

All of these questions are germane to planning the site for development or conservation or both. For example, if fire is common in the landscape, designers must find a way to protect any proposed development on this site from fire hazards. If the site adjoins conservation land or if its forest is one of only a few natural outposts in an agricultural landscape, it may offer important conservation values. On the other hand, if the site borders a metropolis, it may be the next logical place for orderly growth. Box 1-1 identifies some key ecological issues for land use professionals to consider when planning a site.

The simple example shown in these maps illustrates a major theme of this book: context always matters, and without understanding this context it is impossible to create a plan that adequately safeguards humans and natural ecosystems. As landscape ecologist Richard Forman wrote in the preface to his book *Land Mosaics:* "It is simply inept or poor-quality work to consider [land] as isolated from its surroundings. . . . Moreover, because we know this is wrong . . . the practice is unethical."[9]

Box 1-1
Understanding the Ecological Context of Your Study Area

In developing a plan, certain aspects of a site, area, or region are critical to keep in mind:
- *Past processes*—both human and natural—that have brought the site to its current condition
- *Future processes*—both human and natural—that are likely to or might affect the site in the future
- *Ecological details of the site*, including the dominant plant and animal species that will affect the future of the site
- *Areas surrounding the site*—built, agricultural, and natural—where many of the processes that will affect the site in the future will begin (and where many of the processes that begin within the site will have their greatest effects)

Safeguarding Human Communities: Ecological Due Diligence

When people move to a new neighborhood, they usually consider not only the condition and amenities of the house or apartment they are thinking of buying or renting, but also whether the neighborhood is safe, convenient, and welcoming. Planners, designers, and developers all attempt to create neighborhoods and living spaces that are attractive in these respects.

Some "ecological neighborhoods" are safe and welcoming, providing such ecosystem services as clean water and flood control as well as natural areas to replenish the human spirit and protect native species. Other ecological neighborhoods, however, are not so benign: such hazards as forest fires, floods, hurricanes, and native predators may put their residents' safety, welfare, and property at risk. The effects of these mistakes, which situate human communities in ecologically inappropriate areas, are easily recognized after disasters, such as the Southern California fires of 2003 and the great Mississippi River floods of 1993. Christina Chance, a Southern California resident whose house was narrowly spared by the 2003 fires, captured this concept succinctly: "After you have weathered a fire, you learn how to select your home and your community."[10]

Respecting Natural Processes That Cross Boundaries

While human descriptions of landscapes, such as comprehensive plans and engineered site plans, often contain sharp, straight-line boundaries, nearly all other

Figure 1-3. The red-legged frog (*Rana aurora*) requires several different types of habitat, including small pools and moist woods, to complete its life cycle. These habitats may span several properties or even towns, but the frog has no knowledge of such human boundaries.

organisms perceive ecological systems as having leaky, fuzzy boundaries. For instance, the red-legged frog (*Rana aurora*) of the U.S. West Coast will, over its lifetime, use a variety of habitats, including small pools for growth as a tadpole and breeding as an adult, moist woods as its primary adult habitat, and the paths it travels between these sites. The frogs have no knowledge of the human-created property lines or jurisdictional boundaries that run through these habitats, although they may have to deal with human features on the landscape, such as roads and buildings (see Figure 1-3).

Even a natural boundary that seems clearly defined, such as the shoreline of a pond that divides land from water, is a porous barrier for many organisms. Frogs, toads, salamanders, dragonflies, damselflies, caddis flies, mosquitoes, and many other organisms spend the early part of their lives in the water and the later part on dry land, returning to the water to breed (for one example, see Figure 1-4). The entire sport of fly-fishing is built around two aspects of permeable ecological boundaries. Those who fly-fish create their lures so as to mimic adult caddis flies, mayflies, stoneflies, and other insects that spend their juvenile stages living under water and that return to water to lay their eggs. The artificial flies are intended to mimic these creatures because trout capture much of their food out of the water, eating flying adult insects.

Figure 1-4. Like many animals, the red-spotted newt (*Notophthalmus viridescens viridescens*) spends part of its life in freshwater habitats and part of its life on land. The red eft, the juvenile stage shown here, lives in moist forests, while the younger larvae and the adults are aquatic. The newt thus requires healthy aquatic and terrestrial habitats (and connections between them) to complete its life cycle.

Just as land use plans often show sharp boundaries even though natural boundaries are usually imprecise, they also tend to portray only one desired future scenario for a site or community, though in actuality the ecology of any area—even a city—is an unfinished book that can have any of a number of endings. Because of unpredictable events—whether global climate change, massive storms such as hurricanes or tornados, biological invasions such as kudzu or the Asian longhorn beetle, or just the ongoing ecological changes that take place in any system—the ecological future of an area is never certain. For example, no plan could have predicted with certainty which parts of our friends' subdivision in Colorado would be destroyed by fire, although an ecologist may have predicted that fire in this area was likely.

To account for natural processes and uncertainties when we plan, we must first seek to understand them. A recent study of Arizona's Desert View Tri-Villages Area conducted by landscape planner Frederick Steiner illustrates how *ecological due diligence* can inform land use planning.[11] The study emphasizes the importance of context, including not only maps of the Tri-Villages Area but also satellite images, maps, and elevation models of the surrounding landscape. It reviews the area's land use history and possible future influences, discusses external impacts on the Tri-Villages Area (such as major climate patterns), and evaluates how local events may affect nearby watersheds. In short, Steiner describes the ecology of the Tri-Villages Area by beginning with the study area itself and then extending outward in four dimensions: across the landscape, down into the groundwater and soils, and into the past and the future. Reflecting ecological as well as human uncertainties, the study describes not just a single future planning outcome but a range of possible futures.

How can land use professionals create meaningful plans when the future is uncertain, boundaries are porous, and ecological events are often unpredictable? The first requirement is to recognize that ecologically based planning, like land use planning in general, rarely has a single correct solution—although it usually has many "wrong" solutions.

Second, planners and designers can seek out and use ecological information while understanding that much of this information is incomplete or limited in its predictive powers. In this regard, we can draw a parallel to other types of planning analysis, such as a market feasibility study. In such a study, data are collected on past real estate market trends and factors that are likely to affect future trends; models may be created and predictions made. Planners and developers must then make a decision based on the information in the study, recognizing that other factors—known, unknown, and unknowable—may all affect the ultimate marketability of the project.

Third, land use professionals should recognize the difference between *considering* an ecological variable in their plan and *controlling* it. Because ecological processes are uncertain, it is appropriate to build in a margin of safety when it comes to protecting people from the natural world and protecting the natural world from people.

Finally, and most importantly, planners and designers must ask the right questions about the ecological factors occurring within, impinging on, and emanating from their site. Throughout this book, we ask and answer these important ecological questions in order to provide a sound framework for improving the ecological compatibility of readers' future plans or developments.

2

An Introduction to Ecology and Biodiversity

Southeastern Arizona is one of the most beautiful parts of North America, with stunning deserts interspersed among pine-covered mountain ranges. The watershed of the San Pedro River, undammed along its entire 140-mile (225 km) length, stands out in this landscape for its exceptional biological richness (see Figure 2-1). In fact, this watershed of 3,700 square miles (9,600 square km) is arguably as biologically rich as any region of its size in the continental United States or Canada, with almost 400 species of birds, 82 species of mammals, and 43 species of reptiles and amphibians—all in an area smaller than Connecticut.[1] By comparison, the entire United States contains just 768 bird species, 416 mammal species, and 514 reptile and amphibian species.[2] The San Pedro watershed may be the most sought after spot in the United States by bird-watchers, and it is widely recognized among biologists as a jewel. But what does it mean to say that an area is biologically rich? And, once we determine that an area is biologically important, then what?

Biodiversity: The Stuff of Life

Biodiversity is the term used by conservation biologists to describe the entire diversity of life—encompassing all of the species, genes, and ecosystems on earth (or within a given area, as in the biodiversity of the San Pedro River watershed).[3] In practice, biodiversity is sometimes measured simply by counting the number

Figure 2-1. The San Pedro River of southeastern Arizona is undammed along its entire 140-mile (225 km) length. This is a perennial stretch of the river that runs year-round.

of species found in an area (known as the area's *species richness*), as in the brief description above of the San Pedro's biodiversity. However, a more precise measure would also consider the number of different ecosystems present as well as the *genetic diversity* found within individual species. In addition, community structure (the proportions and arrangements of species on the landscape) and ecological and evolutionary processes are generally considered important aspects of biodiversity. In short, the definition can be quite complex, and species richness often is not a very good proxy for a true understanding of an area's biodiversity.

As it turns out, the San Pedro watershed not only is species rich but also contains a high level of biodiversity according to the more complex definition presented above. The watershed includes a great variety of *ecosystems*, different groupings of living organisms along with their nonliving environment. Grasslands, desert scrub, high-elevation forests, oak and mesquite woodlands, and riparian (streamside) vegetation are all examples of San Pedro ecosystems (see Figure 2-2).

In addition, given the physical layout of the landscape, with distinct mountain ranges known as the Sky Islands (see Figure 2-3) separated by expanses of low desert and the river itself, high genetic diversity is likely across the watershed. Genetic diversity is typically greater in regions consisting of geographically isolated subregions (such as the Sky Islands) than in homogeneous regions of a similar size. Thus, at a variety of levels, the San Pedro is quite biodiverse, which makes it interesting to ecologists and conservationists alike.

Figure 2-2. The San Pedro River basin contains a diversity of ecosystems. This photograph was taken from desert scrub looking toward riparian forest bordering the river in the distance.

The Study of Biodiversity: Ecology and Its Subdisciplines

Planners and designers may have several reasons for wanting to understand the biodiversity of the site, area, or region where they are working. From a purely practical standpoint, land use professionals often need to comply with planning or regulatory requirements that necessitate an understanding of local ecosystems and biodiversity. Economic considerations are a second reason to understand local biodiversity, which can either help bring in revenue (e.g., through tourism) or carry unexpected costs (e.g., damage caused by an insect pest). Other land use professionals work to understand and conserve nature because they are ethically motivated or are driven by the wishes of their constituents or clients.

The study of biodiversity begins with basic natural history: an examination of the living world around us. Today, we often think of natural history as the material found in field guides and dusty museums, but the roots of this discipline are as deep as humankind's history. Humans became the most widespread vertebrate in the history of life not through our speed, strength, venom, or beauty but, rather, by understanding our habitats and being able to adjust to them and modify them better than any other species. For most humans who have ever

Figure 2-3. Two of the Sky Island mountain ranges of southeastern Arizona appear in the distance. The plants and animals living on these mountains have been isolated from similar organisms on nearby mountains, leading, in some cases, to the evolution of new species.

lived, not knowing the natural history and ecology of one's native ecosystem has meant dying young.

A list of the species that inhabit a site or region, such as a bird list for the San Pedro, is one of the most basic types of data that natural history provides. Natural historians would also conduct fieldwork to determine how numerous each species is, when each species is present (what seasons of the year as well as what times of day the species is active), and how different species interact. A good natural historian might also begin to analyze these patterns further, asking, for example, what species one might expect to find at a location but that are no longer present and what observed species one would not expect to be there (i.e., *nonnative species*).

These basic observations about the *biota* (all the living organisms) of an area form the starting point for the field of *ecology*, a wide-ranging scientific discipline that seeks to examine, explain, and predict how species interact with one another and with the nonliving world. Since the earliest days of the discipline, ecologists have studied why individual species live in certain areas but not in others. Charles Darwin and Alfred Russel Wallace, working in the mid-nineteenth century, wrestled with this issue decades before the term *ecology* was coined, and one of the classic works in ecology is entitled *The Distribution and Abundance of Animals.*[4] Some of the key questions that ecologists might ask about the San Pedro watershed appear in Box 2.1.

Box 2-1
Key Ecological Questions to Ask about a Region

- *What organisms and ecological communities* occur in the region, or, phrased another way, what elements of biodiversity are found there? (*Communities* are distinct groupings of plants and animals that cohabitate throughout a region—essentially the living components of ecosystems.)
- *Why* does this area contain *so many species and ecological communities*?
- *What biological* and *physical processes* help *determine which species and communities* are found in the watershed?

Within the field of ecology numerous subdisciplines focus on different aspects of species and the ecosystems where they live. Assume for a moment that you are proposing a development (or designing or reviewing a proposed development) in an area of the San Pedro watershed that is rumored to contain Sonoran tiger salamanders (*Ambystoma tigrinum stebbinsi*), which are listed as endangered under the U.S. Endangered Species Act. You need to know whether these salamanders actually exist on the site and, if so, how to design with their habitat needs in mind (as well as how to comply with the Endangered Species Act). Discussed below are some of the different types of biologists who could help answer these questions.

Taxonomists specialize in the identification of a specific group of organisms. Ecologists would turn to a taxonomist for a positive identification of the salamander. The taxonomist could confirm whether a salamander found on the site is a Sonoran tiger salamander or some other, non-endangered subspecies of tiger salamander that has been introduced to the area. Clearly, proper identification is crucial for the land use planners, landscape architects, and developers involved in this situation, because the salamanders at the site may or may not be federally protected.

Behavioral ecologists would study the territorial and migratory behavior of individual salamanders so that developers could know which parts of the site the animals use.

Population ecologists would focus on the entire local population of Sonoran tiger salamanders, studying fluctuations in the numbers of salamanders at the site and comparing the genetic makeup of this population with that of other populations.

Community ecologists would examine the interactions between the salamanders and other species in their community. They would ask which species eat the salamanders, which ones the salamanders eat, and which ones compete with the salamanders for food and other resources. This subdiscipline is also highly relevant for planners and designers, because it helps predict what would happen to the functioning of an ecological community if certain species were removed, added, or restored.

Ecosystem ecologists would study the functioning of the entire ecosystem—the biotic community plus the nonliving land, water, and air on which they live and depend. An ecosystem ecologist would focus on the flows of nutrients and energy through the ecosystem in which the salamanders live and would attempt to develop accurate models of the ecosystem's functioning. In this case, for example, an understanding of the effects of nutrient enrichment could help protect the salamander's aquatic habitats from being degraded by fertilizer runoff or sewage discharge.

Landscape ecologists would consider the patterns that exist across the landscape—namely, how the salamander's brook and wetland habitats connect with, or are isolated from, similar habitats nearby—to determine the possibility of migration among populations.

Conservation biologists would integrate knowledge from the preceding disciplines with an understanding of the legal, economic, ethical, and public policy aspects of the issue at hand to develop solutions for particular planning, conservation, or development projects. Thus, while ecologists and conservation biologists both focus on biodiversity and ecosystem functioning, the two disciplines have differing emphases, with conservation biology applying basic ecological science to address conservation challenges. To protect rare and endangered species, conservation biologists must know which species are present in a given area, how

Box 2-2
Some Questions to Inform a Regional Conservation Assessment

- What species in the region are *endangered*, are *threatened*, or have been *extirpated* in historical times?
- What are the *causes* of this endangerment, and how can these causes be eliminated or mitigated?
- What can be done to *protect* healthy habitats and populations within the region?
- What can be done to *restore* the region to its previous functioning?

their populations are doing, how they interact with other species, how material and energy flows affect ecosystem functioning, and how patches of natural habitat are laid out across the landscape. For example, a conservation biologist studying the San Pedro watershed might ask the questions shown in Box 2-2, which we will return to repeatedly throughout this book.

Why Protect the Natural Environment and Biodiversity?

To ask whether and why humans should protect nature is as profound a question as asking the purpose of human civilization on planet Earth. To answer such difficult questions, some individuals may look to economics, others to political expediency, others to aesthetic considerations, and still others to their own values. Since you are reading this book, you may already have some reasons of your own for wanting to protect the natural environment, and perhaps the pages of this book will add some new reasons. But our main purpose in discussing the value of biodiversity and functioning ecosystems here is not to convince the reader of their value but to equip the reader to articulate to others why conservation should be part of a particular plan. To make this case, the pragmatic conservationist presents at least two of the many arguments for conserving nature: an economic or practical argument that appeals to politicians and business- and engineering-oriented individuals, and an ethical argument that avoids discussions of money and appeals directly to human intuition.

For land use planners and the constituents and politicians to whom they must answer, the most compelling "practical" reason for conserving biodiversity is undoubtedly to protect nature's valuable *ecosystem services*—those ecosystem functions that provide economic utility to humans, such as flood control, water purification, and nutrient cycling. The dollar value of these services to society is tremendous and, in many cases, if natural ecosystems did not provide them, local and state governments would need to spend large sums to accomplish the same thing. For instance, trees within the city limits of San Antonio, Texas, were estimated to provide the city annually with $115 million in stormwater management benefits and $22 million in pollution reduction benefits (since trees absorb air pollution).[5] Similarly, wetlands and watershed lands provide such ecosystem services as water cycling, nutrient cycling, pollution attenuation, and flood control, which can save the public millions—or, in the case of New York City's water supply system, billions—of dollars compared to engineered alternatives. In fact, a study published in the scientific journal *Nature* estimated the value of ecosystem services worldwide at $33 trillion per year—almost twice the gross national product of all the world's economies combined.[6] In reality, the value of ecosystem services to mankind is infinite, for without them humans would go extinct in short order.

Proximity to nature also increases the desirability and value of property, a factor that may increase the profitability of real estate development and the attractiveness of towns, cities, and regions. As the Chicago Wilderness Coalition states on its Web site: "Protecting nature in our region has economic benefits. To remain competitive [we] must offer a comparable quality of life to that offered in other metropolitan areas—and if possible, a better one. An important aspect of quality of life in and around our city is access to nature."[7] Particularly important to developers is the fact that people are increasingly willing to pay a premium to live near natural areas: for example, the Rocky Mountain Institute found that 48 percent of Denver residents were willing to pay more to live near a park or greenbelt in 1990, compared to 16 percent in 1980.[8] In Tucson, Arizona, researchers estimated that a single-family house near wildlife habitat would command a price premium of $4,576 (averaged across five districts in the city) compared to a comparable house a mile farther from the wildlife habitat. Proximity to a golf course resulted in a premium of only $2,215.[9] In the city of Guelph, Ontario, a survey of residents revealed that 90 percent think the city administration should do more to encourage wildlife conservation, while 46 percent indicated a willingness to pay additional tax to fund this activity.[10] Such statistics indicate a strong public mandate for politicians and government officials to include conservation as an important part of their work.

Several other economic benefits of conservation relate specifically to the value of biodiversity. The earth's "biological capital" of species and genes is the ultimate source of all our food as well as many other essential products, including fiber, building materials, pharmaceuticals, and useful chemicals. If these arguments seem to justify protecting nature's cornucopia only in the tropical rainforests, consider that some of our most economically valuable species, especially timber trees, are native to North America. Humans will continue to depend on wild genetic strains of these species to create improved varieties for our use. A more tangible economic argument for many planners is that native biodiversity attracts tourist and investment dollars by helping to define a community's identity and by contributing to local quality of life. People will spend money to see elk and redwood trees, not raccoons and Norway maples. In addition, evidence shows that at least some minimum amount of biodiversity is necessary to maintain the valuable ecosystem services discussed above and that higher levels of biodiversity offer "insurance" that such services will be maintained in the future.[11]

For many people, though, the most compelling reasons to conserve biodiversity cannot be reduced to dollars and cents. Religious faith is the foundation of a conservation ethic for many people, who believe that the Earth has a sacred wholeness that humans must not destroy for their own shortsighted purposes.

Environmentalist teachings are found in religions as diverse as Christianity, Islam, Buddhism, Hinduism, and Judaism. From an ethical standpoint, some people argue that we have a moral responsibility to future human generations to pass along a world that is as ecologically intact, highly functioning, and full of wonder as the one we inherited ourselves. Others feel that humans have a moral obligation to protect the natural world for the sake of other species, irrespective of any benefit that humans may derive.

On a more personal note, many of us can vividly recall times when we have been close to nature: walking through a hushed forest at dusk, marveling at the sudden blooming of desert flowers after spring rains, or even grinning at the antics of seals at the zoo. Moments like these fill us with joy, serenity, and, at times, awe. Even if we do not have this wealth of nature in our daily lives, we seek it out—during vacations to national parks, at our windowsill bird feeder, even on the Discovery channel. It pleases us to know that nature is out there: beautiful, wild, mysterious, and unreliant on people for its existence. Scholars call this the "aesthetic" argument for protecting biodiversity, but it is about more than just beauty, as the anecdote in Box 2-3 illustrates.

Native versus Non-Native Biodiversity

Those who are committed to protecting biodiversity and functioning ecosystems for the reasons just discussed are immediately faced with a thorny question: Given that the term *biodiversity* refers to pretty much all of life on earth (or all of the life in a given location, such as the San Pedro), is all biodiversity equally good? The answer to this question is a resounding "no," as we will explain.

Recall for a moment that the biodiversity of a place depends not just on the number of species in that location but also on the diversity of genes, communities, and ecosystems there and in relation to the larger context—in other words, on how different the place is biologically from other places. Thus, widespread cosmopolitan species and *non-native species* that are found across much of the globe (these are also known as "tramp species," an indication of how they are valued) add less valuable biodiversity to an area than do unique native species; in fact, they often detract from biodiversity when they squeeze out native species. For example, the bullfrog, which is not native to the San Pedro valley, is spreading throughout the region and crowding out such native species as the Yaqui chub (a fish listed as federally endangered) and the Chiricahua leopard frog (which has been proposed for listing under the U.S. Endangered Species Act). Even more threatening are invasive plants, such as red brome and cheatgrass, which cover the landscape and change the frequency and intensity of fires, resulting in large-scale changes to native ecosystems.[12]

Box 2-3
Living in a Land without Quetzals

We must decide what kind of world we want to live in. We can, perhaps, live moderately healthy and moderately fulfilling lives in an ecologically degraded world; hurricanes and floods may devastate human communities, but we can rebuild what nature destroys. We can, perhaps, find technological methods to fend off crop pests and diseases or, in the worst case, find replacements for specific crops that succumb. Will the loss of individual species, even such spectacular organisms as redwoods or right whales, destroy many human lives? Probably not. But what kind of world do we want? The following experience of ecologists Marcy and Bob Lawton illustrates this issue.

On a break from their graduate research in Monteverde, Costa Rica, the Lawtons traveled through parts of rural Guatemala. In a remote section of the countryside, they met a family who had been walking many hours from their home: their son was very ill, and the father was carrying the boy on his back to get to a doctor. Both families stopped to take a break from their walking and spoke for a while. The *campesinos* had never been out of their home district in the mountains and were interested in the lives that the Lawtons lived far from Guatemala. As the two biologists described their home and lives in Chicago, the Guatemalan father asked if there were any quetzals in Chicago, for the quetzal (*Pharomachrus mocinno*) is one of the most magnificent birds of the Western Hemisphere and was considered sacred by the Mayans (see Color Plate 2). When Bob said that there were none, the father asked why anyone would want to live where there are no quetzals, and he edged away from the northerners.

As it turns out, quetzals require mature forest that contains decaying or dead standing tree trunks for their nests. In addition, they migrate through several different types of forest during the course of the year, and they typically refuse to cross open expanses of land that have been cleared by humans. Quetzals are rare because they require a variety of different healthy habitats, including rare habitats such as cloud forests. In short, quetzals are not only beautiful birds but also sensitive indicators of healthy forest regions.

The Lawtons knew this, for Monteverde, where they did their research, is home to a healthy population of quetzals, and they recognized the truth of the *campesino*'s words. Why indeed would anyone want to live in a habitat that was degraded to the point that it could no longer support quetzals? On hearing that the two biologists did not lead lives devoid of quetzals, that they lived in a community full of the birds, the relieved *campesinos* began a conversation that lasted most of the night.

The vast majority of the world's people will never be within a thousand miles of a quetzal, much less live in a community full of the birds. But every habitat has its own version of the quetzal, and probably several: species that are emblematic of their native habitat, that are sensitive to environmental changes, and that make us glad to be alive when we see them. There is a rightness to life in the Central American highlands where there are quetzals that is far better than life in highlands where the birds are now missing. So, too, ecosystems everywhere that are full of their native creatures and that function well create better lives for their human inhabitants. We could live in a world without quetzals and fig trees, moose and sugar maples, sandhill cranes and big bluestem grass, peccaries and saguaro cactus, manatees and longleaf pines, sea otters and Douglas-firs—but, as the *campesino* asked, why would anyone want to live there?

Figure 2-4. Lady slipper orchids depend on bumblebees for pollination. If bumblebees disappear from a habitat, so, too, will the lady slipper orchids.

As a result, when we speak of biodiversity throughout this book, we are generally referring to *native biodiversity*—populations, species, and ecosystems that are indigenous to a given area and were not transported there by humans. As scientists now understand, native biodiversity is not an "à la carte menu" where certain desirable species can be protected while others are neglected. Many species play specialized roles in their native ecosystems—as pollinators, seed dispersers, predators, or parasites—and to maintain one species in such a specialized relationship, we must maintain the other partner as well. To protect lady slipper orchids, we have to protect the bumblebees that pollinate them; to protect Oregon silverspot butterflies, we have to protect the single violet species they feed on (see Figure 2-4). Native species often coevolve to survive in one another's presence, but when nonnative species arrive, they rarely match the function of the native species they displace. For example, a study of birds in Cheyenne, Wyoming, revealed that native bird species generally avoid using non-native trees for feeding and nesting and, instead, select native tree species.[13] Similarly, a healthy wetland of native cattails and jewelweed might support such native animals as red-winged blackbirds and muskrats, but a wetland full of such beautiful but invasive non-native species as purple loosestrife fails to offer the food and shelter that these species need.

For many people, the importance of native biodiversity is personal, aesthetic, or spiritual. It is wonderful to be surrounded by the richness and diversity of life, as any gardener or zoo visitor can attest. But to be surrounded by healthy native ecosystems and species is something truly special, as bird-watchers, botanists, and other naturalists know. Just as many planners value the unique local flavor and sense of place imparted by small, independently owned businesses in their community and may try to prevent these businesses' wholesale replacement by chain stores, so, too, are people across the continent reconnecting with the unique natural history of their home regions. Chicago, for example, has become the locus of major volunteer efforts to re-create the prairie and savanna habitats that once covered Illinois, and these volunteers take great pride in reestablishing these nearly vanished ecosystem types.[14]

While "Biodiversity!" has become a rallying cry for conservationists, the term alone does not do complete justice to what they really want: healthy, complete, functioning native ecosystems populated by native species—preferably a full complement of them—with as few non-native species in the mix as possible. Although a garden may contain more species than a nearby patch of native habitat, conservationists would put scarce resources into protecting the native habitat, not the garden.

Factors That Contribute to High Biodiversity

Biologists have long recognized that biological diversity is not evenly distributed across the globe. Tropical regions contain the largest numbers of species in nearly all taxonomic groups, while subtropical, temperate, and polar regions contain successively fewer species (see Color Plate 3). In general, different groups of species inhabit each climate zone, although some (such as wolves, coyotes, mountain lions, and white-tailed deer) range from the Arctic to the tropics, and others (such as many songbirds and shorebirds) migrate from one zone to another.

Within a given region, areas that contain a variety of elevations typically contain more species than areas that do not vary in elevation. For example, mountainous regions in subtropical areas can include suites of organisms typical of subtropical, temperate, and Arctic zones, thereby including a very diverse group of species in a small geographic area. In addition to the temperature changes that come with changes in elevation, north-south oriented mountain ranges in North America typically exhibit striking differences in rainfall, with their eastern slopes being much drier. Such mosaics of differing temperature and moisture patterns create a variety of distinct habitats, which can support more species than a homogeneous area of similar size.

Heterogeneous regions not only *support* biodiversity in their different habitats but also *breed* new biodiversity. Most *speciation*—the evolution of a new species from existing ones—takes place when a single population is split into two or more isolated populations. This can occur, for example, when cool, wet mountain ranges are separated by hot, dry lowlands or when habitats are isolated on either side of an impassable canyon or mountain range. Over time, the isolated populations will evolve separately and may diverge so much that even if the two populations reunite later they may exist as distinct species that do not interbreed.

The San Pedro region is a biodiversity hot spot for all of these reasons: it is distinctly subtropical, contains a wide range of habitats spanning vastly different elevations, and exhibits widely differing moisture regimes.[15] In addition, the isolated mountain ranges of the area, known collectively as the Sky Islands, have led to the evolution of distinct species.

Humans: A Part of Nature or Apart from Nature?

Humans have inhabited most parts of North America for millennia. Scientists believe that humans first reached North America between 13,000 and 18,000 years ago and had spread to every habitable part of the continent by 5,000 years ago. Wherever they lived, humans affected the ecosystems they inhabited, and vice versa; in fact, most North American ecosystems have more or less coevolved with humans. What, then, does it mean when we say we want to "preserve" nature, keep an area "pristine," or restore an ecosystem to its "original condition"? The following discussion examines these questions by considering the history of the San Pedro watershed and its implications for today's planning and conservation challenges.[16]

Early human activity in the San Pedro watershed (prior to 10,000 years ago) probably had little impact on the river but may have played a role in the extinction of mammoths, mastodons, and other large fauna. If hunting was instrumental in these animals' demise (as many scientists believe), early Native Americans would have fundamentally altered the ecology of the San Pedro and surrounding regions. The next major human-induced ecological change probably occurred about 3,000 years ago when people first settled in permanent communities and began farming and cutting wood for fuel and building materials. Although small in scale, the vegetation clearing and use of irrigation that enabled the adoption of a sedentary lifestyle began to affect the river and its hydrology.

From the 1600s through the mid-1800s, a mix of Spanish settlers and missionaries, sedentary Sobaipuri peoples, and raiding Apache tribes inhabited the San Pedro. During this time, the Spaniards first introduced cattle and other livestock to the area, animals that would ultimately have a major impact on the watershed. When the Apaches periodically drove the Spaniards off their ranches, some of the herds became wild, and feral cattle populated the valley for centuries.

But the major impact of cattle came in the 1880s, when ranchers brought large herds into Arizona from drought-stricken Texas and California. Hundreds of thousands of cattle in this arid landscape proved to be too much: they overgrazed the grasslands so that, when it rained, little vegetation remained to temper the flow of water and hold the soil in place. The San Pedro and its tributaries filled with rushing water that created deep channels in the parched soil known as *arroyos*, some of them as deep as ten to twenty feet (3 to 6 m). The river, which had once run broadly across the surface of the land, now dug deeply into trenches in many places, rendering the possibility of recovery much more remote.

Around the same time that European and Native peoples were introducing domestic livestock, they were removing another important species: the beaver (*Castor canadensis*). Beaver on the San Pedro were once so plentiful that early trappers called it "Beaver River." The dams of these large rodents helped give the river its characteristic slow flow, with large marshy expanses known as *cienegas*, where the river spread into a slowly flowing sheet up to a mile (1.6 km) across. By the early nineteenth century, the beavers were trapped out, and as their dams disintegrated, the slow-flowing, marshy aspect of the river changed. Hunting and habitat changes also removed grizzly bears, wolves, pronghorn antelope, and three-foot (0.9 m) long Colorado squawfish from the river and its valley. But it was the loss of a single key native species, the beaver, and the addition of a single non-native species, domestic cattle, that changed the ecosystem most profoundly.

In the late nineteenth century, copper and silver mining around the San Pedro required large amounts of water and wood, which led to the deforestation of both the riverside habitats and the nearby Sky Islands. The loss of tree cover worsened the erosive effects of rainstorms. At about the same time, large-scale irrigation for agriculture began, with cotton becoming the most important crop in Arizona early in the twentieth century. Earlier inhabitants of the area, such as the Sobaipuri, had irrigated corn, bean, cotton, and squash crops, but the scale of the new irrigation, coupled with the cattle and mining effects, led to further problems, such as arroyo creation. Today, agriculture accounts for about three-quarters of Arizona's water use, while rapidly expanding human communities require more water each year (for example, Sierra Vista, Arizona, the largest city in the San Pedro watershed, grew 465 percent from 1970 to 2000).[17] Water use by humans has resulted in a 2.2 billion gallon (8 billion L) annual water deficit in the San Pedro watershed, with most of this water being pumped from underground aquifers that are hydrologically connected to the river.[18] Overpumping has caused many formerly perennial sections of the river to become ephemeral in recent years, and in some areas trees are dying due to lack of water as the water table falls.

The picture of the San Pedro presented at the beginning of this chapter was that of an ecosystem rich in beauty and biodiversity, a place that still seems pristine in many ways. Yet, the region's history tells a different story, one of significant human impacts stretching back at least 10,000 years and affecting almost every aspect of this ecosystem, from its plants and animals to its soils and water. Does this history mean than the San Pedro is somehow spoiled or not worth conserving? Certainly not. Almost no ecosystem in the world is unaffected by the influence of humankind; only the type and degree of influence varies. Thus, while few places are "pristine" in the sense that they are untouched by humans, many are highly valuable because they provide humans with important ecological functions or services or contain large amounts of biodiversity.

In addition to helping humans understand their relationship to native ecosystems, the ecological history of a region, such as that of the San Pedro, can guide conservationists and land use planners as they seek to identify and restore valuable aspects of an ecosystem that have been lost. In the San Pedro, conservationists are trying to reverse some of the more serious human-induced ecological changes of the past by allowing beaver to recolonize the river and by improving cattle management practices. The goal, obviously, is not to reestablish some "original" prehuman ecosystem complete with mastodons; it is to restore elements of the ecosystem that existed prior to the nineteenth century—a time when humans were present and influential on the landscape but not highly destructive to native plants and animals, streams, and soils.

As illustrated by this restoration effort, many people in southeastern Arizona now recognize the biological and cultural value of the San Pedro River valley as well as its fragility. Twenty groups within the watershed have joined together to form the Upper San Pedro Partnership, which is developing a conservation plan for the river. Articles such as novelist Barbara Kingsolver's paean to the San Pedro in *National Geographic* and the efforts of such groups as The Nature Conservancy and American Rivers have also brought the river national and international attention.[19] But the people of the San Pedro watershed will need to actively manage population growth, land use, and water use in the region if they are to protect this beautiful and important river valley, which has supported human communities for millennia.

3

When Humans and Nature Collide

Imagine Exponentia, a booming city of the early twenty-first century. A hundred years ago, Exponentia was a town of barely 5,000 residents; today, it has more than 100,000, with most of that growth taking place in just the last half-century. A large proportion of the city's residents have high-tech jobs, and many of them appreciate the easy access that the city has historically had to beautiful natural areas. As a result of its recent growth, however, the town-become-city now extends well out into the neighboring farmlands, rangelands, and mountains and has become part of a larger metropolitan complex (see Figure 3-1). Exponentia is fictional, but cities like it can be found across North America; as you read the next few paragraphs, imagine your local version of Exponentia and fill in the relevant details.

Planners are familiar with many of the human challenges that accompany rapid growth, such as the need to fund additional roads, schools, public safety services, and water and sewer infrastructure. But how does urban growth affect native species and habitats? The most obvious effect of the city's expansion is the loss of native habitat. This is a zero-sum game with three players: natural habitats, agricultural lands, and urban land uses. As one land use expands—typically, human-inhabited areas—one or both of the others contract. Granted, these are not completely mutually exclusive categories; for example, lightly used rangelands and sparsely inhabited regions can serve as good habitat for some native species. But, by and large, every acre of the landscape can be assigned to one or another of the categories, and the unmistakable trend—and one that shows no sign of changing—is that native habitat has been shrinking over time.

As the four diagrams of Exponentia shown in Figure 3-1 illustrate, human development is not likely to occur in all areas equally. Development proceeds rapidly on relatively flat sites with well-drained soils, since these make good building sites. Development is slower to reach remote, steep, or poorly drained lands, although homes may appear on hillsides and along ridgetops if local ordinances allow. So, in this hypothetical example, while only about half of the total area has been developed in the past fifty years, most of the flat lowlands have been lost, while the hillsides remain relatively untouched.

Consequences of Human Settlement

As human settlements spread and our activities expand, we affect native biodiversity in many ways. Urban and agricultural land uses destroy and fragment native habitats; our homes, machines, and industries pollute, degrade, and alter the land, air, and water; we harvest (and often overharvest) native species from their habitats; and we accidentally or intentionally introduce non-native species. For example, since European settlement of North America, nearly all of the continent's tallgrass prairie has been converted to agriculture. Most of the states and provinces originally containing tallgrass prairie have lost 98 percent or more of their prairie area.[1] Human impacts affect different regions in different ways, but the cumulative effect—multiplied across landscapes and regions—is to change the Earth in profound ways that are virtually irreversible on human time scales. The remainder of this chapter explores these impacts, laying out the major ecological challenges that this book will help readers address.

Habitat Destruction: Taking up Space

Habitat destruction occurs when native habitats are replaced by human land uses, such as housing, commercial developments, and farmland. When this happens, resident plants and animals perish. Any animals that do survive the conversion may seek refuge in adjacent areas, if suitable habitat exists, but these refugees may be unable to find adequate food, shelter, or territory if the habitat is already occupied and may perish as well. But not all examples of habitat destruction are alike in their consequences. The short-term ecological effect of habitat destruction depends greatly on its *thoroughness*, while the long-term impact depends also on the *permanence* of the changes.

The thoroughness of habitat destruction can be thought of as a continuum. At one end of the spectrum are places like lower Manhattan or large-scale monoculture farms, where native habitats have been completely obliterated. Small ves-

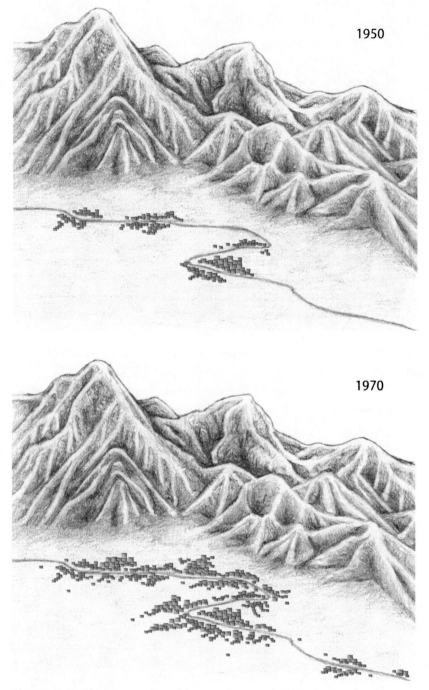

1950

1970

Figure 3-1. This time series of figures shows urban expansion for the hypothetical city of Exponentia from 1950 to 2000. As shown in this series, development tends to occur first on prime, flat, productive sites, moving later into more remote areas and those with environmental constraints.

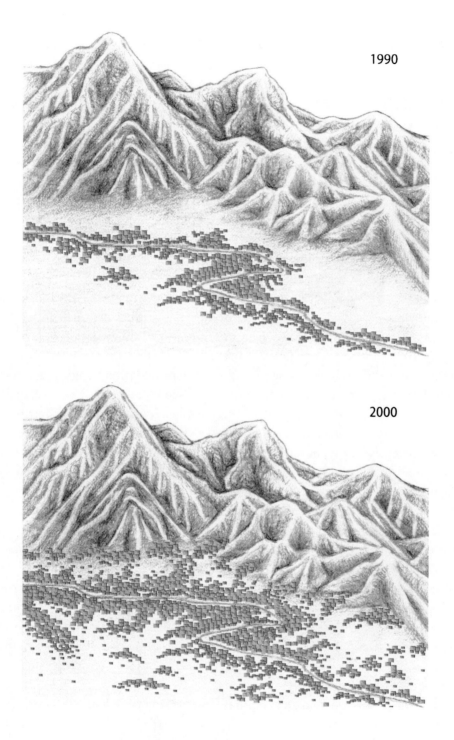

tiges of open space may remain, but they are probably nothing like the native habitats of the area. At the other end of the spectrum are human land uses that retain large areas in their natural condition—for example, a campground situated within a native forest or a lightly cut woodlot. In the middle are suburbs, parks, golf courses, college campuses, and low-intensity agricultural areas such as pastures. The thoroughness of habitat destruction in these areas varies greatly depending not just on the number of buildings constructed or the amount of pavement laid but also on the amount and quality of native vegetation retained. Measures commonly used in planning and development such as "percent green space" are poor indicators of habitat retention because they fail to differentiate intact native habitats from turfgrass and other manicured vegetation, which are often a biological wasteland for native species.

The permanence of human land use changes depends both on the nature of the changes and on the ability of the ecosystem to recover from them. In some cases, the native habitats can regenerate naturally and relatively easily following human land use changes. For example, much of the northeastern United States is heavily forested today, even though most of this region was actively farmed 100 or 150 years ago. Dirt roads, croplands, pastures, wooden houses, and even old railroad beds can all be reclaimed by nature within decades, as can be seen throughout the forests of New England (see Figure 3-2). These regenerated forests are not exact replicas of the presettlement forests, but their basic structure and function are intact, as are most of their dominant plant species.

In other cases, humans have changed the land and its ecology so greatly that restoring it to its original condition may be virtually impossible. In metropolitan areas, where we have paved much of the landscape, the likelihood that large-scale regeneration will occur within several generations is becoming more and more remote. Farming can also alter the land on a near-permanent basis. In many arid regions of western North America, intensive irrigation with groundwater has led to soils becoming overly saline from the small amounts of salt that are naturally found in groundwater. A 1996 report from the U.S. Natural Resources Conservation Service found that at least 48 million acres (19 million ha) of cropland and pasture are currently affected by salinization, an area equivalent in size to the state of Nebraska. The report notes that "reclaiming saline soils economically is difficult, if not impossible. Salinized soil is lost to agricultural production, at least in the near term."[2]

We are certainly not suggesting that humans stop paving or irrigating altogether but, rather, that planners and designers strive to limit activities and changes that alter the land in severe and long-lasting ways. As the examples above illustrate, land use changes that significantly alter an ecosystem's physical substrate—soil—tend to be less reversible (or take longer to reverse) than

Figure 3-2. This house near Lords Hill in central Vermont was abandoned many years ago. As in so many places throughout eastern North America, the forest has grown up around the house, covering what was once farmland.

those that do not.[3] In addition, some ecosystems respond more severely than others to outside perturbations (such as human activity) and tend to return to their predisturbance condition more slowly once the perturbation ends. For example, ecosystems where plant growth and soil formation are slow—such as deserts, tundra, and alpine ecosystems—tend to take longer to regenerate after a disturbance. Finally, different biotic communities regenerate at different rates; the basic structure of a prairie ecosystem may coalesce within several years (assuming that the soils are in good shape), whereas an old-growth redwood forest might take a millennium to form.

Although conservationists sometimes speak of extinction as the only permanent change that humans can effect, other impacts can change the landscape for many generations. Planners, designers, and developers should be especially careful about creating changes in nature that will not be undone in our grandchildren's lifetimes.

Habitat Fragmentation: Being a Bad Neighbor

Habitat *fragmentation* occurs when urban and agricultural land uses divide native habitats into discontinuous patches. A close examination of Figures 3-1a through 3-1d shows that the native habitats around our hypothetical city,

Exponentia, did not disappear in wide swathes all at once; instead, they were nibbled away incrementally and discontinuously as individual developments expanded outward. When formerly contiguous native landscapes become broken into isolated patches, several ecological problems can occur. In general, the smaller a habitat fragment, the smaller the populations of resident species it can support. Small populations are at much greater risk of extinction than large populations, and once a population is extirpated from an isolated patch of habitat, the site's isolation decreases the chance that it will be recolonized.

Fragmented landscapes also have a high proportion of *edge habitat,* where natural lands are influenced by adjacent urban or agricultural areas. These edge areas are unsuitable habitat for many native species because they tend to have a different microclimate and vegetation structure than *interior* areas as well as suffering detrimental impacts from adjacent human land uses, such as noise, dust, and agricultural chemicals. Also, the edge zone is often attractive to predators and thus is a dangerous place for many native species. In fragmented habitats, many open spaces that appear to contain native ecosystems may actually have limited habitat value because they have such a high proportion of edge. The process and effects of fragmentation are discussed in much more detail in Chapter 6.

Exotic Species: Bringing Unwelcome Friends

Since colonial days, North America has been overrun by *exotic species* (also known as *non-native species*) introduced by humans. The number of exotic species is especially high around ports and other coastal areas that were settled early by Europeans; in these areas, up to a third of the plant species can be exotics (see Figure 3-3). For example, according to the U.S. Geological Survey's *Status and Trends of the Nation's Biological Resources,* the small, cold state of Massachusetts has about as many exotic plant species as much larger and warmer California and Florida—probably because of the hundreds of years that Massachusetts ports have been receiving cargo and plants from around the world (Massachusetts has 1,019 exotic plant species, while California and Florida have 1,113 and 1,017, respectively).[4]

Most non-native species exist in relatively low numbers and do not cause major problems. However, some exotics spread rapidly, outcompeting native species and even altering whole ecosystems. These are known as *invasive species.* In his 1943 essay "What Is a Weed?" Aldo Leopold states that "good and bad are attributes of numbers, not of species."[5] While the definition of a weed is inherently subjective, most invasive species share certain traits that make them especially problematic for native ecosystems. According to Leslie Mehrhoff, curator of the University of Connecticut Herbarium, invasive species tend to have the following characteristics:

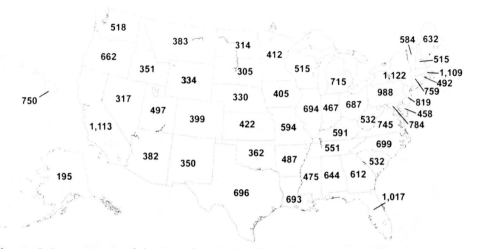

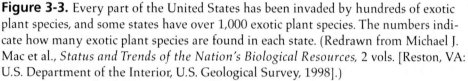

Figure 3-3. Every part of the United States has been invaded by hundreds of exotic plant species, and some states have over 1,000 exotic plant species. The numbers indicate how many exotic plant species are found in each state. (Redrawn from Michael J. Mac et al., *Status and Trends of the Nation's Biological Resources,* 2 vols. [Reston, VA: U.S. Department of the Interior, U.S. Geological Survey, 1998].)

1) Each plant produces large quantities of seeds or propagules;
2) The plants have very effective dispersal mechanisms;
3) The plants are readily established;
4) The plants grow rapidly;
5) The plants compete very effectively.[6]

Some exotic species can cause amazing amounts of ecological mischief, and a consensus is growing among biologists that exotic species are second only to habitat destruction as a threat to North America's native biota. Unlike housing developments and industrial parks, exotic species are often able to infiltrate and overwhelm native habitats before the general public becomes aware of the threat. Many exotic plant species have been imported intentionally, for use either in gardens or in erosion control and land reclamation projects—and some species, such as kudzu, have been imported for both purposes (see Box 3-1). Unfortunately, as international trade and travel increase, the problem of exotic species is likely to worsen. Although only a small proportion of the many exotic species that reach the shores of North America successfully establish populations, the flow of species is so great that every year brings new problems.

Habitat Degradation and Pollution: Fouling Our Nests

Like all living organisms, human beings create waste materials. We breathe out carbon dioxide and water vapor, and we excrete nitrogen compounds and undigested food. When few humans live in an area, our wastes are simply part of

Box 3-1
A Few Notorious Exotic Species

Kudzu (*Pueraria montana*), a native of eastern Asia, is a perennial vine of the legume family. The plant was first brought into the United States in 1876 for display as an ornamental vine at the Centennial Exposition in Philadelphia; in 1935, the U.S. Soil Conservation Service pressed this hardy vine into service to halt erosion on farmland and along roadsides, paying farmers to plant it. Eleven years later, kudzu covered some 3 million acres across the South, an area the size of Connecticut. In 1970, the U.S. Department of Agriculture listed the plant as a common weed, and today more than 7 million acres in twenty-five states are infested with it.[1]

While kudzu, with its blanketing, choking appearance, is impossible to miss, other invasive exotic species, such as garlic mustard (*Alliaria petiolata*), can sneak into an area virtually unnoticed. Some invasive species continue to be welcomed by the general public even long after biologists become aware of how damaging they can be for native species. For example, purple loosestrife (*Lythrum salicaria*) is widely planted as an ornamental even though it can escape cultivation and take over wetland areas with impressive and dismaying speed. Fifty percent or more of the native plant biomass in a wetland area can be replaced by loosestrife, which crowds out rare and endangered native species and disrupts the life cycles of many animals that depend on native plants. In some cases, entire wetlands can be covered by purple loosestrife.[2]

Saltcedar trees (several species in the genus *Tamarix*) not only replace native wetland plants in the arid West but actually change the physical habitat. Their deep roots appear able to draw more water out of the soil than the native species they replace, and they concentrate salts from the water in their leaves. Since they are deciduous, when they lose their leaves, the high salt content leaches into the surface soil, creating conditions that are inimical to many native plants. Finally, saltcedar grows in riparian zones and wetlands, disrupting these fragile and ecologically critical habitats.[3]

Animals, too, can run amok when introduced to favorable habitats. Gypsy moths (*Lymantria dispar*) were introduced to the Boston area in about 1869 to establish a silk moth industry on this continent (the project failed entirely). When the moths escaped from the backyard of Ettiene Leopold Trouvelot, the French painter and amateur entomologist who imported them, they began ravaging the neighborhood. Early attempts to control the spread of the species using scalding water and burning kerosene proved fruitless. In 1981, gypsy moth caterpillars defoliated 12 million acres throughout the northeastern United States, and their range keeps spreading.[4]

NOTES

1. R. Westbrooks, *Invasive Plants, Changing the Landscape of America: Fact Book* (Washington, DC: Federal Interagency Committee for the Management of Noxious and Exotic Weeds, 1998), http://www.denix.osd.mil/denix/Public/ES-Programs/Conservation/Invasive/intro.html.

2. Westbrooks, *Invasive Plants*.

3. National Park Service, "Saltcedar," http://www.nps.gov/plants/alien/fact/tama1.htm (accessed July 25, 2003); The Nature Conservancy, "Element Stewardship Abstract for Tamarix," http://tncweeds.ucdavis.edu/esadocs/documnts/tamaram.pdf (accessed July 25, 2003).

4. U.S. Forest Service, http://www.fsl.wvu.edu/gmoth/ (accessed April 14, 2000; Web page no longer available); National Agricultural Pest Information System (NAPIS), "Gypsy Moth Fact Sheet," http://www.ceris.purdue.edu/napis/pests/egm/facts.txt (accessed June 29, 2001).

normal ecosystem functioning, as are the wastes of other large animals. But when we aggregate into cities and concentrate large volumes of waste, or when we create and apply novel chemical pesticides or spread huge amounts of fertilizer on our crops and lawns—then we cause problems.

The effects of pollution on biodiversity are sometimes readily apparent. For example, Lake Erie and Boston Harbor both experienced radical ecosystem changes and the loss of native species because of pollution from sewage and industrial waste, although both have subsequently recovered significantly after the pollutant sources were addressed. But pollution also affects ecosystems in more subtle ways, including by:

- altering the chemical balance of ecosystems in ways that favor invasive exotic species or affect the competitive balance between native species
- weakening organisms so that they are more susceptible to natural threats
- eliminating certain pollution-sensitive species, often leading to cascading effects on other species
- reducing the structural diversity (i.e., the number of suitable subhabitats) within ecosystems.[7]

Overharvesting of Natural Populations: Being Gluttons at Nature's Table

Much of nature's economy is based on the "harvesting" of one species by another. Except for plants, which harvest their own energy from sunlight, most of the species on Earth get their energy by feeding either on living organisms (as herbivores and carnivores do) or on dead organisms or biological waste products (as decomposers and detritivores, such as bacteria, fungi, and some insects, do). In fact, much of evolution consists of adaptations by species to become either more efficient in their harvesting of other species or better at escaping being harvested.

When a few thousand humans fish in a river the size of the Columbia or search for nuts and berries in a forest the size of Delaware, we function like one of several large-bodied, effective predators and herbivores in the ecosystem. However, when we employ advanced technology, even the nineteenth century's relatively simple technology of trains, telegraphs, nets, and traps, we become something quite different: we can cause the extinction of what was possibly the most numerous bird species ever to live on the planet, the passenger pigeon (*Ectopistes migratorius*). With today's technology—fishing boats equipped with sonar, global positioning systems, and highly effective nets; or chainsaws and logging trucks—we can come close to wiping out species in any ocean or forest.

Global Climate Change: Changing the Rules of the Game

Even in areas where careful land management practices have kept floods and erosion at bay, planetwide events may cause problems. The Earth's climate appears to be warming significantly, almost certainly due to the increase in greenhouse gases that humans have released into the atmosphere since the start of the Industrial Revolution. Greenhouse gases, such as carbon dioxide (CO_2) and methane (CH_4), are generated by various human and natural processes, especially by the burning of forests and fossil fuels. In North America, electricity generation, transportation, and industrial production (in that order) account for most greenhouse gas emissions.[8]

While climate scientists are not yet certain what effects global climate change will have at any given site, they are developing a strong consensus about the overall pattern of effects. One of the more profound anticipated consequences is the rise of sea levels, which would inundate low-lying coastal areas. Sea level rise will result from three trends: the melting of the Antarctic ice cap as the global climate warms (thus adding more water to the oceans), the expansion of the water in the oceans as the temperature rises, and the creation of large icebergs that drop from the Antarctic ice cap into the ocean. If especially large icebergs calve off into the ocean, they will cause an immediate rise in sea level, just as the water level rises when a person gets into a bathtub. This is not mere speculation. In March 2000, the largest iceberg seen in four decades split off from the Ross Ice Shelf in western Antarctica. The berg was almost the size of Connecticut and measured 185 miles by 23 miles.[9]

Climate scientists predict that, if atmospheric CO_2 levels continue to rise as they have over the past 150 years, most of the United States will experience a 3°F to 10°F (2°C to 5.5°C) temperature rise by the year 2100—in contrast to the 1°F rise that occurred during the twentieth century.[10] The warming effects in northern regions such as Canada and Alaska are expected to be even greater.[11] But the predicted results of global climate change go far beyond a simple warming. Many regions will experience significant drying as warmer temperatures cause more water to evaporate from the land. As a result of the extra moisture in the air, some areas will see increased rains—especially an increase in the very heavy rains that cause flooding.[12] The distribution of ecosystem types is also expected to change significantly as a result of the changes in temperature and moisture regimes. Although strong consensus exists among climate scientists that significant changes will take place, different computer models yield different predictions about the exact changes that will occur and how these will affect different parts of North America.

The rapidly changing climate will cause problems for many species as the climatic zones to which they are adapted either disappear or shift more quickly than the species can move. Although some species that reproduce and disperse rapidly will be able to expand or move their ranges as the climate changes, few tree species will be able to migrate quickly enough to keep pace with rapid climate changes. Some habitats, such as the highland forests of the Sky Islands in the San Pedro watershed, could disappear entirely if the climate becomes too warm; their current inhabitants might then go extinct if there is no cooler place to which they can migrate. In addition, some ecologists are concerned that native species will not be able to move their ranges because human land uses will block their way. Such obstacles may render many nature reserves unsuitable for the species that they were intended to protect. For example, in North America, large east-west expanses of agricultural or urban land may impede the migration of forest species that would otherwise be able to expand their ranges northward to adapt to a warming climate.

Land use professionals should expect the effects of climate change to hit home during the twenty-first century. Planners and other local government officials may face new challenges related to mitigating damage from storms, flooding (especially in coastal areas), and other natural hazards; maintaining viable public water supplies as local conditions become drier; and keeping residents safe from wildfire in drier climates.[13] In regions where large parts of the economy depend on the weather, climate change may be a serious economic threat; for example, warmer temperatures in northern New England may threaten the ski industry as well as possibly undermine fall tourism and spring maple syrup production.[14] To protect ourselves from a warmer climate and more extreme weather events, we may spend more on cooling, insurance, and public safety.

For most or all of the problems posed by global climate change, technological solutions will be available—but at what cost? Does it make sense to create an environment that is increasingly hostile to human survival and then spend money to find clever ways to engineer around these self-inflicted problems? An increasing number of world leaders think not and have already taken steps to slow the rate of increase of greenhouse gas emissions into the atmosphere, with the goal of eventually stopping and then reversing the increase altogether. But even if we take immediate action to reduce greenhouse gas emissions, a lag of several decades or even centuries will occur before some of the effects of the reduction of greenhouse gases are felt. During this time, warming will continue along with the increase in severe weather patterns, and some climatic changes may be effectively irreversible.[15] Efforts to reduce greenhouse gas emissions have begun to take root at the local level throughout North America. Numerous state, provincial, and municipal governments across the continent have drafted climate change action plans that include such steps as making buildings more energy efficient, encouraging modes of transportation that are less reliant on fossil fuels, and even planting trees to remove CO_2 from the atmosphere. Another way of reducing greenhouse gas emissions—high taxes on gasoline—has proven very effective in Europe, where the average fuel efficiency of vehicles is much higher than in North America.[16]

Powerful Effects of Local Human Activity

As we will discuss in Chapter 4, natural habitats are in a constant state of flux: new plant material grows and soils are formed until a disturbance such as a large fire or storm comes along to destroy much of the living and dead plant matter (biomass) or to wash away soils. Over time, however, the total plant biomass in most regions remains roughly constant, and the same can be said for the total amount of soil. In contrast, humans in many areas create a constant, ongoing loss of plant matter from the ecosystem by cutting forests and keeping them from regrowing or by using natural landscapes as pastureland, allowing cattle, goats, and sheep to graze in a way that prevents the plant cover from regenerating. The loss of forest, shrub, or prairie cover from an area is in itself not unnatural, as all regions experience some type of disturbance or another. What is unnatural—and so difficult for nature to recover from—is the unending pressure that humans sometimes apply. As a survey of some of the earliest sites of agriculture and civilization reveals, such pressures can have effects that last for millennia.

In the 1920s and 1930s, spurred by the catastrophic soil erosion of the Dust Bowl era, Walter Clay Lowdermilk of the U.S. Soil Conservation Service conducted field studies of several cradles of civilization to see how early farmers had managed their soils.[17] He discovered that a number of the areas that are today deserts, such as portions of Israel, Egypt, Lebanon, Iraq, and China, suffered from severe soil erosion after several centuries of agriculture and animal husbandry. He found a few places in each of these currently desert regions that had been protected from overfarming and overgrazing, such as the sites of ancient temples and monasteries. These sites held soils that were still able to support native vegetation much as it was thousands of years ago.

In China, Lowdermilk found that deforestation along the upper reaches of the Yellow River had led to a massive accumulation of silt in the river's course and a concomitant rise in the river's level. This rise required the building of huge dikes to keep the river within its banks, but in 1852, the river burst through its restraints and killed millions who lived within its floodplains, all as a result of excess forest cutting upstream. Elsewhere in his travels, Lowdermilk discovered regions where soils on steep slopes had been carefully conserved for centuries or longer—in some cases, by farmers annually carrying baskets of soil on their backs from the lower portions of hillside fields to the upper, more erosion prone reaches. Similar patterns have held in recent years; deforestation and other land use changes in upstream areas have increased the severity of flooding downstream, as occurred along the Mississippi River in 1993 and in the Nicaraguan lowlands during Hurricane Mitch in 1998.[18]

Perhaps more remarkably, human land use patterns can change local and regional climate over short time scales, sometimes in profound ways that affect the viability of native ecosystems and local economies. Many of these effects are linked to agriculture, which can change temperature and moisture conditions by removing native vegetation or irrigating dry land. On the high plains of northeastern Colorado, for example, the conversion of grasslands to irrigated and dry agricultural fields appears to have led to cooler, wetter conditions both in the farmed areas and in distant mountain regions.[19] In southern Florida, extensive draining of natural wetlands to plant vegetable, sugar, and citrus crops may have led to an increased frequency and severity of winter freezes, one of which (in 1997) resulted in losses of more than $300 million and the displacement of 100,000 migrant farm workers.[20] This unintended consequence of agricultural cultivation is ironic considering that farmers moved into southern Florida in the first place to avoid damaging winter freezes. Cities can also essentially generate their own weather systems, as their dark paved surfaces and rooftops absorb solar energy and create *urban heat islands.* Compared to nearby rural areas, cities were found to be 1°F to 6°F (0.6°C to 3°C) warmer and have 5 to 15 percent less sunshine, 6 percent less relative humidity, 20 to 30 percent lower wind speeds, and 5 to 15 percent more precipitation (including thunderstorms driven by local heat convection).[21]

As long as human beings actively counteract their impacts on the landscape, we may be able to prevent broad-scale degradation for a time, but as the floods of China, Nicaragua, and the United States, and the deserts of the Middle East, reveal, it may be impossible to avoid a reckoning. The effects of humans on the landscape have been recognized for millennia, as Plato, writing in 360 B.C., lamented: "There are remaining only the bones of the wasted body . . . all the richer and softer parts of the soil having fallen away, and the mere skeleton of the land being left . . . now losing the water which flows off the bare earth into the sea. . . . There may be observed sacred memorials in places where fountains once existed."[22]

Part Two

THE SCIENCE OF ECOLOGY

In his essay "Must We Shoot Deer to Save Nature?" conservation biologist Jared Diamond poses a difficult but common dilemma by relating the story of Fontenelle Forest, a 1,300-acre (530 ha) nature reserve near Omaha, Nebraska.[1] Here, in the absence of native predators such as wolves, deer have become so plentiful that they have eaten most of the seedlings and underbrush, changing the forest's ecology profoundly and limiting its ability to regenerate. Suburban and exurban communities throughout North America face similar challenges when deer populations spiral out of control, causing not only ecological changes but also dangers and nuisances to humans ranging from increased incidence of Lyme disease and deer-vehicle collisions to crops and gardens devoured by these herbivores. At Fontenelle Forest and elsewhere, decision makers must choose from among uncomfortable options: do nothing and allow the deer to ravage native vegetation, or intervene by killing or sterilizing native animals that have obvious public appeal.

To address such ecological challenges, land use professionals need to understand how populations and ecosystems function. The next three chapters present a brief introduction to the science of ecology, focusing on those subdisciplines that are most relevant to planners, designers, and developers.

One effect of the deer population in Fontenelle Forest, if not controlled, would be to change the mix of species in the forest as mature trees gradually die and are replaced mainly by those species that are unpalatable to deer. In Chapter 4, we discuss this phenomenon of ecosystem change over time, which can result from such factors as the interplay of different species, the influence of human activities (e.g., farming and logging), and the effect of physical events (e.g., fires and storms). These changes may be rapid or slow, predictable or unpredictable—but all play major roles in shaping the ecology of a given area.

Especially relevant to the issues at Fontenelle Forest is knowledge about how deer interact with other species in their environment and what causes deer populations to rise and fall. Such questions are addressed by the fields of community ecology and population ecology, which are the focus of Chapter 5. These subdisciplines are especially relevant to land use professionals working in locations with rare, endangered, or other sensitive species, where, for example, it may be important to determine whether a proposed development would undermine the viability of a local population of a sensitive species.

Finally, the management of a given species at a given location, such as deer in Fontenelle Forest, will depend greatly on the landscape context. In Chapter 6, we examine the workings of entire landscapes: how the arrangement of different land uses affects their functioning, how the connectivity or fragmentation of natural areas influences the viability of different species, and how energy and nutrients flow through the landscape. These topics relate directly to land use and offer planners and designers specific recommendations for improving the ecological compatibility of their projects.

4

Change through Time

Here's a pop quiz. Look at the two maps in Figure 4-1 for a moment. Which map represents the landscape of central Massachusetts in 1830 and which depicts the same landscape in 1985? Also, what trend can we discern for the future of this landscape? When one of the authors showed these two maps to his seven-year-old son, the boy, like any well-indoctrinated child of a conservationist, said that the map showing the forested landscape was the older map and that the road-covered, deforested map was the recent one. But he was wrong—today's central Massachusetts landscape is largely forested, while the landscape of 1830 was mostly deforested by its human inhabitants.

To understand the processes that have created the North American landscape of today, let us consider the history of central Massachusetts in detail. This history is worth studying not because it is exceptional but because it is so ordinary: the concepts it reveals apply almost anywhere.

An Ecological and Land Use History of Petersham, Massachusetts

In the minds of many people, natural *ecosystems* are stable and steady, hardly changing over time, like the rocks underneath them. In recent years, however, ecologists have begun to develop a more dynamic concept of ecosystems. An ecosystem, whether it is an ancient forest or a human-modified system such as

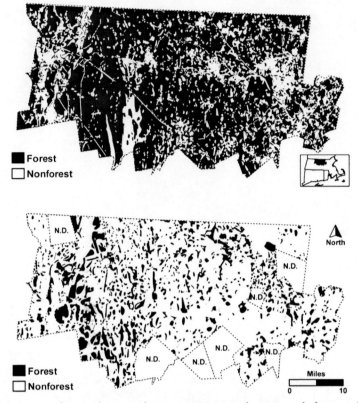

Figure 4-1. Maps of central Massachusetts in 1830 and 1985, with forests shown in black. Which map represents which date? See the text for the answer. (Images courtesy of John O'Keefe and David Foster, from John F. O'Keefe and David R. Foster, "An Ecological History of Massachusetts Forests," in Charles H. W. Foster, ed., *Stepping Back to Look Forward: A History of the Massachusetts Forest*, pp. 19–66 [Petersham, MA: Harvard Forest, 1998].)

those found in central Massachusetts, has both a specific history that has shaped what we see today and internal dynamics that will shape its future structure and composition.

Petersham, a small rural community in central Massachusetts, was first settled by Europeans in 1733, but it had a long and complex ecological and human history before that.[1] Approximately 15,000 years ago, glaciers covered Massachusetts and the regions to the north. Up to a mile thick, these vast expanses of ice scoured the landscape, scraping the existing soil from the bedrock. In the process, this glacial action brought large quantities of sand and rock to the landscape. As a result, the soils of this region are young (less than 15,000 years old), thin, and rocky.

As the climate changed and the glaciers receded, the first of several waves of ecological communities migrated into the area that would one day become Petersham. The first community to arrive as the glaciers receded 13,000 years ago

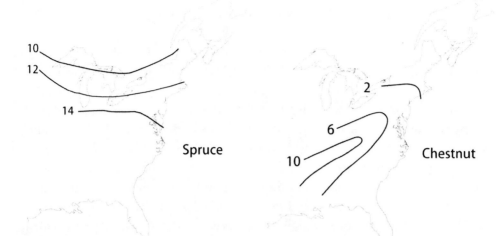

Figure 4-2. Different tree species migrated northward in North America at very different rates after the glaciers began receding at the end of the last ice age 15,000 years ago. As these maps show, spruce trees moved north much earlier than chestnut trees. The numbers on these images represent the northernmost extent of each species that many thousand years ago (i.e., the "2" represents 2,000 years ago). (Maps redrawn from Margaret B. Davis, "Quaternary History of Deciduous Forests of Eastern North America and Europe." *Annals of the Missouri Botanical Garden* 70 (1983): 550–63.)

was tundra, much like the communities of northern Canada today. Some 1,500 years later, spruce-fir forests arrived, which were replaced in turn about 2,000 years later by pine forests. Over time, as the climate warmed, species were able to expand their ranges northward, and other species that were adapted to warmer climates moved in from the south to displace them (see Figure 4-2).

About 10,000 years ago, at roughly the same time that pine forests reached the area, humans entered the scene. Two thousand years later, several deciduous tree species, including oaks, birches, and beech, arrived and gained a strong foothold, beginning the deciduous forests that have dominated the region ever since. By about 3,000 years ago, chestnut trees had moved into central Massachusetts, thus completing the modern suite of tree species that persisted until recently.

In approximately 1,000 A.D., Native Americans began practicing agriculture in the region, growing corn in addition to gathering wild plants and hunting. Beyond producing the obvious effect of clearing patches of forest to plant crops, these peoples used frequent low-intensity fires to improve habitat for game species, a practice that significantly affected many of the region's forests.

When European settlers began populating Petersham, the region's forests consisted mostly of white pine and hardwoods, such as oak, chestnut, hickory, beech, and red maple. But in the 100 years after European settlement, much of the town was deforested: first by subsistence farmers (from about 1750 to 1790) and then by farmers engaged in commercial agriculture (from 1790 to 1850). By 1860, only about 15 percent of Petersham was forested (as shown in Figure 4-1b). Pastures dominated the landscape of that period, with the richest soils being tilled for crops. However, beginning in the mid-1800s, with the opening of farms and ranches in the Midwest and the West and the development of rail transport between these distant areas and the urban markets of the East, many farms in New England were abandoned—and Petersham was no exception. By 1900, approximately 50 percent of the town was once again forested. Stands of white pine covered many abandoned fields and pastures, while other open-land specialists—gray birch, aspens, and cherries—filled other abandoned farmlands.

The turn of the century brought vigorous cutting of the white pines, which had quickly reached a harvestable size, but the overall trend of natural forest re-growth continued; by 1937, 80 percent of the town was forested. The very next year, 1938, brought a catastrophic natural disturbance that rivaled the impact of the settlers' clearing. A fierce hurricane swept through New England, blowing down many of the regrowing stands of forest, especially those dominated by white pine. The composition of Petersham's forests was changing as well because of the chestnut blight fungus (*Cryphonectria parasitica*), which was accidentally introduced from Asia around 1900. By 1940, the blight had virtually eliminated the once-prominent chestnut trees from Eastern forests. Today, at the start of the twenty-first century, the fields created by the settlers and the blowdowns caused by the hurricane are again hidden by forest, which blankets almost 90 percent of Petersham's landscape (see Figure 4-3).

At the same time that these ecological changes were occurring, human valua-tion and use of Petersham's ecosystems were also changing. For example, a 1952 town planning document focused on the ways that residents could derive greater income from forestry and farming in different sections of the town.[2] By 2003, lands that had once been valued mainly for their production potential were con-sidered important for scenic character, recreation possibilities, wildlife habitat, and watershed protection. With these values in mind, the town's 2003 master plan focuses on ways to guide and manage the exurban growth spilling out from Boston in a manner consistent with the town's historic rural landscape.[3]

As this brief history illustrates, Petersham's ecology has been constrained and shaped over time by the interplay of environmental and human factors, in-cluding the arrival and disappearance of glaciers, land use practices of Native Americans and European settlers, hurricanes, and ecological interactions. Many of these changes occur on time frames that affect the work of planners and de-signers, and understanding these changes can help predict the possible futures of

Figure 4-3. Modern-day Petersham, Massachusetts. This landscape was mostly farmland in the 1800s but is now once again mostly forested.

an area. Other ecological changes occur over much larger time frames, as discussed in Box 4-1.

Ecosystems Change Predictably, Sometimes: Effects of Climate and Succession

Ecosystems constantly change, but two types of change stand out as being especially predictable. The first of these has to do with climate change—previously, the climate change that accompanied the melting of the glaciers and, currently, the warming of the Earth caused by human greenhouse gas emissions. On the scale of millennia, ecologists would expect that, as the glaciers receded from the midlatitudes of North America, a specific sequence of different ecological communities would migrate into the ecological vacuum the glaciers left behind. One would expect tundra to appear first, followed by conifer-dominated forests and later by largely deciduous forests. A further prediction would be that, as the glaciers continued to move north, each community would follow them northward, being replaced by other communities moving in from the south.

The ecologists' predictions would be based in part on the patterns that exist today. Just south of the glaciers in Alaska and northernmost Canada lie the tundra communities, with the great northern spruce-fir forests just south of the tundra and hardwood forests farther south. Given that healthy populations of a variety

Box 4-1
The Long-Term Context: Extinctions and Fluctuations through History

The Earth has been gaining and losing biodiversity since the early days of the planet when life first appeared. In the nearly 4 billion years since, biodiversity has flowered. Uncounted species have evolved, diversified, and gone extinct; new combinations of species have formed into new types of ecological communities, many of which have disappeared; and mutations have created new genes, most of which have vanished without a trace. The Earth's biodiversity is like those fabled pots of simmering soup on the back burners of stoves in French kitchens: the pot stays the same, always simmering, but the ingredients and combinations within are ever changing.

By examining fossils, especially those of hard-shelled marine organisms such as mollusks, biologists have learned that even as life is always evolving new forms, species are also continually going extinct. Studies of fossilized marine invertebrates indicate a typical "life span" for these species of about 1 to 10 million years. For terrestrial vertebrates, species persist for an average of about 1 million years; in other words, roughly 1 out of every 1,000 terrestrial vertebrate species goes extinct per 1,000 years.[1] Thus, the Earth's living mantle continuously experiences a constant gentle background rate of extinction as individual species disappear from the pot of life.

Five times in the history of life, the Earth's biota has undergone a mass extinction qualitatively different from background extinctions. The most famous of these was the extinction of the dinosaurs, which occurred at the end of the Cretaceous period, some 65 million years ago—

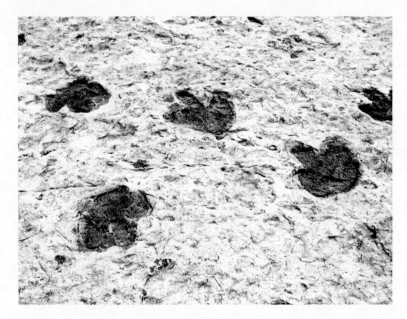

Figure 4-4. Dinosaurs inhabited the Earth for more than 150 million years but went extinct about 65 million years ago. All they left behind were fossils and footprints, such as these from Colorado.

although the most profound extinction actually happened much earlier, at the end of the Permian period, about 225 million years ago (see Figure 4-4). During that event, as many as 95 percent of the marine species alive became extinct, along with a high proportion of the terrestrial species. All of these mass extinctions occurred long before the appearance of humans on the planet and were probably caused by a variety of events. The Cretaceous die-off of the dinosaurs (plus many other species) appears to have resulted from an asteroid impact near the Yucatan Peninsula, which kicked up a vast cloud of dust. The dust obscured the sun, killing most of the world's plants and causing the extinction of many plant-eating animals as well as the predators that fed on them. The Permian extinction may have been caused by fluctuations in the climate and sea level at a time when all the continents were combined into the single supercontinent Pangea, although recent reports may implicate another asteroid or meteorite crash as well. Paleontologists have learned from the fossil record that it takes perhaps 10 to 100 million years for the Earth's biota to recover from a mass extinction.[2]

Clearly, loss of biodiversity is a fact of the Earth's history both in ever-present background extinctions and in rare but powerful mass extinctions. However, today a novel force is causing extinctions and loss of biodiversity across the planet: human dominance of the Earth. Unlike earlier mass extinctions, which were caused by geological changes or extraterrestrial bodies, this mass extinction is caused by one of Earth's species. Early on, as humanlike apes evolved in Africa, their effect was probably no different from that of other predators. Over time, though, as the human population grew and its use of technology increased, so did its effects. Today, as the dominant vertebrate on the planet, humans have an impact on biodiversity far beyond that of any other species past or present. Once again, the great ladle of mass extinction is dipping into the soup pot of life on Earth and removing a major portion of the contents.

Documenting the present rate of extinction is difficult because it is hard to prove the absence of any particular species, but many conservation biologists have estimated the current extinction rate at perhaps 1,000 times the background (prehuman) rate.[3] However, since biologists typically record a species as extinct only if it has not been observed for at least fifty years, we will not know until much later the magnitude of today's effects on the Earth's biodiversity. Even then, omitted from the tally will be numerous species that humans never recorded, classified, or even observed before they went extinct.

How much biodiversity will be left when the first species-caused mass extinction event ends? And how long will it take the planet to regain its previous level of biodiversity? The events of the next few decades, as the human population reaches 8 to 10 billion in the mid-twenty-first century, will define how much of the Earth's biodiversity survives. Native ecosystems and ecological communities can often recover, given time and space in which to flourish, but once species go extinct they are lost forever. Can we prevent the loss of so much of the planet's biological wealth? Or will we stand by helplessly as extinction after extinction moves across the face of the planet?

NOTES

1. Stuart L. Pimm et al., "The Future of Biodiversity," *Science* 269 (1995): 347–50.

2. Edward O. Wilson, *The Diversity of Life* (Cambridge, MA: Harvard University Press, 1992), p. 330.

3. Wilson, *The Diversity of Life.*

of plant species existed safely to the south and east when the glaciers were at their greatest extent, these migrations of general community types were reasonably predictable.

If global warming is indeed as powerful as current predictions indicate, then ecologists expect that the current ecological communities of Petersham will once again start moving northward while warmer climate communities, such as more southerly forms of oak-hickory forests, will move into the region.[4] These predictions are based in part on an understanding of how plant communities in areas south of Petersham changed as the glaciers receded and local climates warmed. In this way, understanding the past 15,000 years of change will help us predict some of the ecological changes of the next one or two centuries.

The effects of climate appear fairly straightforward: if local conditions become warmer (or colder, or wetter, or drier), then ecologists can predict with some accuracy the types of vegetation changes that will occur. Like everything else in ecology, though, such predictions are neither guaranteed nor precise. An ecologist who knew only the composition of North American plant communities of 13,000 years ago would almost certainly not have been able to predict accurately the communities of today. It turns out that many of the common plant assemblages that we know today, such as the Northern Hardwood Forest or the Beech-Maple Forest, did not exist in the same form 13,000 years ago. Instead, the species that comprised those earlier communities were rearranged into different combinations that form the patterns we see today. Thus, our proto-ecologist might have correctly predicted the broad patterns we see today—tundra in the far north, spruce-fir forests south of the tundra, and various hardwood and softwood forests still farther south—but not the exact species composition of the plant communities we now observe.

A second type of relatively predictable change is *succession*, the process by which the ecological community of a given location changes over years and decades. Succession occurs as different species colonize a site and are later replaced by other species. As farms were abandoned in Petersham, for example, seeds from nearby woodlots and forests settled on the old pastures and tilled fields. As ecologists would expect, annual herbs quickly colonized these sites, soon to be replaced by perennial herbs and shrubs. These were, in turn, replaced by so-called *pioneer* tree species—such as white pine, gray birch, aspens, and cherries—which were brought to the site by huge numbers of easily dispersed seeds and grew rapidly into young forests. Under the protective cover of this new forest canopy, another set of tree species began growing. These *late successional species*, such as oaks, hickories, chestnut, and sugar maple, germinate and grow well in shady conditions, unlike the pioneer species. Over a period of decades, the late successional species replaced many of the pioneers, leading to a mature forest.

Succession operates in generally the same way on forested landscapes world-wide. However, even within a small region, the process is never quite as simple as described here. The vagaries of nature—including unusual weather events, heavy fruiting years (known as mast years), and the spatial heterogeneity of sites—can change the pattern of succession greatly. A careful observer would notice that small populations of many of the early-colonizing species actually hang on through the later stages, just as many late-successional species appear early on as small seedlings that can easily be missed.

Understanding local patterns of succession can help planners and landscape architects predict how a landscape or a specific piece of land might change over 20, 50, or 100 years. The process of succession implies that the landscapes we see today may be very different a generation or three from now—and those planning for the future must recognize that succession may turn shallow ponds into meadows, as they fill with sediment, and turn open fields into forests. If designers want to keep landscapes looking as they do today, they may have to actively manage the land—for example, by dredging ponds and cutting back or burning woody pioneers. In addition to succession, global climate change may profoundly alter the types of plants and animals that live in a given region, requiring further management if we are to maintain anything that resembles today's landscape.

Ecosystems Change Unpredictably, Sometimes: Effects of Disturbance

While patterns of succession and ecological change in response to major climatic trends are reasonably predictable, *disturbances* that disrupt ecosystems are much less predictable, at least over small geographic scales and short time periods. A disturbance is any event that "resets" the successional clock by changing the environmental conditions or resources available to the biota. Disturbances can be natural physical events, such as hurricanes, landslides, or fires; natural biological events, such as pest or disease outbreaks; or human-induced events, such as plowing, logging, or mining. Disturbance events of all types and scales tend to open up habitat that is suitable for pioneer species by making available the light, water, nutrients, or bare soil that these species require.

To understand the effect of different disturbances on biotic communities, it helps to classify them according to scale, intensity, and frequency. For example, a localized disturbance, such as a single tree fall that creates a gap in the forest, has far different ecological effects than a widespread disturbance, such as the 1988 Yellowstone fire that burned over a million acres (400,000 ha) in and around the park. Similarly, a grassland ecosystem will respond differently to an occasional large-scale disturbance, such as a fire or pest outbreak, than to a chronic large-scale disturbance, such as cattle grazing. In many cases, intense or chronic disturbances not only alter the balance of species in an ecological community but also create longer-lasting effects by, for example, changing soil characteristics or removing key species from the system altogether.

The term *disturbance* is perhaps an unfortunate choice, but it is the one ecologists have historically used. As the late ecologist William Drury notes in his book *Chance and Change: Ecology for Conservationists*, many early ecologists viewed nature as generally being in balance and described those events that upset this balance as "disturbances."[5] More recently, ecologists have recognized that certain types of disturbance are a natural part of an ecosystem's development through time. For example, because of repeated disturbances (and the subsequent succession) at different scales, few natural forests are even-aged stands, in which all the trees germinated at the same time. The repeated and random effects of disturbance and succession—known as the *disturbance regime*—give forests and other ecosystems their mottled appearance of trees and stands of many different ages. Young and old forest patches create very different microclimates and microhabitats, resulting in a diversity of ecological conditions that supports more species than could be accommodated in a more homogeneous even-aged forest. Thus, ecologists now view ecosystems as containing not just a single biological community but, rather, a shifting patchwork of communities in different successional states, all held together by a common disturbance regime.

Types of Natural Disturbances

This subsection discusses the causes and consequences of several types of natural disturbances, which are organized according to the four basic elements that ancient Greek scientists recognized—earth, air, fire, and water—plus a fifth element, the biota. Following this discussion, we turn our attention to how land use professionals can apply a knowledge of disturbance processes to improve planning and development outcomes.

EARTH

The land provides its own disturbances, such as volcanic activity and earthquakes. Volcanic eruptions can wipe the ecological slate completely clean, leaving a sterile ash- or lava-covered landscape behind. But perhaps the most common form of earth disturbance is the landslide, in which a portion of a hillside gives way and slips, dragging down both small understory plants and mature trees. Frequently, all that is left behind is mineral soil with little organic matter—an open territory for pioneer species to colonize (see Figure 4-5).

But even in the case of a huge disturbance such as the Mount St. Helens

Figure 4-5. Landslides open up bare soil in forested areas, as shown in this photo from Monteverde, Costa Rica.

eruption of 1980, which generated the largest landslide in recorded history, a surprising number of ecological "legacies" remained to help ecosystem recovery.[6] Underground animals, such as ants, gophers, and moles; plants that were protected by snow; and roots and bulbs that rode along the top of the landslide all contributed to a remarkably quick, albeit patchy, recovery of the ecological community, to the surprise of ecologists studying the 200-plus square miles (500-plus square km) of drastically disturbed habitat.

AIR

Windstorms, such as the great 1938 hurricane that leveled so many of New England's forests, are a potent type of disturbance. But the effects of wind function at a wide variety of scales. One of the authors recalls leading a group of graduate students on an introductory walk through a forest. At one point, the group heard a noise like a loud train approaching, followed by the unmistakable sound of a tree falling in the forest. Later in the day, the group met up with another group of students from the class who described hearing the same wind and watching as a large tree was uprooted and landed right in front of them. Such tree falls occur all the time, but no individual tree fall is predictable. Most forests that have not been cut by humans contain a variety of age classes that include seedlings, saplings, mature trees, and dying trees; over time, individual tree falls and their resulting gaps help create the patchwork of different-aged trees that is typical of most forests.

While meteorologists can predict that a hurricane will hit a given portion of the eastern U.S. seaboard at some point over the next 50 or 100 years, they cannot predict the track, severity, or effects of a specific hurricane more than a few days in advance. When a severe storm hits, it may flatten thousands of acres or hectares of forest, or even more. These areas then begin growing large, even-aged stands, such as the ones that sprang up after the devastating 1938 hurricane. In sum, while no scientist can predict the precise local effects of winds or large storms, ecologists can say with confidence whether a given forest will eventually suffer disturbance from winds—either locally, as the students experienced, or over a wide region, as in the 1938 hurricane that ravaged so much of New England.

FIRE

Many native ecosystems, such as Ponderosa pine forests, pitch pine–scrub oak forests, and prairies, are subject to frequent fires. From a forester's point of view, a fire can destroy vast amounts of valuable timber in a very short time. From an ecologist's point of view, a fire can create ecological conditions that help maintain a natural community in a specific state or return it to a specific state. In many types of grassland, for example, trees will begin to grow if frequent fires do not occur to kill the woody vegetation. In time, grasslands left unburned may develop into savannas or even forests.

The Ponderosa pine forests of the American West are a good example of what happens to many forests in the absence of regular fire. Low-intensity fires, which historically occurred every decade or so in many Ponderosa pine forests, help clear away any buildup of brush. Without such fires, brush accumulates and provides fuel for major fires. Two human-instigated processes can increase the amount of brush in these forests: foraging livestock decrease the prevalence of grasses that would naturally outcompete young Ponderosa pines, and human suppression of wildfires leads to an increase in the number of pine saplings.[7] In part because of these human management practices, massive wildfires generally burn across portions of the West every few years; recent examples of Ponderosa pine fires include the Los Alamos, New Mexico, fire of 2000 and the 2002 Hayman fire in Colorado, which burned about 50,000 and 137,000 acres (20,000 and 55,000 ha), respectively.

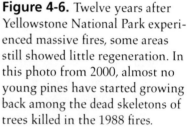

Figure 4-6. Twelve years after Yellowstone National Park experienced massive fires, some areas still showed little regeneration. In this photo from 2000, almost no young pines have started growing back among the dead skeletons of trees killed in the 1988 fires.

In contrast, by clearing out the understory of forests, low-intensity fires enable certain plant and animal species to thrive. If the humus layer (leaf litter and top soil horizon) of the forest has not been badly burned, vast numbers of herb, shrub, and tree seeds lying quietly in the soil seed bank may sprout right away.

By killing the mature trees of the forest canopy, some large fires greatly increase both the amount of sunlight reaching the forest floor and the availability of nutrients such as phosphorus and potassium, which are contained in the ash of the burned trees. These changes lead to rapid growth by any seeds that survive underground as well as from trees that can sprout from stumps. Some of these fires, however, are so hot that they destroy the seed bank, and the forest can regenerate only when seeds arrive from sources outside the burned area. This was the case in some parts of Yellowstone National Park that suffered especially heavy burning in 1988 and were not displaying much tree regeneration even twelve years later (see Figure 4-6).

WATER

Flooding can occur at many scales, with important ecological effects taking place at scales ranging from a few square yards to thousands of square miles. The great floods along the Mississippi and Missouri rivers in 1993, which breached more than 1,000 levees and damaged property in nine states, were a powerful reminder of just how large a disturbance water can create. In general, heavily silted floodplains are prime territory for pioneer species and, in less heavily flooded spots, for species that prefer moist soils. Farmers make use of the rich silt that covers a floodplain after a flood; in fact, the major grain crops are all essentially early successional species that get a little help from farmers who disperse their seeds into prime disturbed habitat: newly plowed fields.

Flooding on a small scale can also be critical to the mix of species present in a given area. Mary Dunn Pond in Hyannis, Massachusetts, is one of the world's best examples of a coastal plain pond. A rare suite of herbaceous flowering plants thrives along the shore of the pond, but this community survives only with the aid of periodic flooding. During especially dry years, evaporation shrinks the pond, opening up new territory for the shoreline plants. Young pitch pines soon grow up along the former shoreline, decreasing the habitat available for the herbaceous shore community (see Color Plate 4). If the water level in the pond rises when the pines are still just a few years old, they die—yielding precious shore habitat back to the flowering plants. If, however, the drought continues and the pines begin to mature, they can withstand flooding much better, and the pond shore community may become squeezed between the pines and the rising water. In this situation, both flooding and drought are critical for the long-term health of the pond-shore plants.

BIOLOGICAL

A *biological disturbance* is a discrete or ongoing event in which the proliferation of a plant, animal, or disease organism profoundly alters the functioning of a natural community. Outbreaks of the exotic gypsy moth (*Lymantria dispar*), for example, were so bad throughout northeastern North America during the late 1970s and early 1980s that they had the impact of an elemental force of nature. One of the authors vividly remembers walking through a Massachusetts forest one June day during those years when the trees were almost completely bare—it looked like late autumn. In those forests that still had some leaves, early summer walks were accompanied by a sound like gentle rain: the continuous dropping of thousands of pellets of frass, or insect excrement. Although most healthy trees are able to withstand up to a few years of defoliation, long-term gypsy moth infestation has the potential to kill many trees.

While exotic organisms frequently cause biological disturbance, since native species have not evolved survival strategies to cope with them, biological disturbance also occurs regularly in the absence of introduced exotic species. On a small scale, trees in a forest may succumb to any number of different insect pests or viral diseases, causing them eventually to die and create a gap in the forest canopy. On a much larger scale, ecologists have found strong evidence that hemlock trees (*Tsuga canadensis*) virtually disappeared from eastern North American forests approximately 5,000 years ago, almost certainly because of a pest or disease to which the hemlocks had little or no resistance.[8] Hemlocks began to reappear about a thousand years later but never regained their earlier dominance in these ecological communities.

INTERACTIONS AMONG DIFFERENT TYPES OF DISTURBANCES

Distinguishing among earth, air, fire, water, and the biota as sources of disturbance can be arbitrary because the categories often interact to create powerful disturbances. High winds frequently accompany heavy rains, and their effects may be multiplied because waterlogged soil does not support trees well. Winds also fan fires, making them more intense.

Rains that happen to follow a major fire can cause severe erosion and flooding because the vegetation cover that normally holds the soil in place will be mostly gone and the ground surface may have been baked into a hard sheet by the fire.[9] Just this combination of fire and rain occurred in Colorado in 1996 when heavy rains fell two months after the Buffalo Creek Fire burned 12,000 acres (5,000 ha). The resulting flood caused $15 million in property damage, killed two people, and clogged and fouled Denver's water supply.[10] Exotic species invasions can either weaken native plants so that they are more susceptible to other disturbances or, in the case of exotic grasses in dry lands, increase the frequency of fire.

How Species Respond to Disturbance

From an ecological standpoint, most natural disturbances should be viewed not as something bad but rather as an integral part of ecosystem functioning. A prairie without fire may not remain a prairie, as trees take over the landscape. River floodplains thrive with the occasional inundation by nutrient-rich silt that comes with floods, and they may suffer when flooding ceases. Coastal plain pond shores lose their characteristic suites of species when water levels remain constant, and forests that do not experience landslides and windthrow become less diverse because pioneer species have no place to grow. In fact, disturbances are so integral to the ecology of most regions that many organisms have evolved adaptations that either help them cope with the common disturbances of their region or actually require such disturbances.

COPING WITH DISTURBANCE

If an ecosystem regularly experiences a certain type of disturbance, then the plant and animal populations living there need to adapt to either resist or recover from these disturbances. Redwood trees (*Sequoia sempervirens*), for example, have very thick bark and can sprout from their roots or dormant buds under the bark, allowing these trees both to resist fire and to regrow after catastrophic fires.[11] Similarly, the great prairies of central North America have been subject to fire for millennia, and prairie grasses are excellent fuel for ground fires when they are dry. Summertime lightning storms start fires naturally, while archaeological and historical evidence indicates that Native Americans used fire as a method to manage populations of game animals.[12] Most prairie grasses respond quite well to burning: the flames clear away the dead aboveground leaves, allowing more sunlight to reach the new leaves that sprout from the growing portion of the plant, which survives underground. Many tree species that can otherwise live in these regions, however, do not respond well to fire. In fact, it appears that regular fires may have helped move the boundary between prairie and forest well to the east of where it would have been in the absence of fire.

In other ecosystems, several tree species benefit from fire. In the northeastern United States, oaks, hickories, and red maple sprout well from burnt stumps following fires that wipe out many less fire-resistant trees, such as hemlock, beech, sugar maple, and yellow birch.[13]

Animal species, too, have evolved in response to disturbances. For instance, the imported red fire ants (*Solenopsis invicta*) that have afflicted the southeastern United States for much of the past century are native to the Pantanal, a huge flooded grassland in Brazil. There, in response to the periodic flooding of their underground nests, the ants have developed the ability to form large floating balls from their aggregated bodies, protecting the queen and her young from the flood. This ability to fend off the effects of floods protects them against a simple home remedy that can destroy other pest ants: pouring water into their nests.

REQUIRING DISTURBANCE

Since disturbance is such a regular feature of many ecosystems, numerous species have evolved to require some form of disturbance in their life cycle. Some tree species, such as the sequoia (*Sequoiadendron giganteum*), sprout only when they land on bare mineral soil following a fire.[14] Similarly, many individuals of lodgepole pine (*Pinus contorta*) and pitch pine (*Pinus rigida*) actually *require* that their cones be subjected to very high heat in order to open and release their seeds.[15] In the absence of fire, these individuals are left with their cones closed and their seeds trapped, so that the trees do not reproduce at all. In a sense, the grasses and herbs of the tallgrass prairie also require fire for their ecological survival, for without fire these prairies would be invaded by trees and would eventually become savanna or even closed-canopy forests. Other species, such as the Eastern hemlock, require different forms of disturbance to complete their life cycle. Hemlock saplings may survive for centuries in heavy shade, only maturing when a tree fall opens a light gap in the forest canopy.[16]

Disturbance in the Context of Human Communities

The preceding discussion explains how natural disturbances are helpful, if not essential, for ensuring the survival of individual species as well as the long-term persistence of whole ecosystems. However, some disturbances—especially certain types of human-induced disturbances—can harm an ecosystem because they exceed its ability to regenerate within a short time frame. This could be the case, for example, with a large and destructive forest fire intensified by heavy fuel loads resulting from decades of human fire suppression, or with a logging operation that clear-cuts a native forest and replants the land with a fast-growing, non-native tree species. In either case, it may take decades between the end of the disturbance and the reestablishment of the native biota.

Large human-caused disturbances may even alter the abiotic (nonliving) components of the ecosystem so profoundly that regeneration of the native biota is virtually impossible. For example, the erosion and salinization of topsoil in agricultural regions throughout the world has resulted in soils in some areas that are so depleted that they can no longer support the native biota they once did. These soils may take hundreds or thousands of years to build up to their previous depth and level of fertility. On a smaller scale, paving and surface mining operations are two additional types of human-caused disturbance likely to result in very long-term alteration of ecosystems, absent deliberate human efforts to restore sites to their former condition.

It is important to note that not all natural disturbances are "good" and not all human-caused disturbances are "bad" in terms of sustaining native ecosystems. Some catastrophic natural disturbances, such as a volcanic eruption or the asteroid impact that is believed to have caused a mass extinction 65 million years ago, can have enormous costs—economic as well as ecological—and surely humans should avoid creating disturbances of this magnitude if at all possible. Conversely, some human-caused disturbances, such as light forestry and shifting cultivation with long fallow periods, are small in scope and have little negative impact (and sometimes even have a positive impact) on native ecosystems. Where human disturbances mimic natural disturbances, they tend not to have undue negative effects. In general, though, organisms have evolved to live with the types of "background" (i.e., noncatastrophic) natural disturbances that regularly occur within their habitats, but not with large-scale, intensive, human-caused disturbances. In the broadest terms, then, planners and designers can help protect native species and ecosystems by seeking to maintain or replicate natural disturbance processes while limiting human-caused disturbances to those that fall within the range of perturbations that native species have evolved to tolerate. We expand on this principle and its applications in the section on land management in Chapter 9.

An understanding of natural disturbance processes is important not only to promote conservation goals but also to safeguard human communities. For many land use professionals, natural disturbances are the monster lurking in the closet: they are dangerous and can strike at any time, but many plans and designs seem to pretend that they do not exist. Natural disturbances are chancy: no ecologist or meteorologist can say with certainty whether or when a particular disturbance will strike a given location. However, with knowledge of the ecology and history of an area, scientists can offer useful insights and some predictions about probable disturbances in a region. By studying the disturbance or climate history of a given region, experts might make any of the following types of predictions:

- There is a 50 percent chance that a category 4 hurricane will strike this city in the next ten years.
- This forest has a 10 percent chance of being affected by a major flood during the next twenty-five years.
- This tree has a 25 percent chance of being uprooted by a windstorm in the next century.
- A major fire will sweep through this patch of prairie every fifteen years, on average.

Emergency management professionals rank the size of many types of disturbance events according to how frequently they recur—for example, a "25-year flood" or a "100-year earthquake." This system is generally helpful, but several caveats must be acknowledged. First, there is rarely enough historical information at any location to know exactly how often very large disturbance events (such as a 500-year flood) recur. Instead, the return interval for large events is extrapolated from the frequency of smaller events using formulas that may not be entirely reliable. Second, return intervals may imply a sense of security that is misleading—for example, "We just had a major flood here, so we probably won't have another one for quite a while." In fact, examples to the contrary abound: portions of the Mississippi River experienced a 100-year flood just two years after the 500-year flood of 1993, while Boston in the late 1990s experienced two 100-year rains in less than three years.

Third, meteorological and ecological predictions assume that local weather patterns will continue to be the same as past patterns—an assumption that becomes less certain as the effects of global climate change take hold. If extreme weather events become more frequent, last century's 500-year flood may become next century's 10-year flood. Finally, it is important to differentiate between the severity of weather events and the severity of their effect on ecosystems and human communities, which is mediated by factors such as land use. For example, a municipal stormwater system designed to accommodate a 50-year rain may become overloaded during a 10-year rain if there has been rapid development and paving in the watershed leading to increased peak surface runoff rates.

As this chapter has illustrated, planners and designers would be wise to consider three types of foreseeable ecological changes in their work: disturbance, succession, and long-term ecological shifts due to climate change. Disturbance processes usually pose the most immediate and tangible consequences for human and ecological communities and are relevant in almost every planning or design project. Fortunately, information on local disturbance processes, such as floods and fires, is often readily available to land use professionals (see Appendix B). Succession and climate-driven ecological changes may be less relevant in heavily urbanized contexts but will be quite important in other situations, such as projects at high elevations or latitudes (where climate is predicted to change most dramatically) or projects that include lightly managed landscaped or open space areas. Examining all three factors is an important part of the ecological due diligence that should accompany traditional planning due diligence in the work of land use professionals.

5

Populations and Communities

Imagine that a developer is proposing a new subdivision in your Northern California planning district and that there are rumors that red-legged frogs (*Rana aurora*), which are listed under the U.S. Endangered Species Act (ESA), live on part of the proposed development site. The developer is aware of this issue and wants to do the right thing legally and ecologically, so together you decide to look for ecological expertise in planning around the frog. You begin with *A Field Guide to Western Reptiles and Amphibians*, a standard, if basic, field resource. The guide's range map for the red-legged frog shows this species occupying a continuous band along most of the U.S. West Coast, including your region (see Figure 5-1). Although it appears from the map that one can find this frog, the largest native frog of the western United States, anywhere along the coastal zone, the accompanying text says that the species "frequents marshes, streams, lakes, reservoirs, ponds, and other, usually permanent, sources of water. . . . When not breeding, may be found in a variety of upland habitats."[1]

The range map is generally correct in depicting where the frog lives (it does not live in Arizona or Idaho), but it is at the wrong scale to help you address the issue at hand—how to plan a subdivision to protect the frogs. To answer this question, you will need a deeper understanding of the frog's ecology. In this chapter, we present key principles that describe the ecology of populations and communities of organisms. These concepts are especially useful for planners, designers, and developers working on a variety of questions, including the following:

Northern Red-legged Frog

California Red-legged Frog

Figure 5-1. This range map indicates that red-legged frogs inhabit Northern California, but planners and designers would need more information to know whether they live on a particular site—and whether the threatened California subspecies, in particular, lives on the site. (Map redrawn from Robert C. Stebbins, *A Field Guide to Western Reptiles and Amphibians,* 3rd ed. [Boston: Houghton Mifflin, 2003].)

- Determining how to comply with state and federal endangered species laws
- Evaluating whether a development proposal will harm a particular population of organisms
- Deciding where to site a nature area or open space set-aside to maximize its value for rare species
- Developing a management plan for locally overabundant species, such as Canada geese or white-tailed deer

Levels of Organization in Ecology

To plan around the red-legged frog, we must first understand which organisms are considered red-legged frogs and which are not. This might sound obvious, but, in fact, the term *species* is one of the most subtle and difficult to define in all of biology. Most introductory textbooks define a species something like this: "all of the organisms that are potentially capable of interbreeding under natural conditions."[2] More advanced books may discuss twenty or more competing definitions of the term. In practice, however, biologists who describe new species use neither the "potentially capable of interbreeding" definition nor the more advanced theoretical constructs but, instead, base their decisions on physical characteristics and, increasingly, on genetic traits. Nonetheless, most ecologists agree that individuals from different species rarely interbreed successfully; if they do interbreed frequently, perhaps they constitute a single highly variable species instead of distinct species. Although the species concept is critical, it is extraordinarily slippery to define both because life on Earth is so diverse and because species are always evolving, making it arbitrary to select a point at which two groups of organisms are different enough from each other that they constitute two different species.

In the example of the red-legged frog, it turns out that the concept of *subspecies* is also important. The map in the field guide actually depicts the distributions of two subspecies—the Northern and California red-legged frogs—both of which overlap your district. This is important from a planning perspective because only the California red-legged frog subspecies (*Rana aurora draytonii*) was listed as threatened under the ESA as of this writing.[3] Taxonomists may delineate subspecies when two or more subgroups within a species exhibit clear physical and geographic distinctions. Individuals from different subspecies can interbreed (good evidence that they belong to the same species), but because of geographic separation the subspecies may be in the process of becoming distinct and may eventually become two different species.

As with the red-legged frog example, most species live in distinct populations. A *population* is a group of individuals of a single species that all live in the same place and that are at least somewhat isolated or distinct from other populations. Because land use professionals typically work in areas smaller than the ranges of entire species, populations are the ecological units of greatest relevance to most planning and design efforts. Because of their geographic proximity to one another, members of a given population are far more likely to interact with other individuals in their population—to mate, compete, cooperate, or undergo territorial disputes—than with members of other populations of the same species. Like most designations in ecology, however, the divisions between populations are not carved in stone, and occasional interactions do occur between members of different populations. However, with increasing human impacts on the landscape—farms, cities, logging sites, roads—natural ecosystems are becoming more fragmented and individual populations are becoming more isolated.

An *ecological community* consists of all of the organisms living and interacting in a given area. The community together with its nonliving environment—soil, water, nutrients, and climate—forms an *ecosystem*. Communities and ecosystems both occur in a wide range of sizes: for example, the bacteria living in a moose's stomach form a community just as the moose and other species of animals, plants, fungi, and microorganisms living in a forest form a community. On land, communities and ecosystems are often identified according to their dominant plant species, but boundaries are not always distinct; instead, there may be a gradual transition between one community and the next. In addition, the boundaries among different ecosystems and communities are often porous. For example, the sandhill crane (*Grus canadensis*) is only a part-time resident in several different ecosystems and communities: the far northern wetlands where it breeds, the Florida and Texas wetlands where it overwinters, and the fields and wetlands through which it passes while migrating.[4]

Population Issues

In landscapes heavily influenced by humans, the boundaries between populations will sometimes be rather easy to distinguish; for example, an eight-lane highway might create an effective barrier that breaks a formerly continuous population into two distinct populations. On the other hand, some species of birds, insects, or wind-dispersed plants may be less affected by the highway and remain as a single population. In the case of the threatened California red-legged frog, such human influences as urban encroachment and habitat fragmentation are causing distinct populations to become further isolated, while preexisting populations are being subdivided into smaller populations.[5] Later in this section, we will discuss why these trends are problematic for the red-legged frog (or any species).

Population boundaries in more natural landscapes are sometimes easy to distinguish and sometimes quite difficult. For amphibians living in a region of dry prairie, each pond will function as a distinct population because it is very difficult for individuals to move between ponds. Similarly, for plants restricted to small rocky outcrops surrounded by forest, each outcrop may constitute a distinct population. On the other hand, in a large region of relatively homogeneous habitat, it will be difficult to distinguish boundaries for wide-ranging species. Creatures that are able to disperse considerable distances, such as the red-legged frog (whose individuals have been noted to move over two miles or three kilometers), may form very large populations if their habitats are close enough for individuals to travel occasionally from one to another.[6]

It would be useful if ecologists could offer a simple description of the geographic area that a given population needs in order to thrive, but these areas vary considerably. For example, the San Francisco forktail damselfly (*Ischnura gemina*) is known only from the Bay Area of California and probably has a range of fewer than 500 square miles (about 1,300 square km), while it could be argued that all of the monarch butterflies (*Danaus plexippus*) of the eastern half of North America compose a single population.[7] In human-influenced landscapes where barriers such as highways and cities impede the movement of organisms, boundaries between populations may be obvious. In other circumstances, land use professionals may need to consult ecologists to determine where the boundaries lie.

Variation among Populations

A careful look at individual populations of any species shows that they are not all alike. Populations exhibit variation in many factors: the number of individuals they contain, the size of the geographic range they cover, and the quality of the habitat they occupy. In addition, populations tend to differ genetically from one another—sometimes in significant ways. This genetic variation is starkly apparent at the Seneca Army Depot in Romulus, New York, which has a unique population of more than 200 white deer.[8] These white deer are the same species as ordinary brown white-tailed deer (*Odocoileus virginianus*) found outside the depot, but the security fencing that was built around the facility in 1941 has isolated the population inside the depot from the larger population of white-tailed deer in the region. Over time, the recessive gene for white coloration expressed itself through the chance probabilities of genetics to become a common gene within the fenced-in population.

Genetic variation among different populations can also indicate that a population is fine-tuned in its adaptation to its local environment. For example, populations at the southern end of a species' range may be better adapted to a warm climate, while those at the northern end of the range may have a greater tolerance for cold. Genetic diversity within a species is critical for the species' long-term survival because it increases the chance that at least a few populations of that species will be adapted to respond to novel challenges or threats, such as changing climate or the introduction of new diseases or pathogens.

Interactions among Populations

When the opportunity exists for different populations of the same species to interact, the fates of these populations are frequently linked to one another. For example, if a population contains only a few individuals, it is at risk of dying out because of random fluctuations in population size. But individuals from other populations in the region may recolonize the nearly or completely vacant site, in what is called the *rescue effect*. In addition, migration from one population to another typically increases the degree of genetic diversity *within* each population (because new genetic information is brought in) while decreasing the diversity *between* populations.

The topic of interactions among populations has become an important issue for conservation biologists. One way to conceptualize the situation is to think of a group of linked populations—called a *metapopulation*—within which many of the individual populations are small and vulnerable to dying out.[9] If one were to represent each population with a light and watch the metapopulation over time, one would see individual populations winking out (as the species was extirpated at a given site) and coming back on again (as sites were recolonized by individuals from other populations within the metapopulation). In the process of ecological planning—such as habitat conservation planning on a development site or designing a new nature reserve—it may be important to study the metapopulation dynamics of one or more critical species. No easy guidelines exist, but in a given case, it is certainly possible that a nature reserve may contain too few populations of what was once a healthy metapopulation to keep the species from going locally extinct throughout the reserve (see Figure 5-2).

Not all populations in a metapopulation function the same way. Most importantly, populations differ from one another in their net reproductive capacity: some populations, known as *sink populations,* do not produce enough young to maintain themselves, and they survive only because of immigration from nearby *source populations,* which produce more young than they can accommodate within their own habitat patches. It is not possible to determine source-sink relationships by the size of the population or the size of the habitat it inhabits; just because a population contains many individuals and appears healthy does not mean that it is a source (see Figure 5-3). Conversely, small populations can be sources of new individuals because of such factors as higher reproductive capacity or higher survival rates (perhaps because of higher quality habitat).

Determining which populations function as sources and which as sinks is quite difficult. Even a multiyear study of the population sizes in different habitats will probably not give the researcher insight into source-sink dynamics. Instead, one must study individual organisms and their movements over time to see which populations are importing individuals and which are exporting them. Because such efforts require that different individuals be recognizable, the researcher must either physically mark individuals (perhaps with leg bands or dots of paint) or find genetic markers to distinguish different populations—and then track individuals over a period of years. The labor involved in such studies makes them rare.

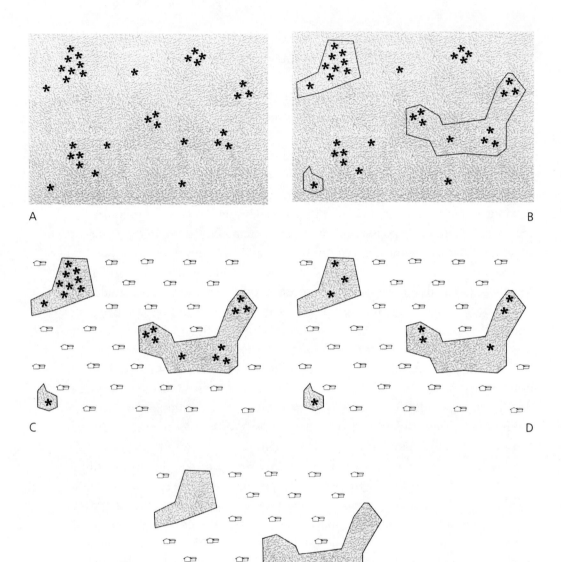

A

B

C

D

E

Figure 5-2. This series of diagrams illustrates how metapopulations may change over time as humans settle the landscape and fragment native habitat. (a) A healthy metapopulation consisting of roughly thirty populations that occasionally interact. (b) Nature reserves have been created around some of the populations but not others. (c) The land outside the reserves is developed, eliminating many of the populations. (d) Without the influx of individuals and genetic diversity from outside the reserves, the populations within the reserves begin to disappear. (e) This trend soon leads to extinction of all local populations.

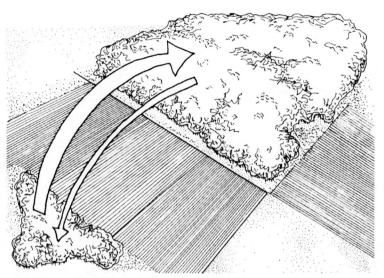

Figure 5-3. Source populations of a given species (such as the population living in the small patch in this drawing) produce more young than they can support, and some of these young disperse to other sites. Sink populations (such as the one living in the large patch) do not produce enough young to sustain themselves and will go extinct without in-migration from source populations. The arrows represent the flow of dispersing young of a species, such as a forest-dwelling bird.

Problems of Small Populations

Small populations are highly vulnerable to several types of randomly occurring problems, none of which typically affect larger populations. Of these problems, the simplest concern the basic demographic characteristics of a population—its sex ratio, birth rate, death rate, and so on.

DEMOGRAPHIC PROBLEMS

Imagine a population of birds—say, the whooping crane (*Grus americana*)—in which each mated pair has an average of two offspring live to adulthood, as would be the case for a stable population. But even though each pair *averages* two offspring reaching adulthood, some pairs have more than two surviving offspring while others have fewer than two. If a population has only a few mated pairs remaining, it is quite possible that most of the pairs will have fewer offspring than usual simply due to random chance. (It is also possible that most of the pairs will have more offspring than usual, but the focus here is on problems that occur when fewer offspring are produced.) If the trend continues for several generations—and this can certainly happen by chance—then the population could disappear. As it turns out, the sole remaining population of whooping cranes living in the wild dropped to fifteen individuals in 1941, putting the entire species at great risk.[10]

Several other demographic parameters are also subject to random fluctuation. Unbalanced sex ratios, for example, can be particularly frustrating for conservationists. Even if a small population is growing and the situation appears to be improving, a couple of years of bad sex ratios can devastate a recovery effort. A few years before it went extinct, the heath hen (*Tympanuchus cupido cupido*) suffered greatly from a skewed sex ratio. Of the thirteen individuals of the entire subspecies still alive in 1927, only two were female and eleven were male—a recipe for extinction, which was this bird's fate in 1932.

Such random variation in demographic parameters is easily demonstrated by flipping coins. On average, half of the coins you flip will come up tails and half will come up heads; if you flip many coins, approximately half will be heads. But if you were to flip two coins, you would be just as likely to come up with two heads or two tails as you would with one of each. This is exactly the problem facing a small population: some of the time, purely through ordinary random variation, either the sex ratio is skewed or the number of offspring produced is lower than usual.

GENETIC PROBLEMS

As human cultures across the globe recognize, it is generally better not to mate with close relatives, and this recommendation also holds true for many plant and animal species. Mating between siblings, or between any two individuals that are very similar genetically, can lead to double doses of rare but lethal recessive traits—or, at the least, to a genetically weakened individual. However, in very small populations, there may be no other option than mating with a relative. Thus, small populations may be especially susceptible to genetic defects that make their descendants less likely to survive and procreate.

As with the demographics of small populations, random events—for example, which individuals mate with each other and which offspring survive—can change the proportions of different genetic traits in a population significantly. This process, known as *genetic drift*, becomes especially powerful in small populations. To use the coins example again, while it would not be surprising to get 3 heads in a row when flipping a coin, it would be shocking to get 300 heads in a row. So, too, genetic drift can lead very rapidly to significant genetic change within a population, purely through random occurrences.

One of the biggest genetic problems in small populations, known as the *founder effect*, occurs when a small group of individuals emigrates from a larger population and establishes a new population. The archetypal situation is one in which several individuals are blown to an island or arrive on a drifting log, where they establish a new population of their species. While each of the individuals may be healthy, the tiny, new founding population almost always contains much less genetic variation than the larger population from which it sprang. This genetic bottleneck means that the new population, even if it increases rapidly, does not have the same genetic flexibility to respond to changing conditions or novel diseases as the larger population. In addition, most of the mating in the new population will occur between genetically related individuals, since they are all descended from just a few common ancestors.

Small populations are also especially prone to randomly losing rare genetic traits through chance alone. Imagine two populations in which a rare trait (say, resistance to a disease) occurs in just 1 percent of the population. In a population of 100,000 individuals, 1,000 individuals will carry the trait, but in a population of 100 individuals, just a single individual carries the trait. Through random events, the small population could very easily lose the trait entirely. At a later point, if both populations are subjected to the disease, only the larger one will have the genetic material that will protect at least some individuals in the population; none of the individuals in the smaller population will possess that gene, and the population will go extinct.

Implications for Planning and Development

The population issues discussed above can be distilled into a handful of guidelines for ecologically based planning and design. First, as we plan human land uses, it is important to understand the patterns of native populations and metapopulations across our home regions. Without this basic knowledge, it is difficult to plan in a way that reduces the threat of local species extinction. Second, we should seek ways to minimize habitat fragmentation. If populations become further divided with roads and developments, they will face a greater risk of dying out and have a lesser chance of ever being recolonized, because of barriers on the landscape. Even if they survive, isolated populations may become genetically uniform without occasional immigration from other populations, making them less resistant to disease or other potential problems. Third, the problems facing small populations are exponentially greater than those facing even medium-size populations, and the costs of remedying these problems escalate rapidly. It is far more efficient to keep populations that are potentially at risk in healthy condition than to wait until they are truly at risk, when we face the alternatives of losing them or incurring large expenses to sustain them.

Ecological Communities

Ecologists viewing a landscape will mentally partition it into different ecosystems—such as a grassland, a woodland, and a lake—each of which will be fairly distinct from the others. This section discusses several key aspects of ecological communities that are especially relevant for planners and designers.

Food Webs and Interactions among Species

Food webs—the feeding interactions among the species of a community—are an important topic in community ecology. No species on the planet exists in isolation, and organisms have only a few methods for obtaining energy and nutrients. To survive and grow, an organism must (1) eat other living organisms, (2) eat the waste or dead bodies of other organisms, (3) be given nutrients or energy sources by an individual, often of another species, or (4) produce its own energy-rich compounds using solar or chemical energy. Regardless of how an organism gets its food, it will most likely at some point have its body digested by others as part of the normal cycling of nutrients and flow of energy through ecosystems (see Figure 5-4).

The food web in Figure 5-4 shows that red-legged frogs feed on algae (when they are tadpoles) and various aquatic invertebrates; they also eat other frogs, mice, and numerous other foods. In turn, the frogs may fall prey to any of a large number of predators—including herons, bitterns, garter snakes, bullfrogs, crayfish, mosquitofish, bass, sunfish, skunks, and foxes—while aquatic beetles and dragonfly nymphs may feed on the tadpoles. Humans also capture the frogs for food (although this practice is now illegal and the size of the harvest has dropped off considerably). Certain species, such as bullfrogs and mosquitofish, also compete with red-legged frogs for specific food sources. Both bullfrogs and mosquitofish were introduced to California by humans for food and mosquito control, respectively, and now threaten red-legged frog populations. Another point of interest in this particular food web concerns the garter snakes, which include the endangered San Francisco garter snake (*Thamnophis sirtalis tetrataenia*). Here, we have a federally threatened frog serving as prey for a federally endangered snake.

From the standpoint of maintaining a functioning ecological community, not all species in a food web are equally indispensable. Some, such as great blue herons, are top predators and as such play a special role in the ecological community. Other species, such as the native red-legged frog and the introduced bullfrog, seem to be in the middle of everything—preying on, competing with, and being preyed upon by many other species. These frogs play a critical role in their community—and, unfortunately, the bullfrogs are just a little more effective in that role than the red-legged frogs, which are being squeezed out by the invaders.

COMPETITION AND LIMITING RESOURCES

Individuals within a community may sometimes compete for a given resource. In many ecosystems, a single *limiting resource* may prevent population growth for one or more species, and competition for this resource can become

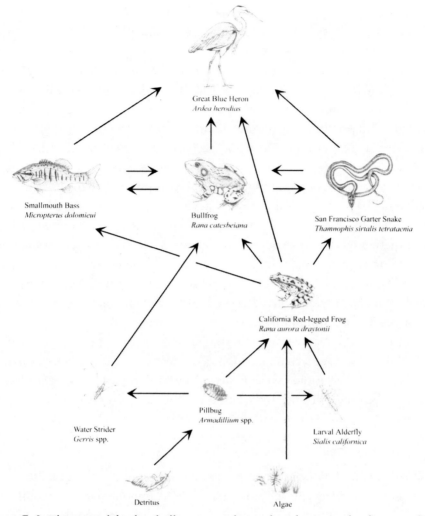

Figure 5-4. This partial food web illustrates relationships between the threatened California red-legged frog and some of the other species in its ecological community. As shown here, the frog feeds on numerous species and is also prey for multiple species, including the endangered San Francisco garter snake.

quite fierce. Common limiting resources include the following:

- Specific nutrients for plants (nitrogen, phosphorus, and potassium are limiting in different ecosystems, which is why most plant fertilizers include these elements)
- Sunlight for plants
- Food sources for animals
- Space for growth (in plants) or for territories (in some animals)

In some ecosystems, when a critical limiting resource for a key group of organisms is added to the system, the species composition and functioning of the ecological community may change quite significantly. Freshwater lakes experiencing *eutrophication*—the process of becoming more nutrient rich—have provided one of the most powerful examples of how the addition of a single limiting resource can change a system rapidly and drastically. Eutrophication of freshwater bodies is common in urban and agricultural areas, where nutrients contained in fertilizer, human waste, detergents, and other pollutants build up in the water. After a great deal of research, especially on lakes in Manitoba, ecologists determined that phosphorus is the key resource in many lakes that limits the growth of algae and cyanobacteria ("blue-green algae").[11] When phosphorus was added to the lakes, huge algal "blooms" developed. When the algae began to die, bacteria that decompose the algae (which had previously been limited by lack of food) experienced their own population booms. Since these bacteria require oxygen to decompose dead plant matter, they quickly depleted most of the dissolved oxygen in the lakes. Low oxygen levels then became limiting for many of the animals that had previously lived in the healthy lake, and many invertebrate and fish species died off from lack of oxygen.

This entire chain began with the addition of a single limiting factor—phosphorus—which caused a chain reaction that affected most of the species living in the lake. Given the serious consequences of eutrophication, land use professionals should be especially careful when designing projects to avoid overloading nearby wetlands and waters with limiting nutrients.

PREDATION, HERBIVORY, AND PARASITISM

Predation, herbivory, and parasitism are quite similar conceptually: in each, one organism gains its energy and nutrients by eating the tissues of another living organism. Predators kill and eat their prey, while herbivores and parasites typically eat only portions of their "prey," leaving it alive. The three interactions can be grouped as forms of *exploitation*.

In many native ecosystems, predators, herbivores, and parasites limit the size of the populations on which they feed. This can be seen as a "top-down" control of the prey populations, as opposed to the "bottom-up" control exerted by limiting resources. Introduced exotic species can wreak havoc on the native biota because they are free from the influence of the predators and parasites that kept them in check in their native habitat. (In fact, one method for controlling exotic species is to import predators and parasites from the exotic species' home ecosystems in an attempt to reestablish natural controls on their populations; sometimes, however, these attempts at biological control backfire, and additional native species suffer.) The effects of predators can be quite complex, however. Sometimes an increase in predator populations can drive down prey populations in a straightforward manner, while in other situations, an increase in predator populations can lead to cyclic or random variation in the numbers of both predators and prey.

Planners and designers should understand predation because humans introduce large numbers of predators—domestic cats and dogs—into their neighborhoods. In addition, we also increase populations of native predators, such as raccoons and coyotes, by offering them steady food sources from our garbage cans and dumps. All four of these predators are *generalists,* predators that feed on many different species. In contrast, predators that feed on only one or a very few prey species are called *specialists.* Unlike predators in natural ecosystems, in human-dominated landscapes cats, dogs, raccoons, and coyotes have a great backup system: most of their food can be provided by humans, so that predator populations are not limited by low prey populations. Even if their prey populations are driven quite low, the predator populations remain high and can have an especially devastating effect on their prey.

A colleague of ours learned about these principles in a graphic manner at her suburban home. She was an avid gardener and a cat lover and eventually had nine or ten cats living in and around her house. After a while, she found that her garden began to suffer tremendous damage from beetle grubs living in the soil. She also noticed that her cats regularly brought her little gifts, many of which were shrews. These mouse-sized mammals are especially effective predators of beetle grubs. As the cats depressed the shrew population, the beetle population rose greatly, to the detriment of her garden.

Those who design and manage human-dominated landscapes need to know yet another key fact about relationships between prey and their predators and parasites. Although most people do not recognize it, humans receive a great deal of free protection against plant-eating insects from wild populations of predators and parasites. Ecologists have long known that in many predator-prey systems, if both prey and predator (or parasite) populations are greatly reduced, then the prey population typically rebounds faster than the predators and reaches much higher levels than previously existed. This phenomenon becomes important when humans apply broad-spectrum insecticides, which kill both the pest insects and the insects that prey on and parasitize the pests. Thus pesticides, if not continually reapplied, can paradoxically lead to increased pest populations by decreasing predator populations.

MUTUALISMS

In addition to feeding on and competing with one another, different species can "cooperate" through *mutualism.* A mutualism between two species might help one or both species acquire or digest food, obtain protection from predators or parasites, or provide a hospitable substrate on which to live. By definition, both species benefit from a mutualistic interaction. For example, treehoppers (sap-sucking relatives of aphids) frequently take part in mutualisms with ants. In this relationship, the treehoppers provide honeydew (a sugary excretion on which the ants feed) in return for protection that the ants supply against predators and parasites (see Color Plate 5).

Species involved in mutualisms are especially vulnerable to extinctions of their mutualist partners. For example, the loss of one or a few bird species may drastically reduce the ability of a shrub species to disperse its seeds, which could lead to the eventual loss of the shrub as well. As illustrated by this discussion, conservation efforts can rarely afford to look only at a single species of interest but must also consider the interspecific interactions that connect the species to the entire ecological community. As humans remove parts of ecological communities either directly or indirectly through their activities, they risk unraveling much of the community structure, often with surprising or detrimental consequences.

Natural Selection: The Engine of Adaptation

The concept that organisms are well adapted to their local conditions has run throughout our discussions of biodiversity and ecology. Populations must respond to all aspects of their local environment: climate and chemistry, predators and competitors, and changes in the distribution of their habitats. The process that helps populations adapt to their physical and biological environment over time is known as *natural selection*. Natural selection helps populations find and capture new food sources, better escape or repel predators, or improve their camouflage, to name just a few examples from the natural world. It is also the process by which populations deal with human-induced modifications of the environment, such as global climate change, the addition of chemical pollutants and pesticides, and the introduction of exotic species into natural habitats.

Natural selection functions through reproductive success; because some individuals within a population possess better adaptations to their environs than others, they leave more offspring on average than the others in the population. As a result, the genes and adaptations of this select group become more common within the population in subsequent generations. Natural selection operates at a variety of speeds: organisms with short generation times (such as bacteria and insects) can adapt within years to changes in their environments, such as the introduction of antibiotics and pesticides.

For species with longer generations, however, selection is a much slower process. Consider the different responses of pest insects and such birds of prey as eagles and falcons to the advent of DDT and other pesticides. DDT was invented in the late 1930s and came into widespread use during and immediately after World War II. By the time Rachel Carson published *Silent Spring* in 1962, she was able to find many examples of pest insects having developed resistance to DDT and other pesticides because these fast-reproducing species had many generations in which to adapt. However, the slow-reproducing birds of prey showed no signs of adaptation to these chemicals, and their numbers dropped precipitously. This example illustrates that organisms with longer generation times—including most species of vertebrates and many vascular plants—will not be able to adapt to many of the profound and rapid environmental changes that humans are creating.

Community Associations

Each species has certain physical and ecological requirements that, taken together, help to define its *niche*. Individuals of alpine species, for example, can survive and thrive in cold and windy conditions, just as individuals of desert species flourish in dry areas with wide temperature ranges. In general, however, desert organisms cannot survive on mountaintops and alpine organisms cannot survive in deserts. Furthermore, even within a given climate regime, different species play different ecological roles, which further help to define their niches. For example, two closely related warbler species may forage for different types of food or search for the food at different heights, creating different niches and avoiding direct competition.

Species that belong to a group of ecologically similar species are said to form a *guild*. To the extent that the species in a guild are largely interchangeable, each species plays a less important role in the community than important predators—such as great blue herons, walleye pike, and dragonflies—do. If one mayfly species, for example, were to disappear from the pond community, the other species of mayfly, mosquito, caddis fly, and other aquatic invertebrates would continue to fill similar ecological roles, including being food for dragonflies.

Especially Important Species

Some species are important in their ecological communities simply because of their sheer bulk; these are known as *dominant species*. For example, several oak and hickory species are dominant players on the ecological stage within many forest communities of the eastern United States. As such, these trees represent a widely available and abundant food source for those herbivores that can adapt to eating the tannin-filled leaves and acorns of oaks or to breaking open the hard-shelled hickory nuts.

Other species, called *keystone species*, play especially large roles in their eco-logical communities even though their populations and biomass may be rela-tively small. If one were to remove a keystone species, the entire community would change in significant ways because the populations of several other species would either explode or crash. Keystone species exert their powerful effects ei-ther by changing the physical environment or by performing a critical function within the food web, as described below. In considering keystone species, however, one should note that there is no clear dividing line between keystone and "non-keystone" species. The relative importance of species in the functioning of their ecosystems spans the continuum from being essential—as in the case of the key-stone species discussed below—to being quite redundant, as in the case of species that fill ecological niches very similar to those filled by other species. (Of course, even a species that plays a redundant role in an ecological community may be worth conserving for many other reasons.)

KEYSTONE SPECIES AS ECOSYSTEM ENGINEERS

Some plant species are not only common within a given ecosystem but also strongly influence the entire ecosystem's functioning. Lodgepole pines (*Pinus contorta*) in the mountainous West, guilds of grasses across the prairies, and hemlocks (*Tsuga canadensis*) in certain forest groves in the East not only domi-nate their ecological communities but also set the basic parameters of their ecosystems. The pines and prairie grasses create settings that welcome fire, and any species living in those communities must tolerate fire or they will not sur-vive. So, too, the hemlocks, which flourish in acidic soil, make local conditions even more acidic as their fallen needles slowly decay, and any plants and animals living in the area must be adapted to the chemistry of these soils.[12]

Several animal species are also known for dramatically modifying their physi-cal environments. For example, in North America, Gopher tortoises (*Gopherus polyphemus*) of the southeastern United States dig holes that significantly change the landscapes where they live, and beavers (*Castor canadensis*) create water bodies and wetlands from formerly dry land. By damming a stream, beavers can quickly turn a few acres or hectares of forest into a pond, creating new habitat for aquatic creatures while destroying terrestrial habitat. Some 100 bird species and 20 mammal species make use of the ponds and flooded meadows that beavers create, not to mention the many plant and invertebrate species that do also (see Figure 5-5).[13] In addition to creating aquatic habitat, beaver activity resets the successional clock: after these animals abandon their dam and lodge, the dam eventually breaks apart, draining the pond, and creating a tract of nutrient-rich mud—the perfect site for a meadow to begin developing. With time, pioneer

Figure 5-5. Beavers drastically change the habitats around them by building dams that create ponds. These ponds eventually fill up with silt, producing a succession of different habitats for native species. (Photograph courtesy of Marco Simons.)

tree species invade the meadow, turning the site into a patch of early successional forest, which eventually becomes mature forest. Thus, over a period of decades, beavers initiate a sequence that provides a series of habitats for species that require ponds, meadows, young forests, or older forests for their survival.

When Europeans first reached North America, beavers were abundant despite some trapping by Native Americans for their pelts; somewhere between 60 and 400 million beavers lived across North America.[14] With the advent of European trade, however, demand for North American beaver products skyrocketed, since many types of stylish hats were made of either beaver skins or beaver felt. By 1900, the beaver population in North America was down to approximately 100,000, and many regions were almost entirely without these industrious rodents and their waterworks. This gap led to drastic changes in the landscape, with far fewer ponds appearing and slowly filling in as meadows and young forest. In the past few decades, populations have recovered somewhat; by late in the twentieth century, the beaver population had reached approximately 6 to 20 million, and their impact on the landscape continues to grow.[15]

KEYSTONE SPECIES AS TOP PREDATORS

Top predators in terrestrial systems often function as keystone species. For example, in places where wolves still remain in North America, they are generally able to keep populations of their primary prey species in check, especially ungulates such as deer, moose, elk, and caribou. Over most of the coterminous United States, wolves have been exterminated by humans through government-sponsored programs and by individual farmers and ranchers. In areas where human hunting has not replaced wolf predation as a control on the wolf's prey (such as many suburban and exurban areas as well as national parks), ungulate populations have increased significantly, with deleterious effects on the vegetation. In contrast, areas that have retained wolves, or where wolves have reappeared either naturally or aided by humans, tend to maintain ungulate herds of a size better suited to retaining healthy vegetation.

An examination of the ecological role of wolves in Yellowstone National Park provides a striking example of their importance as keystone species. In the past, significant debate occurred over whether elk populations increased or remained roughly the same after the last wolves were killed in the park in 1926. Biologists Steve Chadde and Charles Kay studied this question by examining a time series of photographs of the park's vegetation in different locations. The photos revealed that virtually all of the "tall willow plant communities" had disappeared following the extermination of wolves, apparently from extensive browsing by the elk.

The loss of these plant communities had further repercussions, because willow and aspen are especially important to beavers as food and as building materials for dams. Following the elimination of wolves, the park's beaver population dropped precipitously; animals that had been found along nearly every stream in the park in the 1920s were largely absent from the park by the 1950s. Some biologists have surmised that the elk ate most of the beaver's favored foods and that overgrazing by the elk led to poor water quality and rapid silting of beaver ponds. In sum, then, the absence of wolves in Yellowstone appears to have led to rising elk populations, which in turn led to changes in the vegetation of the park, which led to a dramatic loss of beavers. As discussed above, beavers are themselves keystone species, and their near-eradication from Yellowstone has no doubt had significant effects on hundreds of other species.[16] Another chapter in this story is being written today, since wolves were reintroduced to Yellowstone in 1995. With wolves present, the elk have become more wary and now largely avoid the river valleys where they had eaten willow and aspen for decades without fear. As a result, these tree species are reappearing, and so are beavers.[17]

Just as forested regions with wolves or beavers are quite different from those without, the same can be said for other keystone species. When a single keystone species is added to or removed from the landscape, the overall balance of species as well as the abundance of individual species both change considerably.

Planning for Ecosystems, Planning for Species

Faced with the challenge of trying to protect numerous species with limited resources, conservationists have developed several approaches to selecting and prioritizing targets for conservation efforts. Since it would be virtually impossible to prepare and implement conservation plans for every native species within a given area of interest, conservationists instead sometimes focus their attention on selected individual species or small groups of species whose protection might also help protect many other species. Planners and designers may find this approach helpful as well. For example, *umbrella species* usually have large home ranges and often require a variety of distinct habitats. If conservationists are able to protect a reasonably sized population of the umbrella species, such as the grizzly bear, they will also protect populations of many other species. *Flagship species*—large, charismatic species, such as whooping cranes and pandas—can prove especially useful in garnering public support for a given conservation project.

Keystone species are almost always important for conservation, and planners and designers should note whether any keystone species exist (or used to exist) in the ecosystems where they are working. For example, in ecosystems where wolves once kept deer numbers in check but which no longer contain any wolves, land managers must find ways to control the deer population. In some suburban areas, managers have chosen to use birth control on local deer herds, while in more rural areas, hunting by humans may be the only replacement for hunting by wolves. However, not all keystone species are easily replaced. Beavers, for instance, alter landscapes so profoundly and effectively that humans cannot truly mimic their effects. To have the effects of beavers on a landscape, one must have beavers, although, as humans are discovering, these animals can cause a nuisance in settled areas: flooded yards and basements attest to the ability of these ecosystem engineers to alter their surroundings.

Rare and endangered species are frequently selected as conservation targets, often mandated by laws such as the U.S. Endangered Species Act (ESA) and state endangered species acts. However, conservation thinking has evolved significantly since the ESA was passed in 1973. Whereas the ESA focuses on protecting individual species from extinction once they have become critically threatened or endangered, conservation biologists now recognize that often the most efficient way to protect species is to prevent them from becoming endangered in the first place by making sure that healthy, self-sustaining populations exist in healthy ecosystems. Thus, although much attention is still given to small populations of highly endangered species, many conservation organizations and government agencies now focus on protecting (and restoring) healthy examples of native ecosystems. For instance, planners—using such tools as their municipal or county master plan, development regulations, and land acquisition—might seek to protect viable examples of each different type of vegetational community found within their jurisdiction. By doing so, numerous rare as well as common species will be protected in the process.

This discussion highlights the importance for planners and designers of understanding both the ecological communities and the populations of critical species that reside in one's study area. When working to conserve an individual species (such as an endangered or keystone species), population issues, such as demographic factors and metapopulation dynamics, are most important. Yet, each species also exists within the context and supporting framework of an ecological community. Land use plans and designs should aim to protect examples of different ecological communities within a study area while considering how the size and configuration of natural areas will enhance or diminish the viability of populations. This critical issue of landscape configuration and its effect on population ecology is explored further in Chapter 6.

6

The Ecology of Landscapes

Imagine taking a flight across North America on a clear day—from, say, New York to Vancouver—and describing the patterns you observe on the land below. After lifting off, you would fly over industrial and residential landscapes crisscrossed by numerous roads and broken up by the occasional park or greenway. As you left the city behind, forests would begin to dominate, punctuated by farm fields and towns. You might see patches of lighter and darker green, indicating different forest types. Farmlands in the Midwest would appear as a rectilinear grid delineated by roads and hedgerows, while fields in arid eastern Washington watered by center-pivot irrigation might appear as series of green circles against a tan background of scrubland. Approaching the West Coast, you might see a checkerboard of clear-cuts within the old-growth conifer forest.

While these landscapes vary tremendously, all of them can be described as aggregations of three basic elements: *patches, corridors,* and *matrix.* When the landscape is viewed from the air, these become quite apparent, with corridors linking discrete patches in a surrounding matrix (see Figures 6-1a through 6-1c). This pattern of elements is one of the major organizing principles of *landscape ecology,* a relatively new branch of ecology that helps us understand the form and function of features on the landscape. Richard Forman, Michel Godron, and others helped this field coalesce in the 1980s after earlier work by ecologists, geographers, and landscape planners in West Germany and the Netherlands in the

Figure 6-1a. This image shows a large patch of forest plus a smaller patch of developed land within a matrix of agricultural land.

Figure 6-1b. In this photo, a forest corridor stretches between two patches of forest within a matrix of unforested wetlands and farmlands.

Figure 6-1c. Here, small patches of farmland are interspersed in a forested matrix.

1960s and 1970s.[1] Forman's 1995 book *Land Mosaics* provides a more recent synthesis of the field of landscape ecology.[2]

Landscape ecology examines how the spatial arrangement of land uses affects their function for humans, other life forms, and abiotic processes. Since planning and development are first and foremost about the arrangement of land uses within a site or community, this is indispensable knowledge. Landscape ecology also allows us to infer something about natural processes and biodiversity protection issues even when we have little ecological data about the landscape or the species that reside there. Thus, its principles can allow planners and designers to make useful generalizations or reasoned hypotheses in cases when they must make decisions based on incomplete information (which is almost always). Finally, the concepts of landscape ecology can be used for almost any landscape (urban, forested, agricultural) and at almost any scale.

In addition to introducing terrestrial landscape ecology and its relevance to the planning fields, this chapter surveys the other components of landscapes: aquatic ecosystems and abiotic elements. We then integrate these concepts with those in Chapters 4 and 5 to present the ideas of ecological integrity and sustainability—big-picture perspectives that can guide planners and designers in their local projects.

A Word about Scale

Planners and designers work at different scales and in different contexts. For example, a planner may work at the state/provincial, county, municipal, or site level, while a landscape architect might design a planting plan for a single lot or a development plan for thousands of acres or hectares. Ecologists use a separate hierarchy of scales based on biological, not political, organization. Even though there is no "standard" size for biological elements such as habitats and communities, some generalizations are shown in Table 6-1.

Although the term *landscape* is often used colloquially with a variety of meanings, landscape ecologists use it to refer to the area that one can see from a mountaintop or an airplane—an area where a given combination of local ecosystems or land uses is repeated in similar form, usually for tens of miles or kilometers.[3] Examples of landscapes might include the suburbs around a major city, an agricultural valley, or a tract of national forest that is managed differently from surrounding lands. An *ecoregion* encompasses many different landscapes that may be quite dissimilar from one another but that are united by common environmental conditions (such as climate or surficial geology), species, and disturbance processes.[4] Just as planners sometimes work across political boundaries, such as when they work in a multitown watershed area, conservationists often

Table 6-1.

Scale and Context for Planning and Conservation

Scale (size of landscape element)	Political/Jurisdictional (planners, designers, developers)	Ecological (conservation biologists)
Less than 500 acres	Lots, sites, districts, and zones	Habitats
500 to 5,000 acres	Sites, districts, and zones	Ecosystems and communities
10s of square miles	Cities and towns	Ecosystems and communities
100s to 1,000s of square miles	Counties and regions	Landscapes
1,000s to 100,000s of square miles	States and provinces	Ecoregions
9.5 million square miles (land area only)	North America	Continent
57.4 million square miles (land area only)	Earth	Earth

use landscapes and ecoregions—which typically cross political borders—as the primary organizational boundaries for their work.

What is the most appropriate scale at which to plan? The answer, actually, is "all of them." As planners know, it is often possible to be most successful at a small scale, where one wields the most authority and political power. However, grand achievements usually result only from large-scale visions. This paradox, of course, is the reason for environmentalists' exhortation to "think globally, act locally." Effective conservation does not occur in a vacuum; instead, as emphasized in Chapter 1, each site (or development or habitat) should be considered in relation to its context and at a variety of different scales. So, if you are a planner or designer, first select the scale at which you work from the "Political/Jurisdictional" column of Table 6-1. Then move to the right and look up one row and down one row. These are the ecological scales that should be considered, at a minimum, during planning. In the words of landscape ecologist Richard Forman, planning professionals should "think globally, plan regionally, and then act locally."[5]

Conservation biologist Reed Noss explores the topic of scale in his article "Context Matters: Considerations for Large-Scale Conservation," arguing that the selection of too narrow a context for biodiversity conservation may lead to negative consequences.[6] He describes how the managers of the 563-acre (228 ha)

Sugarcreek Nature Reserve in Ohio increased habitat diversity and species richness within the reserve by replacing maturing forest, which is home to relatively rare forest interior species, with more common habitat types. By reducing the amount of rare maturing forest in the reserve, however, they hurt the cause of biodiversity protection in the broader region.

Form and Function of Matrices, Patches, and Corridors

Imagine viewing your hometown as if you were a deer, an eagle, a tortoise, a salamander, or a beetle. Where do you live? What do you eat? Do you need to travel between different habitats, and, if so, how do you get from one to another? Who is trying to eat you, and how do you avoid them? These questions will help us examine how the arrangement of patches, corridors, and matrices on the landscape affect the species that inhabit them.

Animals have three different types of space needs: space for a home range, migration, and dispersal. The *home range* is the area used by the animal for day-to-day feeding and shelter. For some territorial animals, home range is exclusive, such that only one individual (or pair, family unit, or allied group) of that species occupies any habitat patch at any given time. But for most species, home ranges can overlap. Most animals have a minimum home range requirement and cannot survive long term if they lack this amount of suitable habitat. *Migration* is seasonal movement from one habitat to another, usually along a latitudinal or altitudinal gradient. Migrating animals require adequate habitat for each season as well as a suitable conduit for migration. Finally, *dispersal* is movement beyond the animal's typical day-to-day or season-to-season movement patterns; it is responsible for establishing new populations of a species and for interbreeding between separate populations. While dispersal is not essential for the survival of individuals, it is important for the long-term viability of populations and species. Dispersal, like migration, requires that suitable conduits for movement be available. Dispersal is also important for plants and other stationary life forms.

Matrices

The *matrix* is the dominant land use type or ecosystem in any given landscape. Examples of matrices include corn and soybean fields in eastern Nebraska, temperate rainforest in the Pacific Northwest, or housing subdivisions in suburban Los Angeles. The matrix is usually the most extensive land use type (based on area), but sometimes its dominance is the result of being the most interconnected or most "influential" land use type. For example, in a suburbanizing region, urban development may constitute the matrix even though it covers only

Figure 6-2. In this part of the western United States, the matrix land cover used to be scrub vegetation. In the lower part of the photo, the matrix is now an expanding urban area (with a few small patches of scrub vegetation within the matrix), while in the upper part of the photo, the matrix is still scrub with a few small patches of residential development and forest.

40 percent of the landscape. This is because the urban areas are completely interconnected by roads and exert strong influences on native ecosystems, which have been relegated to residual patches. The matrix can change over time—for example, from agriculture to urban at the edge of a sprawling metropolis, or from old-growth forest to early successional forest in a landscape with extensive clear-cutting. In these examples, what was formerly the matrix would become residual patches or corridors (see Figure 6-2).

Patches

Patches are created by several different processes. The unaltered landscape is naturally patchy because of environmental variability (different soils, microclimate, and water availability) as well as disturbance processes, such as fire, flooding, and windstorms. Humans create patches by developing small outposts in a natural matrix, such as when a few farmsteads are cut in a large forested area, or by changing the matrix so that only remnants of natural habitat remain in a domesticated landscape, such as bits of forest or prairie surrounded by cultivated fields.

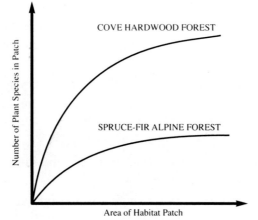
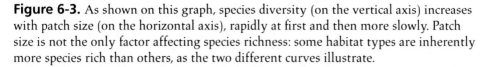

Figure 6-3. As shown on this graph, species diversity (on the vertical axis) increases with patch size (on the horizontal axis), rapidly at first and then more slowly. Patch size is not the only factor affecting species richness: some habitat types are inherently more species rich than others, as the two different curves illustrate.

PATCH SIZE

The size of natural patches affects the number and abundance of species they contain. Ecologists first noted this pattern in the early 1900s and developed species-area curves to plot the relationship between patch size and number of species (see Figure 6-3). In 1967, ecologists Robert H. MacArthur and Edward O. Wilson provided a theoretical explanation for this pattern in their equilibrium theory of island biogeography, which attempts to explain why certain oceanic islands contain more species than others.[7] The theory proposes that the number of species on an island represents an equilibrium between the number of new species colonizing the island and the number of preexisting species going locally extinct on the island. Islands situated near the mainland receive more immigrating species than do distant islands and thus tend to have more species. Similarly, big islands can support larger populations of given species than small islands can. These larger populations are less likely to go extinct over time, implying that large islands can support more species.

During the 1970s, some biologists began to apply island biogeography theory to the design of nature reserves, arguing that, all else being equal, large nature reserves and reserves that are close to other reserves will contain more species than small and isolated reserves. This is an intuitive idea, but a few caveats are worth noting. First, patches of terrestrial habitat are not true islands. The surrounding matrix matters greatly, because this matrix can either enhance species immigration or accelerate extinction. Second, the number of species in a patch depends not only on area but also on habitat type, habitat diversity (i.e., the number of different niches available), disturbances, and other factors.[8] The generalized species-area curves shown in Figure 6-3 illustrate that species richness can differ greatly by habitat type, even for two habitats occurring very near each other.

Finally, the species-area curve is not always a smooth line but may contain "threshold" points for different ecosystems. One important threshold in many ecosystems is the minimum patch size that will support viable populations of predators and large herbivores, which are often keystone species. A patch at least this large may be necessary to preserve an essentially intact example of a particular ecosystem. Thus, while bigger is usually better, conservation planners must also pay attention to habitat diversity, patch context, and size thresholds for different ecosystems.

PATCH SHAPE AND EDGES

The term *edge effect* refers to the different processes that occur at the edge of a patch versus its interior. For example, the portion of a forested tract adjacent to a suburban backyard would tend to be warmer and drier than the forest interior because of sun and wind penetration from the open backyard. The yard might contribute other influences as well, such as pesticides and fertilizers from the lawn, introduced predators such as cats and dogs, noise, and invasive species (see Figure 6-4). While there is no firm rule on how far edge effects extend, sev-

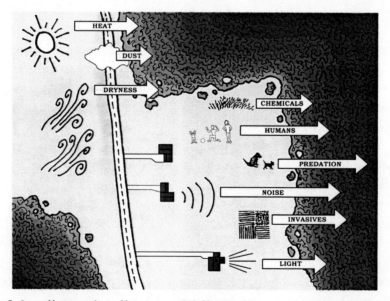

Figure 6-4. Different edge effects extend different distances from settled areas into natural habitats. The length of the arrows indicates the relative distance that each effect extends. (Please note that this diagram is not to scale.)

eral studies offer insight. Microclimate effects—such as elevated wind speed, elevated soil temperature, and reduced moisture—typically extend one-half to one tree height (roughly 30 to 100 feet, or 10 to 30 meters) into a forested patch but were found to extend as far as two to three tree heights (200 to 400 feet, or 60 to 120 meters) into conifer forests in the Pacific Northwest.[9] The extent of the microclimate edge effect depends on the forest type, the amount of understory vegetation, and the patch's orientation relative to the wind and sun.

Patch edges also tend to have different species than patch interiors do. Edges often have a high diversity of species but commonly favor adaptable *generalist* species as well as *multihabitat species* that depend on resources on both sides of the boundary. Examples of common North American edge species include white-tailed deer, raccoon, and skunk, all of which can be found in suburban and agricultural landscapes with abundant edge. By contrast, *interior species* are intolerant of edge conditions and human disturbances, or they require habitat characteristics that are found only in interiors. Examples of forest interior bird species in North America include the northern goshawk, ovenbird, and various warblers and vireos.[10]

The effect of edges on species distribution reveals an important tension among differing habitat management goals. For hunters, edge habitat is often desirable since many game birds and mammals are edge species. For this reason, land managers seeking to improve hunting opportunities have sometimes purposefully increased the amount of edge in a landscape by cutting or burning vegetation. However, edges tend not to contain rare or endangered species and also tend to attract generalist predators, which have been blamed for reducing populations of many rare songbird species, among other animals.[11] The edge effect on species distribution can extend for several hundred yards or meters from a forest edge.[12]

The shape of patches allows us to infer much about their origin and function. Some of these relationships have been studied and confirmed by ecologists, while others are essentially working hypotheses. Rectilinear patches and edges are almost invariably created and maintained by humans, whereas natural edges tend to be irregular, with curves and lobes. Initial studies suggest that curvilinear and lobed boundaries tend to promote wildlife movement *across* boundaries (animals often enter or exit a patch at one of the lobes), whereas straight boundaries promote movement *along* boundaries.[13] Round patches contain more interior habitat and less edge habitat than do elongated or convoluted patches of the same total area. However, lobed and elongated patches tend to be more heterogeneous than compact ones, which may promote greater genetic diversity and better resistance to pests and disease as a result of populations within the patch being partially isolated from one another.

Considering all these factors, what patch shape and what types of edges are optimal from a conservation standpoint? Maximizing native biodiversity requires both edge habitat and interior habitat. However, since edge habitat is usually abundant in human-influenced landscapes, the first priority for nature reserves is generally to protect interior habitat. A round patch with few irregular edges maximizes interior habitat area. Depending on the situation, this basic shape might be optimized according to the factors discussed above. For example, if the area is subject to disturbance processes, such as fire or pest outbreaks, the addition of lobes offers a "risk-spreading" benefit, reducing the chance that a disturbance event will affect the entire patch at once.

Corridors

Landscape ecologists use the term *corridor* generically to refer to any land use that is long and relatively narrow and either connects two or more patches or interrupts or dissects the matrix. Corridors run the gamut from fundamentally natural habitat, such as a strip of forest along a river, to human creations, such as roads, railroads, and pipelines.

Five major functions of corridors have been identified.[14] As *habitats*, most narrow corridors of residual or planted vegetation (such as hedgerows or buffers around a development site) are dominated by edge species that can tolerate inputs and disturbances from the surrounding matrix. However, some corridors are intact natural habitats, such as riparian or ridgeline ecosystems. Corridors act as a *conduit for movement*, not just for animals but also for plants, humans, water, sediment, and nutrients. To the extent that they help plants and animals move across the landscape, corridors often can improve the viability of populations and contribute to conservation efforts. While corridors may facilitate movement for some species or materials, they may act as a *filter* or *barrier* to movement for others. In this way, a corridor can reduce or eliminate interactions between individuals on either side, creating separate populations or, in the case of people, distinct neighborhoods. Finally, corridors can function as a *sink* or a *source* for animals, plants, people, water, air, heat, dust, or chemicals. For example, windbreaks planted in agricultural areas in the 1930s following the Dust Bowl function as a sink for dust particles and often as a source for insect- and crop-eating animals.

Because corridors typically serve different combinations of functions for different species and processes, it is important to tailor the function of any proposed corridor to the intended purpose. The most important factors influencing corridor functions are width, connectivity, and heterogeneity. A corridor of natural habitat that is tens or even a couple of hundred feet (tens of meters) wide will be mostly edge and consequently will be used mostly by generalist species. To allow movement by interior species and many large mammals, corridors must be hundreds to thousands of feet (hundreds of meters) wide to provide adequate buffering from the matrix and adequate long-term protection from disturbances.[15] The appropriate width of stream corridors is discussed on pages 200–1. Connectivity must be evaluated not just spatially (i.e., whether the green ribbon on the map is continuous) but also functionally for the purposes of moving a specific animal or substance.[16] Factors that have been demonstrated or are believed to make corridors better for animal movement include few narrows or gaps, fairly straight configuration, little environmental heterogeneity, little crisscrossing of streams or roads, and shortness of length.[17]

BENEFITS OF HABITAT CORRIDORS IN FRAGMENTED LANDSCAPES

In the popular and semitechnical literature, such as the magazines and Web sites of some conservation groups, corridors are sometimes presented as an answer to most conservation problems. For example, the Web site of Ecotrust, a conservation group based in Portland, Oregon, states that "wildlife corridors are necessary because they maintain biodiversity, allow populations to interbreed, and provide access to larger habitats."[18] The typical argument for corridors goes like this. Before human land uses, such as agriculture and urban areas, came to dominate, the landscape consisted of large blocks of intact habitat that allowed organisms wide freedom of movement. Today's patterns of human land use have fragmented the landscape and cut off patches of native habitats from one another, thus isolating small populations of organisms that were once part of larger populations. These small populations face an increased risk of extinction. The solution, according to many conservation biologists, is to decrease isolation by retaining (or creating) corridors that link patches of native habitat.

The value of corridors for biodiversity conservation is the subject of current debate and research among ecologists. Thus far, scientific evidence for the efficacy of corridors is limited, but at least a dozen studies offer observational and experimental evidence that corridors facilitate movement and dispersal between habitat patches.[19] Given the difficulty of conducting large-scale ecological experiments, most of this evidence relates to plants and smaller animals (insects, birds, and small mammals) on relatively small habitat patches. This, however, is the scale at which most planners and designers work. At the same time, the scientific literature does not yet offer much evidence to support the concerns of some ecologists that habitat corridors are detrimental in certain situations—for example, by enticing animals into habitats where mortality risk from predators or road crossings is higher, or by enhancing the spread of pests, wildlife diseases, and exotic invasive species. Nevertheless, it is worth keeping these cautions in mind. Ensuring that any natural corridors consist of high-quality habitat with native vegetation would help minimize several of these concerns. A greater practical "cost" of corridors is that limited resources will be spent to create corridors of marginal conservation value rather than being used for more worthy projects.[20]

We can gain additional insight on the value and optimal design of corridors by once again thinking of the landscape from the perspective of different organisms. One question is whether corridors are broadly effective—helping a wide range of species—or whether they should be employed specifically to help a given species of concern. In 1999, conservation biologist Andy Dobson and fourteen coauthors representing a diversity of opinions answered this question by suggesting that "the first step in the analysis of corridor capability [should be] the selection of target species. . . . The idea of a generic landscape corridor—connectivity for the sake of connectivity—is more aesthetic than scientific and will generally be dismissed in the hard light of scientific review."[21] As Dobson and his colleagues point out, corridors can be especially useful in carefully targeted conservation efforts, such as helping to sustain populations of species that are migratory or nomadic, or populations that are not likely to be viable in the long term in established nature reserves.

Given the accumulating evidence that corridors can improve the viability of populations, and given the great difficulty and expense of creating corridors after a region becomes developed, it is wise to set aside corridors prior to or during the development of a region. If we wait until we have comprehensive scientific data about what kinds of corridors help what species, it may be impossible or at least prohibitively expensive to "retrofit" a landscape with habitat corridors later. Accordingly, when a major project such as a road or shopping center is proposed that would threaten habitat connectivity, planners and designers should presume that the loss of connectivity would hurt the local biota and take steps to reduce or mitigate this loss unless site-specific studies demonstrate otherwise. On the other hand, when faced with the question of whether to spend limited conservation resources to protect a corridor at a specific location, planners and conservationists would be wise to invest in ecological studies to determine whether the proposed corridor would actually help the target species. If not, resources can be redirected to address a more pressing need.

EFFECTS OF HUMAN CORRIDORS

Numerous researchers have studied the effects of human corridors—particularly roads—on populations and ecosystems. The most important ecological effect of human corridors is as a filter or barrier to the movement or dispersal of native species. This and other effects of common human corridors are profiled below and in Figure 6-5.

Roadkills occur in staggering numbers, with an estimated 1 million vertebrates per day killed on roads in the United States alone.[22] The best way to reduce this carnage is to limit the number of roads—an important goal for conservation-minded planners and developers. Short of closing roads or not building them in the first place, the most successful technique for mitigating roadkills is to install fencing that restricts animal movement onto the road in conjunction with underpasses or overpasses that allow animals to cross the road safely.[23] Underpasses range from shallow tunnels for salamanders and other amphibians to wide swaths of vegetation with the roadway elevated high above (see Figures 6-6 and 7-5e). Prefabricated underpasses (culverts) for amphibians and small mammals are relatively inexpensive and could be incorporated into residential subdivisions or commercial developments where a proposed road will divide a formerly contiguous population or isolate feeding, breeding, or nesting habitats.

Overpasses can consist of raised arches over the highway (in some cases, up to a few hundred feet wide) or bridges covered with natural vegetation that are flush with the surrounding landscape and pass over a sunken roadbed (see Figure 7-5d). Any overpass or underpass system must be paired with effective fencing, berms, or other barriers to direct animals toward the crossing points. Wildlife crossing systems should be designed around the needs of specific target species: the largest animals of interest and the species most sensitive to the road barrier. Accommodating the needs of these species should result in a system that works for most other species. These needs should determine where the crossing structure is placed, whether it passes over or under the road, how large it is, and what material is used for the surface.

In addition to reducing roadkills and enhancing wildlife movement, sensitive road design should address the other major ecological impacts of roads, including altered drainage and hydrology, pollutant runoff, and the spread of non-native vegetation. Regarding vegetation, a recent effort to enhance roadside habitat has involved planting native grasses, flowers, and shrubs rather than non-native species.[24] This movement combines earlier objectives for roadside vegetation management—stabilizing slopes, providing a "clear zone" for errant vehicles, beautifying the roadside, and minimizing maintenance costs—with a new understanding of the potential ecological value of roadside habitats. For example, Iowa's Living Roadway Program encourages and offers grants for planting native species, including restored prairie communities, alongside the state's roads. Roadside managers and ecologists have found that the use of indigenous prairie plants as well as less-intensive mowing and herbicide spraying regimens (or none at all) actually reduces weed and erosion problems while improving habitat for native grassland plants, birds, and insects.[25]

State programs are not the only way to promote ecologically compatible roadside management. Planners at the municipal or county level can encourage or require the use of native roadside vegetation in new public and private devel-

Figure 6-5a. Of all corridor types, *median-divided superhighways* are the most likely to inhibit animal crossings. Such barriers cause populations on either side of the highway to be isolated from one another, making each subpopulation more vulnerable to extinction. The isolation effect applies to birds as well as insects, reptiles, amphibians, and mammals. The edge effect of multilane highways extends anywhere from a few hundred feet for many mammals and pollution-sensitive plants to a mile or more for noise-sensitive grassland birds and other species. Most inhabitants of road edges and medians tend to be edge species and exotics. (*Sources:* H.-J. Mader, "Animal Habitat Isolation by Roads and Agricultural Fields," *Biological Conservation* 29 (1984): 81–96; Richard T. T. Forman et al., *Road Ecology: Science and Solutions* [Washington, DC: Island Press, 2003].)

Figure 6-5b. *High-speed two-lane roads* have the highest road-kill rates because more animals attempt to cross these roads than try to cross superhighways. Many animals are lured to the road or roadside by the prospect of food, salt, a warm surface for basking, or even the water that collects in puddles after a rainstorm. Road-kill rates are expected to be high where a natural movement corridor intersects the road. Road mortality is not likely to threaten populations of most rapidly reproducing animals but can be a major factor for rare or less fecund species, especially large mammals. (*Sources:* Patricia A. White and Michelle Ernst, *Second Nature: Improving Transportation without Putting Nature Second* [Washington, DC: Defenders of Wildlife, 2003]; A. F. Bennett, "Roads, Roadsides and Wildlife Conservation: A Review," in Denis A. Saunders and Richard J. Hobbs, eds., *Nature Conservation 2: The Role of Corridors* [Chipping Norton, Australia: Surrey Beatty, 1991], pp. 99–117.)

Figure 6-5c. A major effect of *secondary roads* is "taking up space" on the landscape. Public roads and adjacent roadsides in the United States occupy roughly 27 million acres, or 11 million hectares (1.2 percent of the U.S. land area), and the "road effect zone" of degraded habitat near these roads encompasses almost one-fifth of the U.S. land area. The use of open roadsides as a conduit for animal movement is the exception rather than the rule, although road corridors do facilitate the spread of certain invasive species. Even a narrow paved road can function as a barrier to movement for many insect and small mammal species. Roads that separate amphibian breeding habitat from adult habitat may have serious impacts on amphibian populations. (*Sources:* Forman et al., *Road Ecology*; Richard T. T. Forman, "Estimate of the Area Affected Ecologically by the Road System in the United States," *Conservation Biology* 14, no. 1 [2000]: 31–35; B. A. Wilcox and D. D. Murphy, "Migration and Control of Purple Loosestrife [*Lythrium salicaria L.*] along Highway Corridors," *Environmental Management* 13 [1989]: 365–70; Richard T. T. Forman and Lauren E. Alexander, "Roads and Their Major Ecological Effects," *Annual Review of Ecology and Systematics* 29 [1998]: 207–31.)

Figure 6-5d. While they are less of a barrier than paved roads for many species, *narrow, unpaved roads* still inhibit movement by many insects and small mammals. Predators are known to travel along unpaved roads with little traffic. Even lightly used forest roads promote human incursions into natural areas for hunting and logging and help spread invasive species, whose seeds often hitch a ride on vehicles. Large mammals, such as bear and elk, are very sensitive to road density. For this reason, some land managers have proposed road closings in natural and seminatural areas to stabilize populations of rare interior species. (*Source:* Bennett, "Roads, Roadsides and Wildlife Conservation.")

Figure 6-5e. *Rail corridors* are rarely completely devoid of native species, but the habitat value of these areas varies greatly depending on how they are managed. Remnant strips of natural vegetation are the most favorable for native species, and rail corridors are often more likely than roads to exhibit such "benign neglect." For example, in agricultural areas of the Midwest, rail corridors contain some of the last remnants of native prairie and have therefore been a critical source of seeds for native plants used in prairie restoration projects. Active and abandoned rail corridors in urban areas can be important ecologically because they are some of the few unmanaged areas within a heavily managed matrix.

Figure 6-5f. Urban and suburban *greenways* combine multiple functions—habitat protection, recreation, nonmotorized transportation, and opportunities for historic or cultural appreciation—into a single corridor. Habitat is generally suitable mainly for edge species due to the narrow width and intensive human use of the corridor. Most greenways in developed areas have narrow spots or are intersected by roads, which greatly limits their value for long-range wildlife movement. Riparian greenways can help filter pollutants and excess nutrients, reduce erosion, and improve stream habitat. (*Source:* Reed F. Noss, "Wildlife Corridors," in Daniel S. Smith and Paul C. Hellmund, eds., *Ecology of Greenways* [Minneapolis: University of Minnesota Press, 1993].)

Figure 6-5g. Unlike roads, *trails and paths* are often used by mammals as conduits for movement. However, heavy use by humans or even limited use by dogs (which leave scent marks) sharply reduces use by wild animals. Well-defined narrow trails have less impact than wide or braided trails because human activities are less dispersed and animals can learn to avoid them. Therefore, in sensitive nature reserves, land managers may want to confine most human use (and all use by dogs) to a portion of the site near the edge. (*Source:* Richard T. T. Forman, *Land Mosaics: The Ecology of Landscapes and Regions* [Cambridge: Cambridge University Press, 1995], p. 174.)

Figure 6-5h. As with roads, *utility corridors* (power lines, gas and oil pipelines, and so forth) contain mainly edge species. Most utility corridors are kept open by regular disturbance from humans, such as cutting or herbicide spraying. Studies show that they inhibit crossing by many mammal, bird, amphibian, and insect species. Ecologically sound management might involve planting with native herbaceous and shrub species that would require less frequent maintenance, provide better habitat for native animals, and create less of a barrier to movement. Also, curvilinear, "soft" edges might encourage animal movement into and across the corridor. (*Sources:* Forman, *Land Mosaics*, p. 174; H. H. Obrecht III, W. J. Fleming, and J. H. Parsons, "Management of Powerline Rights-of-way for Botanical and Wildlife Value in Metropolitan Areas," in Lowell W. Adams and Daniel L. Leedy, eds., *Wildlife Conservation in Metropolitan Environments* [Columbia, MD: National Institute for Urban Wildlife, 1991], p. 255.)

Figure 6-6. Salamanders use this tunnel to cross under a road during their annual migration to breeding ponds. Note the fencing and concrete "funnel" in the foreground of the photo, which guide salamanders toward the underpass and prevent them from accessing the road surface.

opments, while engineers and landscape architects can propose the use of native grass or shrub ecosystems as aesthetically pleasing and low-maintenance alternatives to monocultures of non-native grasses.

Land Mosaics, Land Transformation, and Implications for Planning

Taken as a snapshot at a single point in time, the land displays a *mosaic*, or quilt-like, pattern of patches, corridors, and matrix. This mosaic is created by variability in the environment (e.g., soils, moisture, and topography), natural disturbances, and human activity. However, viewed 10, 50, or 100 years later, the mosaic is likely to look different. Two processes are responsible for this change.

In the absence of human activity, the natural processes of disturbance and succession discussed in Chapter 4 result in *shifting mosaics*, in which individual patches change from early successional to late successional vegetation and vice versa but the landscape as a whole remains in general equilibrium (see Figure 6-7). Since different species rely on different successional stages for light, nutrients, food, and shelter, it is important that there be at least some patches at

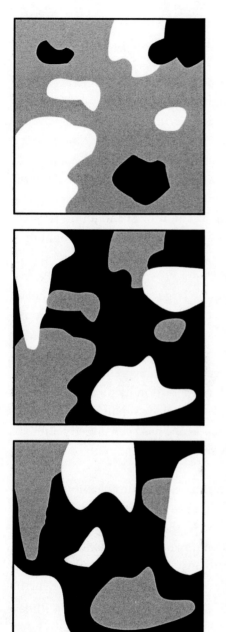

Young Forest

Middle-Aged Forest

Older Forest

Figure 6-7. Even in the absence of human intervention, landscapes change as a result of succession and disturbance. This diagram shows the same forested landscape over time, with fifty years passing from one panel to the next. Individual forest patches mature from young (white) to middle-aged (gray) to old (black), while natural disturbances create new young patches from older ones. Over time, however, the landscape as a whole remains a mosaic with forests of all different ages represented.

every successional stage at any given time. For example, in the forests of northern New England and eastern Canada, moose (*Alces alces*) find most of their food in young hardwood stands where the forest was recently cut or damaged by wind or ice, whereas the moss *Neckera pennata* occurs only in late successional forests in this landscape.[26] A landscape lacking either of these forest types could not support all native species.

Compared to a natural mosaic where succession and disturbance follow each other in a continual cycle, a human-influenced mosaic is more likely to change directionally as the matrix of natural habitat is interspersed with more and more human land uses. Understanding how this happens is useful for planners and designers. Land transformation can occur through several different processes: *perforation, dissection, fragmentation, shrinkage,* and *attrition* (see Figure 6-8).[27] All five of these processes are often lumped under the term *fragmentation* in common parlance, but there are important differences from an ecological standpoint.

Perforation occurs when scattered houses are built within natural habitat or when remote patches of forest are clear-cut, for example. This process rapidly increases the amount of edge and decreases the maximum size of an uninterrupted interior habitat patch. For example, if just ten houses are scattered throughout a remote, forested, 1,000-acre (400 ha) section of a town, roughly 110 acres (45 ha) of edge habitat will be created, assuming a 300-foot (90 m) edge width.[28] Perforation is most troublesome for species that require large patches of interior habitat. At least initially, perforation is not likely to subdivide natural populations, because the matrix of natural habitat remains continuous.

Dissection is caused by roads and other human corridors carving continuous swaths through the matrix. As discussed above, different types of human corridors create barriers for some species but not for others. If individuals of a species are unable to cross the corridor, then the population will be subdivided. This may occur even though less than 5 percent of the landscape has been directly altered. Dissection also creates a large amount of edge relative to the amount of land that is directly altered.

Fragmentation and shrinkage occur when patches of natural habitat become discontinuous from one another. When this happens, the matrix may change from being natural habitat to a human land use. At this point, many if not most interior species will probably have been lost, and many other species will have been divided into metapopulations or reduced to unsustainably small populations that may soon disappear. Nevertheless, the landscape may still provide habitat for generalist species, species with small home-range requirements, migratory birds, and other species that can use *stepping stones* of natural habitat in moving from one core habitat area to another.

Attrition is the final stage of land transformation, during which the residual patches of natural habitat are lost completely. At this stage, even the amount of edge habitat diminishes rapidly, and the biota are likely to be limited to those species that can tolerate human land uses and activities.

The study of land transformation reveals two useful principles for planners and developers. First, the greatest impact to sensitive native species usually occurs early in the land transformation process—by the time one-quarter of a com-

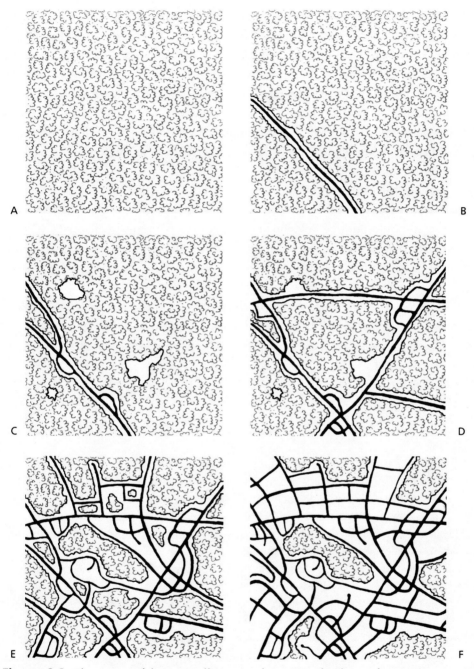

Figure 6-8. This series of diagrams illustrates the various land transformation processes that occur as a result of human settlement. In sequence, they show an uninhabited forested landscape (a), dissection (b), perforation (c), fragmentation (d), shrinkage (e), and attrition (f).

munity's land has been developed. Thus, ecologically based planning should begin immediately, rather than waiting until substantial growth has already come to a town, county, or region. Second, dispersed development is almost always more detrimental to natural communities than is a comparable amount of concentrated development because it accelerates all five land transformation processes: perforation, dissection, fragmentation, shrinkage, and attrition. This principle provides ecological support for clustering development at the site level and especially at the municipal and regional level so that large remnant patches of native vegetation can be retained.[29]

Having reviewed the major concepts of landscape ecology, we can now ask two questions of great relevance to planners and developers: where and in what sequence should land be developed to maximize ecological values? Landscape ecologists Richard Forman and Sharon Collinge have proposed conceptual answers to these questions, and the following discussion is based on their "spatial solution" to land use planning.

Where is the best place, ecologically, to situate any given land use, such as a new housing development, road, shopping center, farm, or nature reserve? Although the answer to this question depends on place-specific variables, landscape

Box 6-1
"Indispensable Patterns" for Biological Conservation

1. *Large natural patches.* Large patches are the only way to protect interior species and species with large home ranges. Large patches are also more likely to allow for a shifting mosaic in which natural disturbances do not affect all the land at once and, thus, several successional stages (with their associated biotic communities) are represented at any given time.
2. *Vegetated riparian corridors.* Naturally vegetated streamsides are essential for protecting many aquatic species important to conservation.
3. *Connectivity between large patches.* The landscape must provide functional connectivity for species of conservation interest—that is, linkages that these species can use for home range movement, migration, and dispersal. Wide, continuous corridors are most likely to serve this function, but stepping stones in a moderately suitable matrix will suffice for many species.
4. *Natural remnants in human-dominated areas.* Within urban or agricultural landscapes, three types of natural remnants should be protected, in order of descending priority: (1) areas of especially high conservation value, such as microhabitats that are rare throughout the landscape; (2) landscape types that provide essential ecosystem services, such as flood control; and (3) remnants of the former natural matrix that provide edge species habitat and human access to nature.

Source: Based on discussion in Richard T. Forman, *Land Mosaics: The Ecology of Landscapes and Regions* (Cambridge University Press, 1995), p. 452.

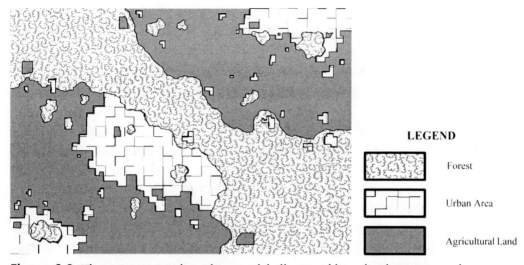

LEGEND

Forest

Urban Area

Agricultural Land

Figure 6-9. The aggregate-with-outliers model, illustrated here, has been proposed as one way to incorporate biological conservation and human land uses at the landscape scale (tens of miles or kilometers across). (Based on Richard T. T. Forman and Sharon K. Collinge, "The 'Spatial Solution' to Conserving Biodiversity in Landscapes and Regions," in R. M. DeGraaf and R. I. Miller, eds., *Conservation of Faunal Diversity in Forested Landscapes* [London: Chapman and Hall, 1996], pp. 537–68.)

ecology can offer a useful generic answer, which can then be adapted to the planning or design questions at hand. At the scale of landscapes, four "indispensable patterns" of natural vegetation must be maintained in order to protect native species and natural processes.[30] These patterns are discussed in Box 6-1.

The *aggregate-with-outliers* model is one possible way of incorporating these four patterns into land use plans.[31] This design proposes that major land uses—such as natural vegetation, agriculture, and urban development—should generally be aggregated to maximize large-patch benefits. However, small outlying patches should also be created to provide for edge habitat, reduce the risk of catastrophic disturbances or pest outbreaks affecting a single patch, increase genetic variation, and provide opportunities for human appreciation of nature. Connectivity for native species should be provided by natural corridors as well as small patches, which can function as stepping stones (see Figure 6-9).

The aggregate-with-outliers model does not apply in exactly the same ways to both natural vegetation and urban areas. As we discuss throughout this book, people in urban and suburban areas benefit from having small patches of natural vegetation sprinkled throughout the developed landscape. In contrast, small patches of urban areas do not improve the functioning of native ecosystems, which are best left in large patches. Once again, these principles (and Figure 6-9) offer a generic solution for ecologically based land use planning—a solution that must be refined based on the details of each place.

What is the ecologically optimal sequence of land transformation? Planners use many techniques to influence the sequence of land transformation—that is, the order in which land is developed or altered. Zoning maps, infrastructure investment programs, urban growth boundaries, development phasing ordinances, incentives, and subsidies all affect the sequence of land transformation. An ecologically based approach to land transformation would maximize each of the four indispensable patterns on the landscape for as long as possible. Thus, development should be aggregated on less ecologically important lands, reserving natural areas that are large and relatively round for as long as possible. Within the land that is converted for agriculture or development, remnant small patches and corridors should also be set aside. Figure 6-10 illustrates how this more ecologically favorable land transformation process might look at 20 percent, 50 percent, and 80 percent of total buildout. Even at the 80 percent stage, the landscape may still support many species of conservation interest in the remaining large patch and perhaps in some of the smaller remnant patches. This is a radically different outcome from conventional urban development (or agriculture), in which nature is relegated to leftover scraps or small parks selected with little regard for regional ecology.

How practical or implementable are these "optimal" land use scenarios offered by the field of landscape ecology? At first glance, the idea of identifying lands for development, agriculture, and natural habitat at the scale of towns or counties appears to be at odds with property rights concerns, not to mention most current practice. However, directing land use in this manner can be accomplished using zoning and planning tools, as has been done successfully in some notable instances. For example, *urban growth boundaries* (e.g., Portland, Oregon) and regionwide *transfer of development rights* programs (e.g., the Pinelands in New Jersey) are both essentially techniques for achieving an aggregate-with-outliers land use pattern at the landscape scale (see Chapter 10 for further discussion of these tools).

Conversely, large-lot zoning (roughly 1 to 40 acres, or 0.4 to 16 hectares, per lot) runs counter to these ecologically based land use solutions because it creates a fine-scale intermingling of developed, agricultural, and natural lands that eliminates the large-patch benefits to be gained by aggregation. While some ecological values can be retained on large residential lots (see Box 10-1 for an enumeration of these), even 35-acre (14 ha) "ranchette" house lots in the western United States were found to have significantly fewer native birds and predators and significantly more introduced predators and plants than nearby ranch lands and nature reserves.[32] Because it is so spread out, ranchette development degrades far more natural habitat than would an equal number of houses in an ordinary suburban development.

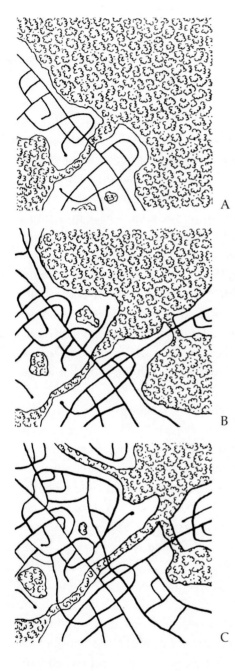

Figure 6-10. This time series of three sketches showing a community at 20 percent (a), 50 percent (b), and 80 percent (c) of maximum buildout illustrates how the land transformation sequence can be improved to maximize conservation values. Whereas the typical sequence of community development results in early and extensive habitat degradation (as shown in Figure 6-8), this improved sequence retains the maximum amount of large habitat patches and corridors at each stage of development. (Based on Richard T. T. Forman and Sharon K. Collinge, "The 'Spatial Solution' to Conserving Biodiversity in Landscapes and Regions," in R. M. DeGraaf and R. I. Miller, eds., *Conservation of Faunal Diversity in Forested Landscapes* [London: Chapman and Hall, 1996], pp. 537–68.)

Even at the scale of individual sites, the ecological benefits of aggregating or clustering development as opposed to distributing it evenly across the site are apparent. For example, if a 640-acre (1 square mile, or 260 ha) tract of land is divided into sixteen 40-acre house lots—a common pattern in the West—76 percent of the tract will be affected by development, assuming a 650-foot (200 m) disturbance radius (edge effect) around the houses. However, if the houses are clustered on one-quarter of the site (on 10-acre lots), only 31 percent of the tract is affected.[33] Subsequent chapters expand further on these design concepts.

Ecosystem Ecology

To review, an *ecosystem* is the sum of the biological community plus the non-living environment that supports it. When British ecologist A. G. Tansley coined the term *ecosystem* in 1935, the field of ecology was just beginning to move from the study of individual organisms' behaviors, functions, and interactions to a more holistic view of nature as a chemical, material, and thermodynamic system as well as a biological one.[34] More recently, ecosystem ecologists have made much progress in quantifying the flows of water, energy, nutrients, and other constituents through the living and nonliving components of ecosystems.

In the economy of nature, organisms acquire and spend several different abiotic "currencies" that are necessary to sustain life. The balance of these components in the environment—their concentration, form, and fluxes—affects biodiversity by helping to determine which species can survive in any given environment. Planners and designers should have a basic understanding of these ecosystem currencies, how human land uses and activities affect them, and what we can do to mitigate these impacts.

Perhaps the most important ecosystem currency is energy. As discussed in Chapter 5, energy moves through *food webs* from plants to herbivores, predators, and decomposers. During photosynthesis, plants store the energy in sunlight as chemical energy by transforming a low-energy form of carbon (carbon dioxide, or CO_2) to various high-energy forms of carbon (sugars and carbohydrates such as glucose) consuming water and releasing oxygen in the process. Animals reverse the process, combining high-energy carbon molecules and oxygen to release the stored energy and generating CO_2 and water as by-products. Without oxygen, animals cannot complete this process of metabolism, and they die. These basic energy transfer processes occur in almost every ecosystem found on Earth.

Nutrients are the chemical substances that organisms need to sustain basic life processes. The most important plant nutrients are nitrogen and phosphorus, which are essential ingredients of proteins, nucleic acids, and other cell components. How much of these elements are present and in what form they occur are both important: plants can absorb certain chemical forms of nitrogen and phosphorus but not others. With the help of nitrogen-fixing bacteria on their roots, legumes, such as clover and beans, convert the abundant but biologically useless nitrogen gas (N_2) in the atmosphere to ammonia (NH_3), which plants can absorb.

Other major nutrients required by organisms include potassium, sulfur, calcium, magnesium, iron, and sodium.

While all of these nutrients are essential for life, in many cases a single limiting nutrient controls how much plant growth any given ecosystem can sustain (see pages 82–84). In most ecosystems, and for most plants, nitrogen, phosphorus, or both are the limiting nutrients—nitrogen more commonly in terrestrial and marine ecosystems and phosphorus more commonly in freshwater ecosystems. When additional amounts of the limiting nutrient become available, the total amount of plant growth (called the ecosystem's *primary production*) can increase dramatically. When humans artificially increase the availability of the limiting nutrient in an ecosystem—such as when they fertilize crops, or when nutrients from sewage enter an ecosystem—plant growth usually becomes more vigorous. (See Table 6-2 for a list of major human sources of nutrient enrichment.) But other changes happen, too. The types and abundances of plant species present may change since some species are better adapted to low-nutrient conditions whereas others gain a competitive advantage in high-nutrient environments. Unfortunately, many invasive exotics thrive in high-nutrient environments and are at a competitive advantage in such places as roadsides and farm field margins.[35] Plant consumption by herbivorous animals may increase in nitrogen- and phosphorus-enriched ecosystems as well, as animals feast on nutrient-rich leaves and sprigs.

In aquatic ecosystems, the effects of nutrient enrichment, or *eutrophication*, can be even more dramatic. Many people who live (or have a summer house) on a shallow lake or pond have given up the thought of swimming there because the water is thick with weeds and algae whose growth has been stimulated by nitrogen and phosphorus seeping out of septic systems. When this plant matter dies, decomposing bacteria can rapidly consume all of the dissolved oxygen in the water body, resulting in fish kills. Eutrophication can also change the species composition of a water body by influencing the competitive balance among plants.

In addition to influencing ecosystem ecology by altering the availability and flows of nutrients, humans affect ecosystems by introducing a wide variety of chemical pollutants. Chemical pollution is perhaps the most important way that human activities affect distant ecosystems, since airborne urban and industrial pollutants can move hundreds of miles. Two types of chemical pollution are most worrisome for North America's ecosystems and biodiversity: acid deposition and ground-level ozone. Acid deposition (acid rain as well as dry deposition) occurs when sulfur dioxide and nitrogen oxides emitted from power plants, industries, and motor vehicles react in the atmosphere to form sulfuric and nitric acids.

Table 6-2.

Major Human Sources of Nitrogen and Phosphorus Enrichment

Nitrogen	Phosphorus
Agriculture • Chemical fertilizers • Manure application and livestock feedlots	Agriculture • Manure application and livestock feedlots • Chemical fertilizers
Atmospheric deposition in precipitation and dust • From agriculture • From vehicle emissions • From industrial sources	Sewage treatment plants and septic systems • From human waste • From industrial discharges to sewage systems • From detergents
Sewage treatment plants and septic systems • From human waste	Other nonpoint sources (lawn and golf course fertilizers, domestic animals, road runoff, etc.)
Other nonpoint sources (lawn and golf course fertilizers, domestic animals, road runoff, etc.)	Other point sources (industrial discharges, runoff from landfills, etc.)
Other point sources (industrial discharges, runoff from landfills, etc.)	

Sources: Patricia A. Chambers et al., *Nutrients and Their Impact on the Canadian Environment* (Hull, Quebec: Environment Canada, 2001); S. R. Carpenter et al., "Nonpoint Pollution of Surface Waters with Phosphorus and Nitrogen," *Ecological Applications* 8, no. 3 (1998): 559–68.

Note: Nitrogen and phosphorus sources are listed in approximate order of importance, and, within each source, subcategories are listed in approximate order of importance. The relative importance of the sources may differ somewhat depending on the landscape context: urban areas generate a greater proportion of excess nutrients from industrial and other point sources of pollution, while rural areas derive a larger proportion from agriculture and atmospheric deposition.

When they fall as rain or airborne particles, these substances acidify soils and waters. On land, acid deposition increases nitrogen availability while leaching other plant nutrients from the soil. This process can upset the nutrient balance of forests, leading to the decline of dominant tree species, especially evergreens. Acid deposition can also reduce biodiversity and natural functioning in freshwater ecosystems that have little natural capacity to neutralize acids. Because of acid pollution, rain in the eastern United States may be lethal to native fish; consequently, for example, at least 20 percent of lakes in New York's Adirondack Mountains and an estimated 9,000 miles (15,000 km) of streams in the southern Appalachians are fishless.[36] Biological restoration of freshwater systems is impossible until chemical pollution has been addressed. Although the 1990 Clean Air Act Amendments in the United States mandated reductions in sulfur dioxide emissions, acid deposition, especially of nitrogen compounds, remains a significant problem.[37]

Ozone is beneficial in the upper atmosphere, where it protects life on earth from ultraviolet radiation, but excessive ozone in the lower atmosphere causes ecosystem damage as well as widespread human health problems, including increased incidence of asthma and other respiratory ailments. Through a complex set of chemical reactions, elevated ground-level ozone levels are caused by human emissions of nitrogen oxides and volatile organic compounds (such as petroleum fuels and solvents). Major effects include reduced growth, leaf or needle damage, and death of tree species, such as Jeffrey and Ponderosa pines in California; pines, spruce, and fir in the Appalachians; and, possibly, sugar maples in the Northeast.[38] In a synthesis of scientific studies on the subject, the World Resources Institute concluded that "ambient levels of ozone are stunting the growth of most, maybe all, conifer and hardwood forests in the eastern United States."[39]

For planners and designers, a basic understanding of an area's or site's ecosystem ecology can contribute to a more environmentally compatible plan or design. At the baseline data collection stage, it helps to identify important flows into and out of the area or site (particularly any aquatic habitats), such as nutrients, sediments, toxins, or heat. Often, these flows can be discerned without doing any field measurements—for example, simply by knowing that the farmer who cultivated the land used large quantities of chemical fertilizers and pesticides. With knowledge of the baseline ecosystem ecology, one can then evaluate whether a proposed plan or project would increase or decrease any flows and, if these changes are detrimental, find ways to mitigate them. Specific examples of such an approach might include planting additional trees to reduce the "heat island" effect of extensive blacktop or using vegetated swales to trap sediment before it enters waterways. While the effects of acid deposition and ground-level ozone exceed the scale of local land use decisions, planners and designers who want to "think globally, act locally" should understand the distant consequences of plans that, for example, will increase vehicle miles traveled or electricity consumption. They may also want to consider how air pollution from local and distant sources may affect the long-term health of the human populations and local ecosystems where they are working.

Freshwater Ecosystems and Their Relation to the Land

Humans have decimated freshwater ecosystems and their native biodiversity perhaps more than any other ecosystem type. This problem has reached a crisis in the United States, which ranks first worldwide for diversity of crayfishes, freshwater mussels, freshwater snails, and several types of freshwater insects. More than two-thirds of the nation's 300 freshwater mussels species are either extinct or threatened, as are 51 percent of its 322 crayfish species and more than 300 of its 801 fish species.[40] This section provides a brief overview of freshwater ecosystems and human impacts on these ecosystems. Some techniques that planners and designers can use to mitigate these impacts are discussed in Chapter 10.

The functioning of rivers and streams as well as the species present differs depending on their size and location in a watershed. A basic knowledge of these differences can help us understand which ecosystem components are most important for protecting biodiversity in any given stream system. For example, riparian vegetation is essential alongside headwaters streams but somewhat less so (although still desirable) along major rivers. Key characteristics and processes are summarized in Table 6-3.

Human insults to freshwater ecosystems are almost too numerous to count, but they can be grouped into direct and indirect impacts. Direct impacts to rivers, streams, and lakes include water withdrawals, dam construction, stream channelization or realignment, dredging, filling, introduction of non-native species, and discharge of pollutants directly to water bodies. These practices are almost always detrimental to native species and should be scrutinized by planners and designers before being endorsed or incorporated into plans. Environmental laws in the United States enacted since the 1970s have sharply reduced the direct discharge of pollutants and have provided for greater oversight of water withdrawals. More recently, an effort has begun to undo some of the harm caused by dams and stream channelization through such projects as the Everglades restoration in Florida and the removal of dams throughout the United States and Canada.

Indirect impacts include the effects on freshwater ecosystems of human land uses in the surrounding watershed. Chief among these is *nonpoint source pollution*, which occurs when human activities increase the amount of sediment, excess nutrients, toxic chemicals, or other pollutants draining to water bodies. This concept is highly relevant since planners and designers can either mitigate or worsen nonpoint source pollution through their land use proposals. The most important effects of land use on freshwater ecosystems and their native biodiversity are summarized in Table 6-4.

Landscape ecology principles of connectivity apply to streams as well as land; the major difference is that streams are essentially a one-dimensional world where organisms and abiotic flows can move only upstream or downstream. This fact makes connectivity of stream systems especially important since there is no other way around for fish and other water-dependent species. Dams are an obvious impediment to movement, but a two-mile-long stretch of stream with no riparian vegetation (and, hence, a warmer water temperature) or the area just below a sewage treatment effluent pipe may be just as much of a barrier for some species.[41] Applying this concept to land use planning suggests that when finan-

Table 6-3.
Stream Characteristics

	Upper part of watershed; 1st- to 3rd-order streams[1]	Middle part of watershed; 3rd- to 5th-order streams[1]	Lower part of watershed; 5th-order streams and higher[1]
Physical Characteristics	Steep gradient; high water velocity; rocky or gravelly bottom; typically up to 15 feet (5 m) wide	Often an alternating pool-riffle structure; bottom may have gravelly, sandy, or silty areas; typically 15 to 50 feet (5 to 15 m) wide	Low gradient; slow water speed; high sediment load; silty or muddy bottom; extensive floodplains; typically over 50 feet (15 m) wide
Water Characteristics	Cold water; often high in dissolved oxygen	Somewhat warmer water	Warmer water; sometimes low in dissolved oxygen
Biological Characteristics	Detritus from land forms the base of the food chain; many stream organisms attach to the bottom to withstand fast current; fish rely on gravelly or rocky streambed for spawning and feeding	Energy inputs include detritus from shore, particles from upstream, and photosynthesis within the water; largest number of habitat niches	Major energy input is particles from upstream; extensive bottom-dwelling animal community

Source: James Grant MacBroom, *The River Book* (Hartford: Connecticut Department of Environmental Protection, 1998).
[1] A 1st-order stream is a perennial stream with no tributaries. A 2nd-order stream is formed when two 1st-order streams join, and so on.

cial resources are limited, stream segments should be prioritized for protection based not just on their innate characteristics but also on their connectedness to the rest of the stream network. Alternatively, the cause of the "gap" can be addressed by removing dams, restoring riparian vegetation, or cleaning up pollution sources.

Aquatic habitat should be considered in all municipal, county, and regional land use plans. A helpful first step is to prepare a map of the area's hydrological network that shows functional gaps, such as dams, areas where streams have been

Table 6-4.

Effects of Land Use on Freshwater Ecosystems and Biodiversity

Problem	Major Causes	Effects on Native Biodiversity
Elevated water temperature	Removal of riparian vegetation; runoff from buildings and paved surfaces	Decline of cold-water algae and insect species; local extinction of cold-water fishes
Eutrophication (enrichment with nitrogen and phosphorus)	Fertilizers, septic systems, animal wastes, atmospheric deposition	Often favors exotic plants over native ones; can lead to fish kills and proliferation of toxic microbes
Pesticide and herbicide pollution	Runoff from farms, golf courses, lawns, and gardens	Death, deformity, and decreased reproductive success for aquatic animals
Pollution from petroleum, heavy metals, other toxins	Runoff from roads and parking lots	Death, deformity, and decreased reproductive success for aquatic animals
Introduction of invasive exotic species	Invasive species transported by boats; natural processes; and release of exotic aquarium animals and plants into the wild	Exotics outcompete or feed on native plants and animals
Elevated peak flow rates and flooding[2]	Impervious surfaces; loss of wetlands and native vegetation	May change the amount and structure of stream habitat niches
Diminished base flow rates during dry weather[2]	Water withdrawals; impervious surfaces	Habitat is eliminated or degraded for almost all aquatic species during droughts
Increased sedimentation and turbidity (cloudiness of water)	Erosion from urban and agricultural lands	Smothers stream-bottom habitats for aquatic insects, crayfishes, mollusks, and snails; impairs fish reproduction
Loss or alteration of riparian habitat	Removal of riparian vegetation	Decline of streambank species; riparian corridors less suitable for animal movement
Loss of organic inputs	Removal of riparian vegetation	Undermines aquatic food chains, reducing abundance of insects and fish

[1] Stream flow consists of base flow that is sustained year-round from groundwater plus surface flow that varies depending on precipitation. In naturally functioning watersheds, vegetation, soils, wetlands, and floodplains act as sponges, limiting peak flow and helping to maintain a level of base flow year-round. When this functioning is impaired, streams are prone to more frequent and more severe floods as well as longer periods of low-flow or no-flow conditions during dry spells.

channelized or piped underground, or long stretches lacking natural riparian vegetation. In the absence of extensive information about local water bodies, freshwater ecosystems are one place where it is often appropriate to rely on indicator species; sensitive freshwater species such as trout, mayflies, and caddisflies often indicate good water quality, while other invertebrates, such as isopods and bloodworms (midge larvae), tend to indicate elevated levels of pollution and fine sediments.[42] In many communities, teams of volunteers sometimes known as "stream teams" gather basic data on water temperature, turbidity, indicator species, and bottom and bank structure. The resulting hydrological map and stream data will help to highlight aquatic habitats of high value, habitats that have been severely degraded, and major threats to aquatic biodiversity. This information, in turn, can be used to inform policies ranging from the location of different zoning districts to site planning requirements to habitat protection and restoration initiatives.

Ecological Integrity and Sustainability

After reading these chapters about the science of ecology, you may feel daunted by the large number of ecological factors relevant for planners and designers, many of which are complex and difficult to evaluate fully. Which of these factors are most important to consider and plan for? How do we know if what we are protecting is adequate to sustain native biodiversity indefinitely? How much nature can we really protect in a world of expanding human population and land uses, and what should be the goals of conservation-minded planners, designers, developers, and citizens? The answer to this last question must be partly personal, based on your own conservation ethic and the mandate of the organization where you work or volunteer. But ecologists have recently offered some scientific insight by developing holistic assessments of *ecological integrity* to meld all of the relevant ecological factors into a single framework. *Sustainability* is the combination of ecological integrity with the human objectives of long-term economic prosperity and social equality. We close our discussion of the science of ecology with a look at these concepts and at the scientific as well as ethical guidance they can offer to planners, designers, and developers.

Ecological integrity is analogous to human health: it is a constellation of factors related to a system's structure, function, and ability to sustain itself in near-optimal condition well into the future. Ecologist James Karr, who pioneered the concept, defines a system with ecological integrity as one that has natural physical and chemical processes and that can "support and maintain a balanced, integrated, adaptive biological system having the full range of elements (genes, species, assemblages) and processes (mutation, demography, biotic interactions, nutrient and energy dynamics, and metapopulation processes) expected in the natural habitat of the region."[43] Ecologist Richard Forman defines integrity as consisting of near-natural levels of four ecological characteristics—productivity, biodiversity, soil, and water—each of which can be measured quantitatively.[44] For both definitions, integrity is defined in relation to native ecosystems unaffected by modern human activity. However, as previously discussed, wild nature is not a static condition but rather the situation where species and ecosystems are free to respond to disturbance and physical change.

Ecological integrity as defined above is often unattainable in landscapes with significant numbers of humans or amounts of human land uses. Thus, for land use professionals, it is often more helpful to think of integrity not as a single condition that any given landscape either achieves or fails to achieve but rather as a continuum between more integrity and less. For example, we may be able to attain a high level of ecological integrity for portions of landscapes (e.g., headwaters streams, rare microhabitats, or small nature reserves) or may be able to improve the integrity of threatened or damaged areas. In addition, integrity is a benchmark against which to measure the ecological impact of proposed plans or designs. Land development would almost certainly become more ecologically sensitive if government reviewers required an assessment of predevelopment and postdevelopment levels of productivity, biodiversity, soil, and water as part of mandatory environmental reviews.

In situations where complete ecological integrity is not attainable because of the scope of human activities on the land, the criterion of *ecological health* may be an appropriate goal of land use professionals. Ecological health requires that human activities on a site avoid (1) irreversible or long-lasting impacts to the land (e.g., soil loss or toxic contamination) and (2) off-site impacts, such as pollution or habitat fragmentation, that might degrade other ecosystems that still possess ecological integrity.[45] Ecological health is still a lofty goal, and one that could have tremendous benefits if it were a standard part of planning and development. But it is also an eminently practical goal that can point the way to specific design modifications, such as minimizing regrading and paving, which both constitute long-lasting impacts to the soil; reducing the demand for fossil fuel energy through effective transportation planning and energy-efficient building design; and utilizing stormwater management systems that minimize pollution runoff and mimic natural hydrological processes.

Stepping back for a moment to examine the very large picture is always risky; we may not like the picture or what is says about our values, our lifestyles, or our work. But if you are reading this book, you are probably willing to examine this important perspective. To state it bluntly, very little of the planning or development now occurring in the United States or Canada is sustainable. The land uses that result from these processes borrow heavily from the future, consuming unrenewable resources at a high rate and depleting renewable resources—such as soil, groundwater, and forests—to the point where they may take hundreds or thousands of years to recover. Our ecological impacts—local, regional, and global—have vastly accelerated the rate of species extinction, and they affect nature in ways we do not yet even understand. Current planning and design practices frequently propagate short-term economic gain while leaving a legacy of problems for future generations. And far too often, they fail to promote social equality, instead magnifying disparities of wealth and encouraging ostentatious consumption at the cost of environmental destruction and continued poverty for the world's poor. Altogether, the Earth's long-term human carrying capacity, assuming U.S., Canadian, or European lifestyles, is probably less than 2 billion people, yet an estimated 8 to 10 billion humans will inhabit the planet by 2050.[46]

This view of global unsustainability speaks to the need for immediate and radical action, yet planning is marked by incrementalism and political give-and-take, and land development is marked by risk-averse formulas for financial success. As a planner, designer, developer, or involved citizen, you stand at the epicenter of this conflict. For land use professionals who want to do the right thing ecologically, this book offers some defensible rationales for doing so: saving money, increasing profit, winning votes, satisfying constituents, improving quality of life, and protecting human lives and property. In most cases, one or more of these reasons will provide a solid basis for incorporating ecological factors into planning and design projects. In other cases, though, the decision to support, pursue, and even fight for environmental conservation and sustainability in one's work and one's life is ultimately a moral one, driven by the desire to live in a way that does not prevent others from living and to preserve nature's magnificent legacy for its own sake and that of future human generations.

Color Plate 1. Three weeks before this photograph was taken, the 10,800-acre (4,400 ha) Hi-Meadow Fire in Colorado destroyed fifty-eight structures, including several houses that could be seen from this deck. Firefighters stopped the blaze just thirty feet from this house. The distant ridge in the photo was completely burned, while the felled pine in the foreground was badly charred.

Color Plate 2. A male quetzal (*Pharomachrus mocinno*). Quetzals are especially sensitive indicators of ecosystem health because they require contiguous forest stretching among several different forest types.

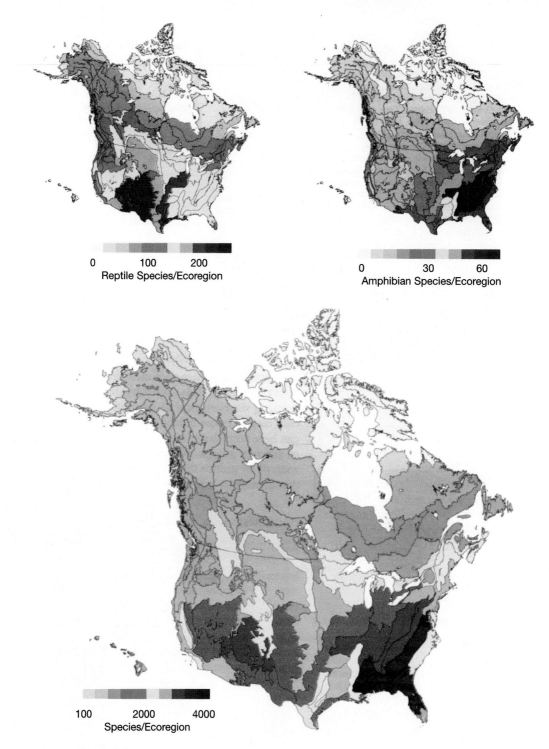

Color Plate 3. In temperate zones such as North America, the number of native species tends to be greater closer to the equator. Within this general pattern, however, considerable variability exists. For example, the hot spot of reptile diversity in North America is the desert Southwest, while the highest amphibian diversity is in the southeastern United States. (*Source:* Taylor H. Ricketts et al., *Terrestrial Ecoregions of North America: A Conservation Assessment* [Washington, DC: Island Press, 1999].)

(a)

(b)

Color Plate 4. Flowers along the shore of Mary Dunn Pond in Hyannis, Massachusetts, live a precarious existence. Several of these species require years of low water to provide growing habitat (see the flowers in the foreground of a) and years of high water to kill encroaching pitch pines (see the dead pine sapling on the right side of b). Too many years of low water or high water may extirpate the pond-shore flowers.

Color Plate 5. The treehopper and ant in this photo are partners in a mutualistic relationship. Treehoppers imbibe large amounts of plant sap and pass much of it as a dilute sugary liquid to ants (see the drop in the middle of the photo). The ants, in turn, protect the treehoppers from predators and parasites.

Color Plate 6. More than a third of Yellowstone National Park burned in 1988. In this photograph from 2000, the burned areas are still quite visible: they are the light patches of dead trees.

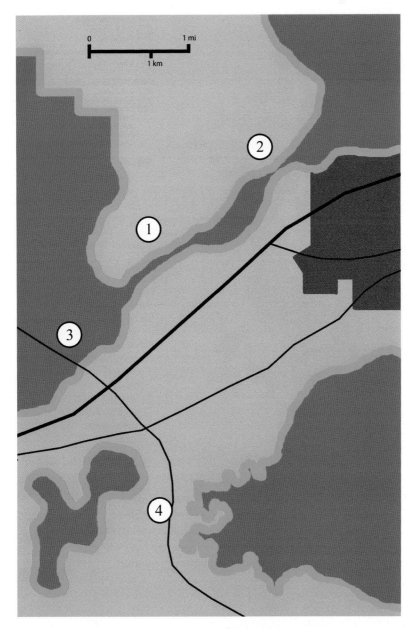

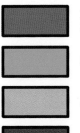
Color Plate 7. Not all reserves are equal, as they vary in size, shape, connectivity, and context. This diagram shows various aspects of nature reserves, as highlighted by the numbers in the figure. Corridors are often useful for connecting reserves (1) (see Chapter 6 for further discussion). Some portions of corridors may be so narrow that they mostly consist of edge habitat (2). "Plump" reserves have a relatively small proportion of edge habitat (3), while reserves with "wrinkled," or convoluted, boundaries have a large proportion of edge (4).

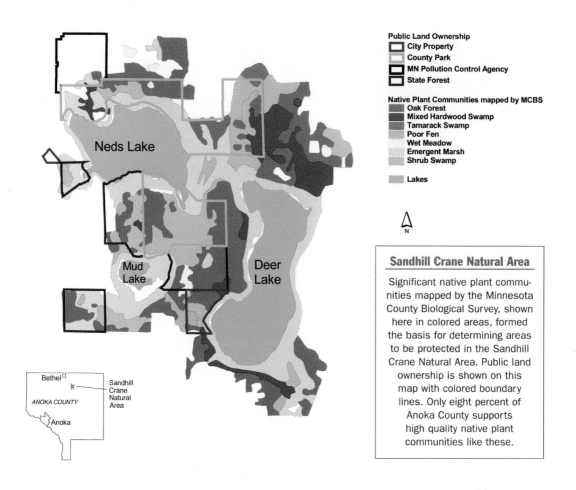

Neds Lake

Mud
Lake

Deer
Lake

Bethel
ANOKA COUNTY
Anoka
Sandhill
Crane
Natural
Area

Color Plate 8. In this example from East Bethel, Minnesota, information on native
plant communities as well as land protection status has been combined to help select
the best locations for new nature reserves to protect sandhill cranes (*Grus canadensis*).
Such ecological analysis is an important part of any long-range land use plan.
(Graphic courtesy of the Minnesota Department of Natural Resources.)

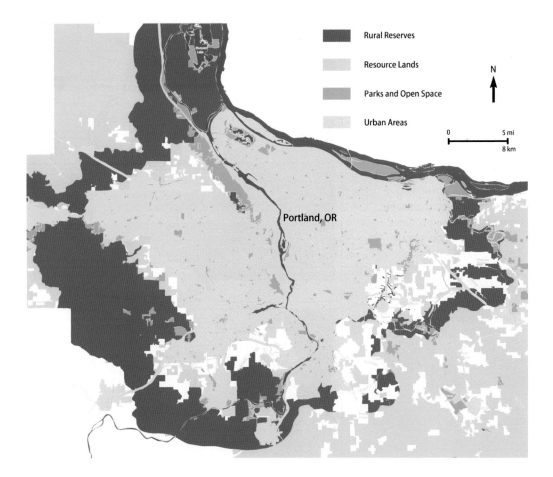

Color Plate 9. The Portland 2040 regional plan, shown here in simplified form, is a long-term, large-scale land use framework similar to a Landscape Conservation and Development Plan (LCDP). Note the aggregation of different land use types at the landscape scale. The rural reserves correspond roughly to the core and secondary habitats of an LCDP, while the resource lands correspond to the intensive production areas. (Map redrawn from the original Portland 2040 plan.)

Color Plate 10. By clustering development within a site and preserving lands shown on the community's greenprint, a conservation subdivision (a) can provide far more ecological value than a standard subdivision (b). Both site plans contain the same number of house lots, but the conservative subdivision retains more native habitats, provides better protection for the stream that borders the site and the tributary that flows through it, and contributes to the area-wide conservation network shown in the greenprint (c). The study site is outlined in black in the lower center of (c).

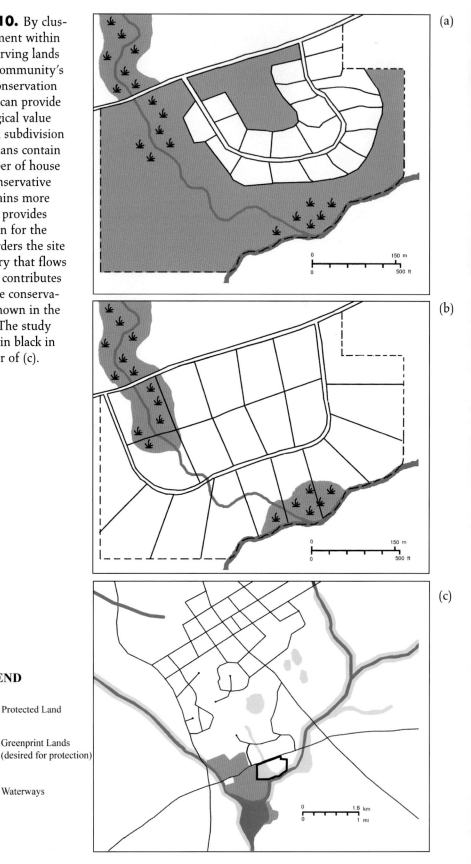

(a)

(b)

(c)

LEGEND

Protected Land

Greenprint Lands
(desired for protection)

Waterways

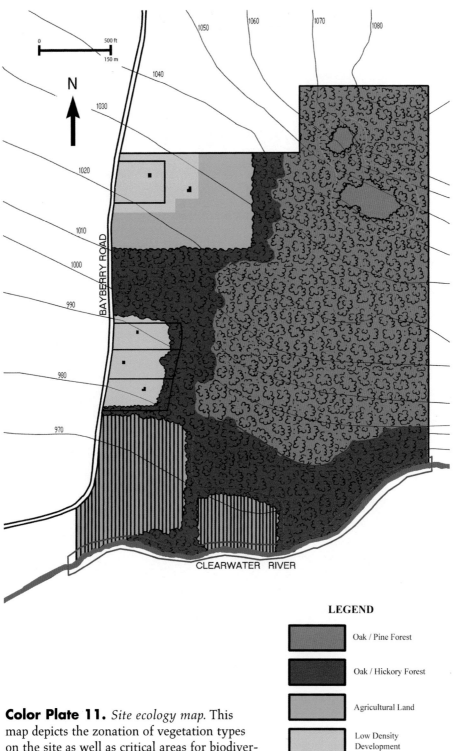

Color Plate 11. *Site ecology map.* This map depicts the zonation of vegetation types on the site as well as critical areas for biodiversity protection, including the stream community, riparian forest community, and limestone glade community.

LEGEND

- Oak / Pine Forest
- Oak / Hickory Forest
- Agricultural Land
- Low Density Development
- Stream Community
- Riparian Community
- Limestone Glade Community

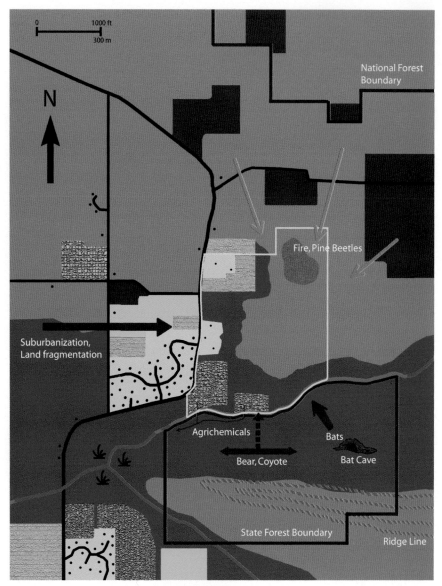

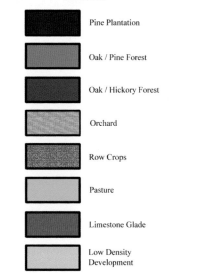

Color Plate 12. *Ecological context map.* This map depicts the site in its broader ecological and land use context. The site itself is outlined in gray. Important outside factors include the surrounding land uses and habitat types, presence or absence of habitat corridors, patterns of wildlife movement, and potential natural hazards.

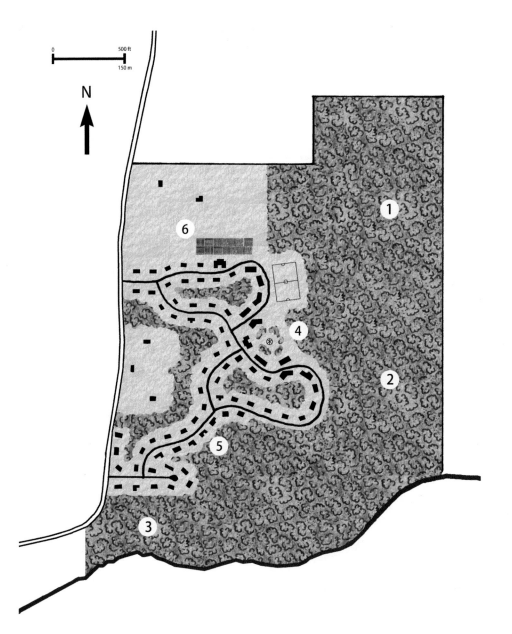

Color Plate 13. *Rural cluster plan.* This ecologically based design contains the same number of dwelling units as the conventional subdivision (ninety-six), in a combination of sixty-three single-family houses and eleven three-unit condominium buildings. Much of the site's ecological value has been retained by preserving the limestone glade (1) and hardwood and oak-pine forests (2) while providing for the restoration of hardwood forest on former agricultural land to create a continuous riparian corridor connecting to habitat east and west of the site (3). To protect homes from the fire-prone oak-pine forest, roads, a playing field, and a village green are used as protective buffers (4). Many of the houses offer backyard access to nature (5), while local food production is provided by community gardens and by the working orchard, which has been protected (6).

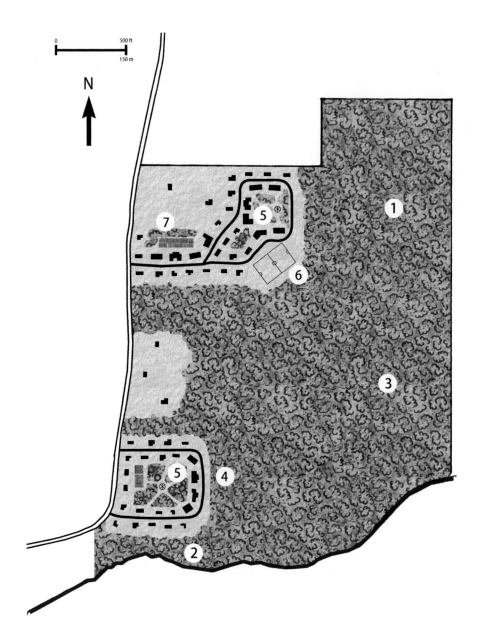

Color Plate 14. *Village cluster plan.* This design achieves even greater ecological protection than the rural cluster plan by placing most of the development on previously disturbed agricultural lands. The ninety-six total units include forty single-family houses plus fifty-six units contained in fourteen four-unit structures. Valuable habitats protected and restored in this plan include the limestone glade (1), riparian (2) and upland hardwood and oak-pine forests (3). As in the rural cluster design (see Color Plate 13), roads, a playing field, and a village green provide fire buffers from the oak-pine forest. Although the density of the developed areas is higher than in the other two plans, residents have easy access to nature (4) as well as to neighborhood open spaces, including two village greens (5), a playing field (6), and community gardens (7).

Legend:
- Critical Habitat
- Rivers
- Roads
- Study Area
- Ridges
- Protected Area Boundaries
- Existing High Density Devel.
- Existing Low Density Devel.
- Wetlands
- Conifer Forest
- Mixed Forest
- Deciduous Forest
- Row Crops & Orchards
- Pasture & Grasslands

0   1 mi
1 km

N

Color Plate 15. *Local ecology map.* This figure depicts land cover, protected areas, critical habitat areas, roads, and streams for the community-scale study area.

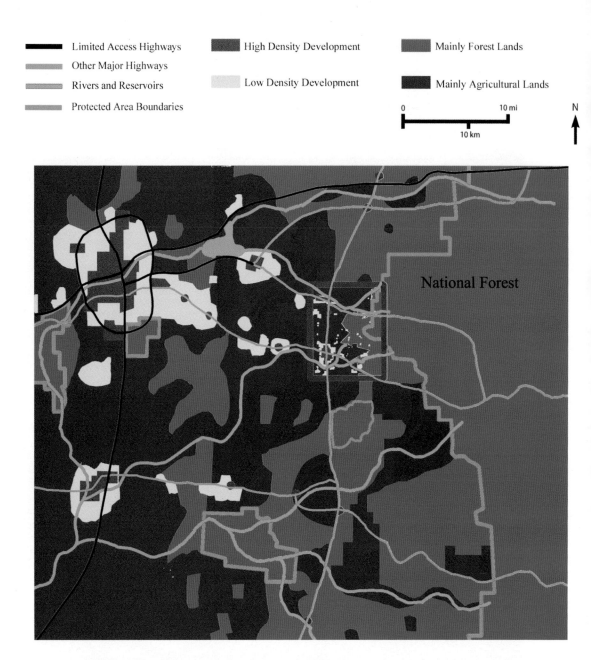

Legend:

- ▬▬▬ Limited Access Highways
- ▬▬▬ Other Major Highways
- ▬▬▬ Rivers and Reservoirs
- ▬▬▬ Protected Area Boundaries
- ▮ High Density Development
- ▮ Low Density Development
- ▮ Mainly Forest Lands
- ▮ Mainly Agricultural Lands

0   10 mi
10 km

N

National Forest

Color Plate 16. *Regional context map.* This map shows the community's human and ecological context. Note the spread of urban development east from the major metropolis, the proximity of the large national forest, and the mosaic of forest and farm lands south of the community that provides limited forest connectivity between protected areas. The red box denotes the area shown in Color Plates 15, 17, and 18.

Legend:

Rivers

Roads

Town Boundary

Protected Area Boundaries

100-year Floodplain

Wildfire Hazard

Wild Predator Hazard

Steep Slopes/Landslide Hazard

0   1 mi
0   1 km

N

Color Plate 17. *Natural hazards map.* This map identifies lands within the community that are most prone to floods, fire, and landslides, as well as areas where large predators are present.

Color Plate 18. *Land use plan.* This sample solution to the community planning exercise depicts recommended future land use. Features include open space protection targeted to the most ecologically sensitive lands in the community (1) as well as small tracts near the towns for human enjoyment (2); the use of transfer of development rights to buffer the national forest (3), conserve additional important habitats (4), and protect productive farming areas (5); and the direction of new development to land around the two major towns (6) as well as designated growth areas outside the towns (7).

Part Three

APPLICATIONS

Conservation biologist D. A. Falk once remarked: "The daily practice of conservation is as different from the world of theory and scholarly research as is the blackboard at a military academy from the battlefield."[1] He went on to note that actual conservation decisions are often influenced by economic, legal, real estate, regulatory, political, and public opinion considerations as much as, if not more than, by conservation science. These remarks are truisms to anyone who has worked in the land use professions, but it is telling that they appear in a book of scholarly scientific papers—a resource that few planners, designers, or developers would have the time or inclination to read and incorporate into their work. Throughout this book, we have tried to bridge this gap between scholarship and practice.

In this spirit, the next five chapters move from the classroom to the "battlefield," examining the ways that conservation science is, and could be, applied to land use planning and design projects. We begin in Chapter 7 with a discussion of conservation planning—the design of nature reserves and buffer areas—and then broaden the focus in Chapter 8 to include other types of natural and seminatural areas serving a range of needs, both natural and human. Chapter 9 introduces the burgeoning field of restoration ecology and discusses how planners and designers can reintroduce natural habitats and processes on degraded lands. This chapter also addresses the flip side of restoration: land management, or preventing degradation in the first place by incorporating ecological understanding into land stewardship.

Chapter 10 focuses on specific planning and design techniques that can improve project outcomes. The book concludes with an opportunity to practice applying the lessons of ecology and conservation biology to a two-part planning and design exercise, replete with much of the messiness of real-life professional practice.

7

Conservation Planning

Conservationists work to protect native species and ecosystems at many different scales, under many different conditions, and for many different reasons. "Pure" conservation planning is often conducted by groups such as The Nature Conservancy—when deciding where to establish a new nature reserve—or the U.S. Fish and Wildlife Service—when determining how to implement the Endangered Species Act. In these contexts, biodiversity conservation is often the sole—or at least primary—goal of conservation planning efforts. But with ever-growing human demands on a finite land base, we believe that conservation planning must be construed broadly to include not only the preservation of nature in relatively pristine reserves but also the integration of conservation values into landscapes that are influenced and even dominated by humans. Land use professionals have a central role to play in conservation planning for these non-pristine landscapes, which make up the majority of North America's land. In this chapter and the two that follow, we discuss the full range of conservation planning efforts under this broader definition. We begin with three vignettes that illustrate some of the issues and opportunities that arise as conservationists and land use professionals attempt to protect and restore landscapes.

One of the most extensive conservation initiatives ever proposed is the Yellowstone to Yukon (Y2Y) project. Begun in 1993, Y2Y is an attempt to link several existing conservation areas into an expanded network of reserves and buffer areas that stretches 2,000 miles (3,200 km) through a 460,000-square-mile (1.2 million square km) region (see Figure 7-1).[1] Dozens of organizations, including

Figure 7-1. The Yellowstone to Yukon (Y2Y) project is an attempt to link existing and proposed reserves in western North America. The proposed reserve network within the project area shown on this map could support a viable population of grizzly bears and many other species.

advocacy groups and mainstream conservation groups, have promoted the Y2Y project or become active partners in it. Y2Y is intended to protect a wide variety of ecosystems across western North America while paying special attention to providing adequate habitat for a large and sustainable population of grizzly bears (*Ursus arctos horribilis*). To achieve this goal, it must not only set aside additional nature reserves but also work with a wide variety of rural landowners across five states, two provinces, and two territories. Given the vast area involved and the different sets of laws, customs, and expectations across the project area, the founders of Y2Y view it more as a "bottom-up" collection of conservation projects at several scales than as a single "top-down" program.

A few hundred miles south of Yellowstone National Park, the Socorro springsnail (*Pyrgulopsis neomexicana*) survives as just a single population on a piece of private property. The world's entire population of this snail lives in a thermal pool less than three feet (1 meter) square and in its associated eight-foot (2.5 m) long outflow ditch. In 1994, the U.S. Fish and Wildlife Service approved a draft recovery plan for these tiny snails, which are less than 0.1 inch (3 mm) in length, calling for a habitat management plan to be created in consultation with the owners of the springs. The Socorro springsnail's beach towel–sized habitat is located entirely on private land, but if this habitat can be protected, and if additional populations can be established in the region, this gravely endangered species will have an improved chance of surviving into the future.

To the west lie the chaparral and coastal sage scrub of Southern California. These very diverse plant communities are part of a Mediterranean-climate ecosystem, one of just five such ecosystems on the planet. The communities contain numerous *endemic species* (species found nowhere else) as well as such threatened and endangered species and subspecies as the Stephens' kangaroo rat and the Coastal California gnatcatcher. The San Diego Multiple Species Conservation Program and the Multiple Species Habitat Conservation Plan of Riverside County represent two far-reaching attempts to protect significant amounts of these rare ecosystems and their endemic species. To do so, the conservation plans spell out not only where land should be set aside to protect critical habitat but also where land can be developed to accommodate Southern California's burgeoning population. Given that land in the area is vastly more expensive than the cost of an equal amount of land in most of the Y2Y project area, the conservation plans draw on a range of legal and financial tools other than the acquisition of nature reserves.

Different Types of Conservation and Open Space Areas

As the preceding examples demonstrate, conservation issues occur at many different scales and in markedly different contexts. Conservation efforts also vary greatly in the extent to which they integrate nonconservation issues and goals; for example, protecting the Socorro springsnail may rely above all on a sound biological strategy for managing the genetic resources of a small population, while the Southern California habitat conservation efforts integrate the multitude of economic, social, land use planning, and political considerations present in a major metropolitan area. Before discussing the mechanics of conservation planning, it is worth establishing a basic typology of natural areas, from strict nature reserves at one extreme to small urban open spaces at the other. The eight categories presented below move in a progression from the most pristine and highly protected natural areas to the least so.

Category 1: Strict nature reserves and wilderness areas. These lands have been set aside to protect native species in a more or less natural setting with little or no human interference. Among conservation biologists (and many other segments of society), a consensus exists that some portions of the landscape should be restricted to minimal human use so that natural processes can unfold unimpeded. Some of these areas are suitable for low-impact recreation such as birdwatching and wilderness hiking, while others may be off-limits to any human use other than occasional scientific monitoring. If these areas are large enough and in good condition to begin with, they may be able to survive long into the future with little human intervention. Examples of this type of conservation area include designated Wilderness Areas within U.S. National Forests—which have no roads, recreation facilities, or resource extraction activities—and Research Natural Areas on U.S. Bureau of Land Management (BLM) lands—which are "managed for minimum human disturbance."[2] These areas fulfill important habitat protection roles as well as serving human needs to experience untrammeled and unmanipulated nature. While these lands tend to be relatively ecologically intact, many of them are missing top predators, such as mountain lions, wolves, and grizzly bears.

Category 2: Reserves actively managed for biodiversity protection. These areas receive more intervention by land managers than those in Category 1, with more manipulation, restoration, or management of particular species or ecosystems. These landscapes, which are managed to protect native biodiversity, may also be compatible with low-impact human uses, including hiking, bird-watching, and nature photography. Many reserves managed by governmental agencies and nonprofit conservation organizations fall into this category.

Category 3: National parks and monuments. These lands frequently play a key role in biodiversity protection, but human recreation and education are also important parts of their mission. Many national parks, such as Yellowstone and the Great Smoky Mountains, function as large, well-buffered nature reserves that can sustain populations of large carnivores or migrating herbivores (hoofed, herbivorous quadruped mammals) as well as numerous other species; these parks also serve the crucial role of exposing the public to nature. Other areas were set aside as parks because they contain extraordinary geological features, such as Yosemite National Park, or represent unique human-shaped "cultural landscapes," such as Mesa Verde National Park in New Mexico. In these areas, biodiversity protection may be an important function even though it was not the original reason for creating the park.

Category 4: Multi-use managed areas. These are true multi-use lands, managed for production (e.g., timber, livestock, and mining), recreation, and biodiversity protection. U.S. National Forests ("land of many uses"), state and provincial forests, and BLM holdings all fall into this category. Although these lands experience heavy human impacts that the previous categories do not, they are often very important for protecting biodiversity or for buffering more strictly protected lands.

Category 5: Working lands. Lands such as managed forests, military bases, farms, pastures, and mining areas serve human needs, but many also contain pockets or even large areas where native biodiversity can thrive—for example, on many small-scale farms, military reservations, or woodlots. On the other hand, large monoculture farms usually offer little value for biodiversity protection. Working farms and forests often play a key role in protecting scenic views and are valued by communities because they help give an area its unique character.

Category 6: Local nature areas. Local nature areas are like the comfortable old shoes or sweaters of one's home or neighborhood—easily accessible places where you can walk your dog, hear a few birds, or see some wildflowers. These are the places that most people will experience as "nature" week in and week out. In most cases, these lands are not great preserves for native biodiversity or sites for ecological research because they are heavily affected by human use and by their proximity to human neighborhoods. This category includes public, non-profit, and sometimes private lands, such as town forests, suburban greenways, local land trust holdings, and private woodlots.

Category 7: Parks, school grounds, golf courses, yards, and other recreational spaces. This assortment of public and private lands is where people stroll among trees, play sports, or relax on a picnic blanket. These areas exist primarily for humans and are managed for recreation, so any native biodiversity that survives is usually incidental. However, if carefully designed and managed, such lands do have the potential to offer considerable habitat value.

Category 8: "Accidental" urban and suburban open spaces. Vacant lots, abandoned and active railroad rights-of-way, unbuildable land within cities and suburbs (e.g., marshes and ledge), and even some stormwater management ponds all represent pockets of nature that may play roles in both biodiversity protection and public access to nature. Although few of these areas are managed for biodiversity, and most will be rather low quality sites for native biodiversity, they gain importance because their surroundings are so heavily built up. As with more formal local nature areas, these places can also offer recreational and educational opportunities for people living nearby.

As is clear from the wide spectrum of lands discussed above, natural areas are created for many different reasons (sometimes for several reasons at once) and serve many different functions. For conservationists and land use professionals, it is important to be precise about what functions one is trying to provide and what type of natural area will best serve these functions. For example, woodlands set aside for general recreation require less buffering than nutrient-sensitive wetlands, while greenways for wildlife movement must be designed differently

Table 7-1.

Values and Functions of Different Types of Natural Areas

Conservation Functions ● Primary function ⊙ Secondary function ○ Incidental function	1: Wilderness Areas	2: Biodiversity Reserves	3: National Parks	4: Multi-Use Areas	5: Working Lands	6: Local Nature Areas	7: Parks and Yards	8: "Accidental" Urban Areas
Biodiversity Protection Functions								
Large, intact ecosystems	●	●	●/⊙	⊙				
Populations of rare species	●	●	●/⊙	⊙	○			
Corridors and stepping stones	●	●	●/⊙	⊙	○	●		○
Habitat for common native species	⊙	⊙	⊙	⊙	○	●	○	○
Economic Utility to Humans: Production and Ecosystem Service Functions								
Agricultural or natural resource production				●	●			
Watershed protection, flood control	●/⊙/○	⊙/○	○	⊙	○	●/⊙/○	○	○
Noneconomic Utility to Humans: Recreational, Educational, and Aesthetic Functions								
Active recreation							●	○
Passive recreation	○	○	●	●	○	●	●/⊙	○
Wilderness experience	●/⊙	○	●	⊙				
Viewshed protection	○	○	●	○	⊙/○	●/⊙	⊙/○	○

than those for bike paths or walking trails. Failure to understand these subtleties can lead to squandering of conservation funds and a failure to meet conservation goals. Table 7-1 offers a simplified matrix showing how well different types of natural areas serve different conservation, economic, and recreational functions. Since conservation functions obviously depend on the specifics of the situation and site, this table is intended not as doctrine but rather to spur critical thought about the various motivations for conserving nature.

The remainder of this chapter and much of Chapter 8 discuss aspects of these eight categories of natural areas that are most relevant to planners and designers. The following subsections discuss nature reserves (Categories 1 and 2), offering guidance to land use professionals on selecting and designing such areas. National parks and multi-use areas (Categories 3 and 4) are addressed briefly at the end of this chapter. Chapter 8 discusses Categories 5 through 8: those types of natural and seminatural areas that are intended to meet a variety of human and ecological goals.

Selecting and Designing Nature Reserves

Despite continual improvements in the theory and practice of conservation science, selecting and designing nature reserves remains something of an art, and thinking on this topic continues to evolve (see Box 7-1). Below we present a four-step process for selecting and designing nature reserves that can guide planners and designers working to create or connect to natural areas at various scales.

Step 1: Creating an Inventory of Conservation Assets, Opportunities, and Threats

The first step in selecting and designing nature reserves is to identify the elements of nature that are present within a particular geographic area, those that are worth conserving, and the ways in which they are threatened. This holds true whether one is seeking to conserve a wide-ranging group of large carnivores (as in the Y2Y project) or a single animal species with a tiny habitat range (as with the Socorro springsnail).

While writing this chapter, we received an e-mail from Jae Choe, one of Korea's foremost ecologists. He began by writing: "I am preparing a paper or plea to try to save the DMZ [demilitarized zone] here in Korea. The reunification of South and North Korea may mean the end of the DMZ."[3] Why should an ecologist worry about the Korean DMZ? As it turns out, during the half-century since its establishment, this 2.5- by 154-mile (4 by 248 km) strip of land has become a de facto nature reserve. True, shells occasionally go into or over it and land mines go off once in a while, but by and large this is an open area that has been left undeveloped for fifty years.

In response to Choe's e-mail, we created a series of questions, which we present in Box 7-2 as a framework that land use professionals can use to inventory, evaluate, and assess the ecological resources and threats to nature in the places where they work. For planners and designers, these questions will usually be asked in the context of a specific planning project; thus, the "study area" could be a single site, a group of sites, a town, county, or other political or jurisdictional entity.

SOURCES OF DATA FOR CONSERVATION INVENTORY AND ASSESSMENT

The questions shown in Box 7-2 require a considerable amount of data to answer, but planners and designers usually have rather limited resources for

Box 7-1
A Brief History of Nature Reserves

Hunting preserves for royalty and sacred groves where hunting and resource collection were forbidden were among the earliest portions of the landscape that humans set aside to remain undeveloped. Hunting preserves were common in Europe throughout the Middle Ages, although in many of the preserves the great predators were hunted into local extinction. Sacred groves and other sacred sites have been set aside by cultures in Africa, North America, and Asia over the centuries.[1]

The next great phase in land conservation began in the late nineteenth century with the protection of "Great Geology" and (to a lesser extent) "Great Beasts." In 1864, the U.S. Congress gave Yosemite Valley to California to be used as a state park, and in 1872, Congress created the world's first national park, Yellowstone National Park (see Figure 7-2).[2] Congress stipulated that the park should "provide for the preservation, from injury or spoliation, of all timber, mineral deposits, natural curiosities, or wonders within said park, and their retention in their natural condition" and, further, that it was "dedicated and set apart as a public park or pleasuring-ground for the benefit and enjoyment of the people."[3] In large measure, then, the motivation for setting aside the park was to protect geological wonders of nature for the enjoyment of humans rather than to preserve biological diversity. According to the National Park Service, other early parks—such as Yosemite (which California gave back to the federal government), Mount Rainier, Crater Lake, and Glacier—were set aside for similar reasons, while preservation of Native Ameri-

Figure 7-2. The 1872 federal act that established Yellowstone National Park as the world's first national park stated that the park was established "for the benefit and enjoyment of the people," as is inscribed on this entry gate.

can ruins was the motivation for creating such parks as Casa Grande and Mesa Verde. However, the growing tourist trade—and the influence of railroad companies—also played a major role in establishing the early parks.[4]

Wildlife conservation was also a motivating force for some of the early North American parks and became increasingly important in the early twentieth century. According to the terms of the transfer for Yosemite, California authorities had to "provide against the wanton destruction of the fish and game found within the said reservation and against their capture and destruction for purposes of merchandise or profit," a clear indication that wildlife conservation was at least part of the goal in protecting Yosemite.[5] By the turn of the century, the Great Beasts began to play a more prominent role in land conservation in the United States, as the following brief chronology shows.

1900   The U.S. government passes the Lacey Act, which prohibits the interstate transport of illegally caught wild birds and mammals. This legislation was in part a response to the massive killing of wild birds for use on women's hats (see Figure 7-3).

1903   President Theodore Roosevelt establishes the first Federal Bird Reservation, the three-acre (1 ha) Pelican Island in Florida.

1908   Congress establishes the National Bison Range (see Figure 7-4).

1912   Congress establishes the National Elk Refuge.

1913   Congress passes the Migratory Bird Act.

By the time the National Park Service Act was passed in 1916, both scenery and wildlife were officially recognized as reasons for setting aside national parks, as this statement from the act makes clear: "The fundamental purpose of the said parks, monuments, and reservations . . . is

Figure 7-3. Around the end of the nineteenth century and the start of the twentieth century, many women's hats were adorned with real stuffed birds. The resulting decline in bird populations helped spur the formation of such organizations as the Audubon Society. This hat from Montana has birds from New Guinea and Southeast Asia.

Figure 7-4. In 1908, as President Theodore Roosevelt grew concerned over the near-extinction of the bison, the U.S. government created the National Bison Range in western Montana. This 18,500-acre (7,500 ha) reserve still exists today and is administered by the U.S. Fish and Wildlife Service.

to conserve the scenery and the natural and historic objects and the wild life therein and to provide for the enjoyment of the same in such manner and by such means as will leave them unimpaired for the enjoyment of future generations."[6]

During the twentieth century, nature conservation became a continually larger and more sophisticated endeavor, beginning with the involvement of several government agencies and, by midcentury, expanding to include nonprofit conservation groups. In 1940, nearly 200 reservations managed by the U.S. Fish and Wildlife Service became known as "refuges" where it was "unlawful to hunt, trap, capture, willfully disturb, or kill any bird or wild animal." However, over the next three decades, legalized hunting (especially of waterfowl) became increasingly prevalent on these refuges and on other, newly created refuges.[7]

During the 1970s, both governmental and nonprofit organizations began creating reserves that focused on the habitat of rare species—not just on charismatic megafauna such as bison and hunting targets such as waterfowl. Since then, the U.S. Fish and Wildlife Service and The Nature Conservancy, to name just two groups, have created dozens and hundreds of reserves, respectively, to protect the habitat of rare and endangered species.[8] In contrast to the large, geology-focused national parks of the past, many of these reserves were established specifically to protect individual rare species, and many were relatively small.

More recently, conservation groups have begun to look at the larger picture, both literally and figuratively. Rather than focus only on rare species, conservationists have recognized that large areas of relatively common ecosystem types also merit attention; if we do not take care of healthy ecosystems today, then tomorrow they may be in far worse condition and much harder to protect, and many of the species they contain may then require active (and expensive) protection. In 1980, for example, the U.S. Congress passed the Alaska National Interest Lands Conservation Act, which added more than 53 million acres (21 million ha) to the National Wildlife Refuge System by creating nine new refuges and expanding seven others.[9] At the start of the twenty-first century, The Nature Conservancy began an ambitious campaign to protect large, high-quality examples of relatively common ecosystem types (so-called matrix habitat) as a way to prevent large numbers of species and habitats from ever becoming rare.

NOTES

1. Anil K. Gupta, "Policy and Institutional Aspects of Sacred Groves: Tending the Spirit, Sustaining the Sacred," http://csf. colorado.edu/sristi/papers/policy.html (accessed July 2, 2001).
2. U.S. National Park Service, http://www.cr.nps.gov/history/npshisto.htm (accessed July 5, 2000; Web page no longer available).
3. Barry Mackintosh, *The National Parks: Shaping the System,* 3rd ed. (2000), http://www.cr.nps.gov/history/online_books/ mackintosh1/sts2.htm (accessed July 2, 2001).
4. Mackintosh, *The National Parks.*
5. U.S. Fish and Wildlife Service, "Short History of the Refuge System," http://refuges.fws.gov/history/over/over_ hist-a_ fs.html (accessed July 27, 2000).
6. From the National Park Service Act (the Organic Act) of 1916, 16 U.S.C. 1, quoted in (and reference from) Michael J. Bean and Melanie J. Rowland, *The Evolution of National Wildlife Law,* 3rd ed. (Westport, CT: Praeger, 1997), p. 306.
7. U.S. Fish and Wildlife Service, "History of the National Wildlife Refuge System," http://refuges.fws.gov/history/index.html (accessed January 31, 2001) and links from this page.
8. U.S. Fish and Wildlife Service, "The 1970s: The Environmental Decade," http://refuges.fws.gov/history/chron/chron_ 1970_fs.html (accessed January 31, 2001); Noel Grove, *Preserving Eden: The Nature Conservancy* (New York: Abrams, 1992).
9. U.S. Fish and Wildlife Service, "The 1980s: Expanding the System in Alaska," http://refuges.fws.gov/history/chron/chron_ 1980_fs.html (accessed January 31, 2001).

collecting and interpreting ecological information. The following are a few possible low-cost as well as more conventional techniques for acquiring and analyzing ecological data. Appendix B provides a list of sources where much of this information can be found.

Remote sensing. Remote sensing data (i.e., aerial photos and satellite images) paired with geographic information systems (GIS) offer large amounts of information at a modest cost and thus are a good place to start, especially when working at scales larger than individual sites. Many state/provincial, regional, and local governments have created GIS data layers that are available to land use professionals for free or for a nominal cost, and data availability is increasing all the time.[4] The most important data layers needed to conduct an ecological inventory include land cover,* various hydrology layers, and any layers that map the occurrences of rare habitats or rare and endangered species. Remote sensing can

Box 7-2
Questions for Planning Nature Reserves

Questions of Ecological Status
- What *habitats and ecosystems* are present in the study area?
- What *important native species*—such as rare, keystone, umbrella, and dominant species—are present? For these species, are the local *populations* viable?
- Are they isolated, part of a larger population, or part of a metapopulation? Are there demographic problems? What *disturbance and successional processes* affect the study area? Will the study area need to be *managed* in the future to meet conservation goals?
- What is the *condition of the ecosystems* in the study area today? What did these ecosystems look like in *earlier times,* and do opportunities for *restoration* exist?

Questions of Human Impacts and Landscape Context
- What is the study area's *ecological context in space?* Key aspects of context include adjacent land uses, nearby protected areas, connectivity of the landscape, and abiotic flows, such as water and nutrients.
- What current and future *human activities* may change or influence the study area's ecology?
- What *legal and regulatory protections* restrict how lands within the study area may be used now and in the future?

also be paired with field assessments to provide "ground truthed" data about local ecosystems. For example, if field studies associate the red-legged frog with pools located in moist forests, then other instances of the same habitat can be flagged as potential (though not certain) red-legged frog habitat.

Scientific literature and agency data and records. Preexisting studies may offer surprisingly good information about the ecology of your study area. In the United States, excellent biodiversity information can be found at states' Natural Heritage programs (originally created through the joint efforts of The Nature Conservancy and state governments), while in Canada, a parallel network of Natural Heritage Information Centres and Conservation Data Centres operate at the provincial level. State, provincial, and federal wildlife departments, local land trusts, conservation organizations, and universities can also be excellent sources of information.

---

* Land cover and land use data both describe the surface cover of the earth. Land cover data usually distinguish among various types of forests, grasslands, or wetlands (e.g., coniferous forest versus mixed forest versus hardwood forest) and are especially helpful for ecological inventories. Land use data often provide more information on human settlement patterns (e.g., differentiating commercial from industrial land) but may lump all types of forest or wetland into a single category. If neither data set is available for your study area, aerial photographs coupled with field surveys can be used to determine land cover.

Field assessments. Field studies by experts, such as ecologists and wildlife biologists, are still the gold standard for obtaining ecological data. General habitat assessments (e.g., characterizing habitat type, prevalence of native versus exotic species, and overall "intactness") can usually be done relatively quickly, whereas painstaking work is often required to study populations of individual species (such as those subject to the U.S. Endangered Species Act). Small and midsize local governments usually have limited resources (if any) for this type of study but can require field assessments to be conducted prior to the development of large or sensitive tracts of land. These site-specific data, in turn, can be added to the community-wide or regionwide ecological inventory.

Local experts. Almost every community has resident experts on the local biology, whether they are professional ecologists, government employees, resident naturalists, or hunters. These people are a rich and often untapped resource, but planners must be cautious about basing a plan on individual opinions, even informed ones. In the 1960s, planners adopted the Delphi method to harness individual expertise while minimizing the risk of error or bias. Like supplicants consulting the oracle at Delphi, planners pose a series of questions to the experts, who are questioned one at a time. Based on the answers, a second round of questions is posed until responses coalesce around a consistent set of themes. Researchers in North Carolina recently used this approach to identify focal species for a habitat planning project.[5] One can envision many other applications of this technique to biodiversity protection planning, such as identifying critical habitat linkages for a region or restoration objectives for a site.

Community bioassessment. One way to obtain inexpensive place-specific ecological information is to mobilize community members to conduct biological inventories and ongoing monitoring. Ecologists have developed a number of simple "rapid appraisal" protocols that encourage citizens to get involved in ecological assessments. For example, one program in New Mexico examined riparian ecosystems using twelve criteria that could be evaluated by nonexperts (including high school students) in less than an hour using only a tape measure, insect screening, and a wristwatch.[6] In addition to providing valuable data, community-based bioassessment methods can increase public participation in and support for conservation efforts.

Step 2: Selecting Conservation Target(s)

Once the conservation inventory has been completed, the next step is the subjective process of selecting goals, or *conservation targets*—those components of biological diversity and ecosystem functioning that are considered most important to conserve. Since different targets will result in different conservation outcomes, it is especially critical that planners and designers are clear about their goals. Otherwise, the newly created reserve may not serve the desired functions.

Conservation biologists Michael Soulé and Dan Simberloff identify three principal types of goals that conservationists may have in establishing nature reserves:

- To maintain the functioning of ecosystem services, such as watershed protection and flood control (as we saw in the example of New York City's water supply in Chapter 1)
- To preserve biodiversity in the aggregate by protecting habitats and ecosystems
- To conserve particular species or groups of species—often "flagship" species, such as charismatic mammals or birds, but also less prominent species[7]

Conservationists frequently recommend selecting conservation targets from more than one of these categories in order to improve the chance that critical biodiversity is protected. For example, as we saw in Chapter 5, devoting resources to protecting an endangered species may be futile if the ecological relationships and environmental conditions that the species requires are lost. On the other hand, focusing only on ecosystem protection might mean that endangered species with unique needs will not be accommodated.

Step 3: Identifying Reserve Locations and Creating Reserve Networks

Once conservation targets have been selected, the next step is to identify possible sites that are likely to conserve these targets from among a list of candidate sites within the study area. Frequently, the list of possible sites will already have been narrowed significantly by such factors as existing land use patterns, land ownership, and political and economic considerations. In many cases, there is no single right answer about where to site a nature reserve, but in other situations, the appropriate location of a nature reserve is constrained to a few sites or even to one. For example, the Jasper Ridge Biological Preserve in Northern California contains a rare type of grassland that is found only on serpentine soils (a geographically restricted soil type), and the Haleakala Volcano on Maui in Hawaii is the only place where the Haleakala silversword grows. No other sites would have served these purposes. At the other end of the spectrum, parks are often created in part to bring humans into contact with common species, such as various small mammals, birds, or wildflowers. For this type of open space, almost any moderately natural and scenic area can work well. Most nature reserves lie somewhere between these extremes: although they could not have been placed just anywhere, their sites were quite possibly chosen from one of several roughly comparable locations.

When designing a network of reserves across a region or landscape (or when selecting the best single reserve given the regional context), two general rules can help.[8] First, the principle of complementarity suggests that one should select areas that are dissimilar so that a broad range of species and habitats is protected by relatively few reserves. Second, the principle of irreplaceability places an especially high value on sites that contain rare or unique native ecosystems that would be difficult to re-create elsewhere if they were destroyed or degraded.

One technique that can offer practitioners guidance on how to select nature reserves from a group of candidate sites is *gap analysis*. This approach uses GIS technology to compile information on the potential or known ranges of numerous species and then compares this information to the current location of nature reserves. Planners can then propose new reserves for areas where large numbers of species (especially rare species) occur outside of protected areas—the conservation "gaps." The Biological Resources Division of the U.S. Geological Survey is currently running a major gap analysis program covering the United States, and its data are available for downloading.[9]

Step 4: Designing an Effective Nature Reserve

The final step—reserve design—involves not only locating the reserve but also determining its size, shape, edge characteristics, and relationship to other features in the landscape. As Gary Meffe and C. Ronald Carroll point out in their book *Principles of Conservation Biology*, "the phrase 'reserve design' is actually something of a misnomer," since conservationists rarely have the luxury of actually designing reserves; instead, they might be able to select from among a range of choices that has been severely constrained by other human demands on the land.[10] But even though "designing" reserves is more feasible in some situations than in others, the guiding principles are useful in all cases. This discussion builds on the concepts presented in Chapters 4, 5, and 6, but with a focus on applying ecological principles to creating effective reserves.

RESERVE SIZE

Conservation biologists frequently recommend that reserves be as large as possible and connected to other reserves, for the reasons discussed in Chapter 6:

- All else being equal, large nature reserves and reserves that are close to other reserves will contain more species than small and isolated reserves will.
- Large reserves can support larger populations of predators and large herbivores, which enable the reserves to be better exemplars of native ecosystem than small reserves.
- Large reserves provide a greater proportion of interior habitat relative to edge habitat and are therefore better at protecting rare and endangered interior species.
- Large reserves can support larger populations of any given species, which can help populations avoid the problems that come from being too small (see pages 79–81).

In addition, large reserves can more easily accommodate catastrophes, such as massive fires and hurricanes, than small reserves can. Such disturbances are natural parts of the ecology of most regions, and they play important roles in re-setting the successional clock (as described in Chapter 4). But if one of these natural disasters were to cover an entire reserve, it would seriously threaten any species unable to tolerate the disturbance or the resulting change in habitat. For example, the 1988 wildfires in Yellowstone National Park burned roughly 36 percent of the park, or 793,000 acres (321,000 ha) (see Color Plate 6).[11] Because only 11 percent of the nationally protected areas in the United States and Canada are larger than 250,000 acres (100,000 ha), most of North America's reserves would have been completely burned by such a fire, leaving no refuge for fire-sensitive species.[12]

This example illustrates the importance of considering disturbance and succession prosesses when designing nature reserves. Conservationists often recommend that nature reserves be at least as large as the *minimum dynamic area*—the minimum area of land needed to be reasonably confident that every successional stage, and the species that rely on habitat at that stage, will continue to be represented as the landscape changes over time.[13] The minimum dynamic area varies greatly depending on the ecosystem but is usually several times larger than the extent of the largest disturbance that would affect the ecosystem (such as a fire, hurricane, or pest outbreak). Although planners and designers usually work at smaller scales than this, the concept is still relevant. For example, a designer choosing where to site a 25-acre conservation area within a 200-acre (80 ha) development site might learn that a 25-acre mature forest in the region is likely to be knocked down by a hurricane sooner or later whereas a 25-acre serpentine glade is unlikely to be completely eliminated by natural processes. Knowing this, the designer may select the glade as a better long-term conservation investment.

While large reserves clearly have many advantages over small reserves, in some situations small reserves are adequate as a substitute for or desirable as a complement to the large reserves. For one thing, not all regions have large areas that can become nature reserves, and in some situations, a small reserve fits the needs of a region or of a given species or small patch of rare habitat (as in the example of Jasper Ridge Biological Preserve). In addition, a series of small reserves spreads the risk of loss from disease or disturbance, especially in situations where no single reserve is large enough to contain the minimum dynamic area.

One way to determine the appropriate size of reserve for conserving a particular species is to consider the amount of suitable habitat needed to support a *minimum viable population* (MVP) of that species. As described in Chapter 5, small populations face several types of demographic and genetic problems that increase their risk of extinction. Population viability analyses attempt to determine the population size required for a given species to keep it from succumbing to such problems. The MVP is usually defined as the number of individuals needed for a population to have a specific probability of surviving a specified number of years; for example, under one definition, a population would need to have a 95 percent probability of surviving for 100 years to be considered viable. When designing a reserve or reserve network with specific target species in mind, it is worth performing such analyses to evaluate whether the reserves will in fact protect a population that has long-term viability. If the population for which a reserve was created goes locally extinct after a few decades, scarce conservation resources may have been wasted. There are no easily applied guidelines regarding the size of MVPs, although they tend to be on the order of several hundred individuals for populations that experience immigration from other populations and several thousand individuals for populations that do not.[14]

ISOLATION AND CORRIDORS

Although conservation biologists generally attempt to make nature reserves as large as possible, constraints such as preexisting human land uses and high land costs frequently prevent the creation of large reserves. Yet, *very* large areas may be needed to maintain many critical aspects of biodiversity, such as intact forest ecosystems and hydrological networks; populations of large-bodied, wide-ranging mammals; and viable populations of other plant and animal species that occur at low densities across the landscape. In particular, many keystone species such as wolves, bears, wolverines, cougars, bison, elk, and caribou require large amounts of habitat, and a reserve that is not large enough to contain viable populations of native keystone species will probably change drastically if these species are locally extirpated.

To help these species survive and to maintain healthy ecosystems in landscapes where there are not enough large nature reserves, conservationists and land use professionals must pay special attention to reducing the isolation of reserves. Creating corridors of natural habitat between reserves can be an important method for reducing a reserve's isolation (as discussed in Chapter 6), and this method has been increasingly used since the mid-1980s. Because conservation biologists refer to a wide variety of entities as "corridors," confusion can arise when different people refer to different types of corridors. Table 7-2 and Figure 7-5 describe a variety of landscape features that have been called corridors. Keeping in mind the caveats discussed in Chapter 6, land use professionals should consider incorporating corridors into their land protection schemes as a way of maximizing the ability of populations to interact throughout the entire landscape and to maintain viability into the future.

RESERVE SHAPE

The shape of a reserve can have a surprisingly large impact on its ability to perform its intended functions. The most important aspect of reserve shape is the relative proportion of edge and interior habitats, because (as discussed in Chap-

Table 7-2.

Types of Habitat Corridors

Type of Corridor and Description	Functions and Benefits
Strips of native habitat, such as hedgerows and greenways, that link habitat patches.	These corridors enable animals to move among habitat patches and are the essence of what many biologists mean when they use the term.
Elongated habitats that follow long, narrow landscape features such as rivers, ridgelines, or rights-of-way.	Although these "corridors" do not necessarily connect larger habitat patches, they may protect important habitats.
A series of stepping stone refuges for migrating birds.	These may be a useful alternative to a true movement corridor for birds and other migratory animals.
Tunnels under highways (or bridges over them) that allow animals to move across the landscape.	These linkages help prevent roadkills and keep populations genetically connected.
Megacorridors, which are essentially large, oblong nature reserves.	Corridors that are wide enough to contain the average home range of large carnivores—up to 14 miles (22 km) wide—may help in large-scale conservation efforts, such as the Y2Y initiative.[1]

Source: Based on Daniel Simberloff et al., "Movement Corridors: Conservation Bargains or Poor Investments?" *Conservation Biology* 6 (1992): 493–504.

[1]Gary K. Meffe, C. Ronald Carroll, and contributors, *Principles of Conservation Biology,* 2nd ed. (Sunderland, MA: Sinauer, 1997), p. 326.

ter 6) edges generally provide inferior habitat from the standpoint of biodiversity conservation than interior areas do. According to the generally accepted wisdom, "plump" reserves—those with a high ratio of area to perimeter—are more effective in the long run than are slender reserves or those with wrinkled boundaries because they have the most interior habitat and the least edge habitat (see Color Plate 7). Large reserves also have a higher proportion of interior habitat than do small reserves.

Small Locally Important Reserves and Large Nationally Important Reserves

Although planners and designers are rarely called on to create new national or state parks or forests (natural area Categories 3 and 4), these reserves are nevertheless often important to the communities where land use professionals work. Many regions, especially in western North America, have considerable area devoted to

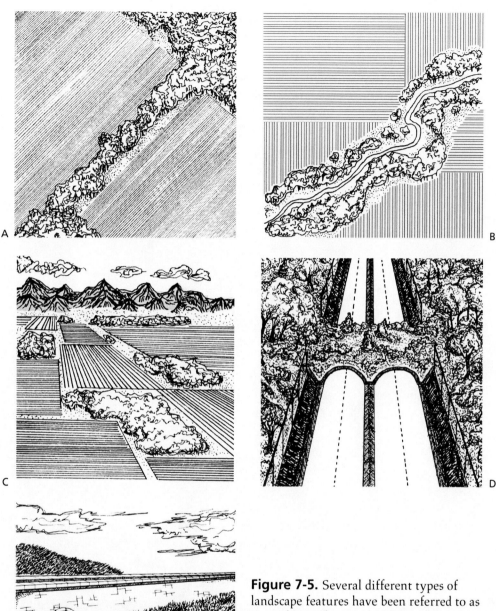

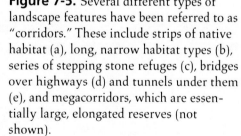

Figure 7-5. Several different types of landscape features have been referred to as "corridors." These include strips of native habitat (a), long, narrow habitat types (b), series of stepping stone refuges (c), bridges over highways (d) and tunnels under them (e), and megacorridors, which are essentially large, elongated reserves (not shown).

various types of parks and multiple use lands in public ownership. As we emphasize throughout this book, it is critical to know what is beyond the edges of one's immediate planning area in order to identify both potential threats and potential benefits. Public lands may offer planners an opportunity to link protected lands within their jurisdiction to larger reserves nearby, thus helping to protect native biodiversity.

8

Nature in the Neighborhood

Throughout this book, we have discussed the importance of large, intact native ecosystems for protecting biodiversity. Large wilderness areas also have a special importance for humans, as evidenced by the strong public support in the United States for protecting wilderness areas in remote parts of the continent, even if the vast majority of the population will never visit them. But while large wildlands are critical, they are not sufficient to fulfill all of North America's conservation needs; since large protected areas will constitute only a modest fraction of the landscape, we must also pay attention to the conservation values of cities, suburbs, farms, working forests, and other managed lands if we are to conserve nature across a full range of settings and scales. Nor do large wildlands offer ready access to nature for the majority of North America's population, which lives hundreds of miles from megaparks such as Yellowstone or Canada's Wood Buffalo National Park.

For most North Americans—and in the work of most planners and designers—nature on a day-to-day basis means the smaller natural and seminatural areas located close to our homes. These are the lands found in Categories 5 to 8 of our natural lands typology in Chapter 7: working lands, local nature areas, parks and recreation areas, and "accidental" urban and suburban open spaces. In this chapter, we explore these local natural and seminatural areas, beginning with a discussion of the values and functions they provide and then considering how land use professionals can improve the planning and design of such areas. We conclude the chapter by reviewing the costs and benefits of interspersing humans and nature and by suggesting ways to minimize the danger to human communities from nearby natural systems.

Values and Functions of Local Natural Areas

Local natural areas can provide significant conservation value for native species and ecosystems, even within an urban or suburban context. Humans, too, can enjoy both economic and noneconomic benefits from these lands, as described below.

Protecting the Local Natural Environment: Conservation in Ordinary Places

Although large parks are critical for protecting certain elements of biodiversity, such as large carnivores, most of the Earth's species are small animals, plants, fungi, and microorganisms that can survive quite well in small patches of natural habitat. Insects, arachnids, small vertebrates, and herbs and grasses can reach population sizes that have long-term viability in just a few acres or hectares, as long as the correct type of habitat is available.[1] Human activity in heavily urban or agricultural areas may, however, destroy exactly these small patches of habitat that are so critical for the organisms that specialize on them.

Wetlands are an especially powerful example of this phenomenon. Between 1780 and 1980, the coterminous United States lost more than half its wetlands while California, Illinois, Indiana, Iowa, Kentucky, Missouri, and Ohio all lost more than 80 percent of their original wetlands. Florida alone has lost more than 9 million acres (about 4 million ha) of wetlands. Many species require wetland habitats for some or all of their life cycle, so protecting these habitat patches is critical if biodiversity is to be conserved within the matrix of the human-dominated landscape. For example, 154 of the 214 vertebrate species (72 percent) observed in Florida's Econlockhatchee River Basin use wetlands exclusively or in conjunction with uplands to complete their life cycle.[2] Similarly, other organisms require specific types of habitats that occur only in small patches on the landscape, such as acid, alkaline, or serpentine soils. To protect these organisms, it is necessary to conserve the special habitat types on which they rely.

For species that utilize more common habitats, such as woodlands, grasslands, and shrublands, the ability to survive in urbanized landscapes is closely related to the size of the available habitat patches. Here, the concept of species-area relationships that we discuss on pages 99–100 becomes important. Table 8-1 illustrates the observed relationship between the size of urban habitat patches and species diversity for different groups of animals.

Table 8-1.

Sample Species-Area Relationships for Habitat Patches in Urban Landscapes

Number of Species on Different-Sized Habitat Patches

Patch Size (Acres)	Woodland Birds (Massachusetts)	Woodland Birds (Czechoslovakia)	Chaparral Birds (California)	Land Vertebrates (Czechoslovakia)
2.5	No Data	6	2	9
5	24	14	3	14
10	27	21	3	21
20	31	29	4	33
40	36	36	5	51
104	43	46	6	95

Source: Based on Lowell W. Adams and Louise E. Dove, *Wildlife Reserves and Corridors in the Urban Environment* (Columbia, MD: National Institute for Urban Wildlife, 1989), p. 15, tab. 1. Data in this table are derived from five different studies, each of which examined several different-sized habitat patches in a single region to compare the number of species from one or more animal taxa.

Obviously, it matters *what* species are present in a habitat patch, not just how many. Here, too, size is important. For example, in patches smaller than about twelve acres (5 ha), the bird fauna is likely to consist primarily or exclusively of habitat *generalist* species, such as jays, house wrens, catbirds, robins, blackbirds, and cardinals. Edge-sensitive, forest interior bird species—including migratory, insectivorous songbirds such as the ovenbird, veery, and several species of warblers, vireos, and flycatchers—begin to appear when patch size reaches about fifteen to twenty-five acres (6 to 10 ha), but some species require even larger patches (up to a few hundred acres or hectares).[3] A study of parks in Seattle revealed that urban woodlands of roughly 100 acres (40 ha) can support a bird fauna similar to that in much larger rural reserves as long as native forest vegetation is maintained.[4] Size is not the only factor influencing the viability of urban habitats for native species; connectivity, human disturbance, and vegetation management are also critical, as we discuss later in this chapter.

Remnant habitat patches in urban areas are especially important because they represent the last refuge for many species in a given region. Some of these habitat patches show up in odd places, such as cemeteries. For example, the Mt. Auburn Cemetery in Cambridge, Massachusetts, is a favorite spot for birdwatchers, and more than 200 bird species, including many migratory species, have been observed here.[5] This is no accident: In the 1800s, the cemetery's owners and designers deliberately planted tree and shrub species that they knew would provide food and cover for a wide variety of birds. Similarly, salt marshes and wetlands within large cities, such as New York, Philadelphia, and Washington, D.C., play important roles as stopover points for migrating shorebirds and waterfowl.

Even many rare species can survive in metropolitan areas. For example, New York City's Parks and Recreation Department has established a successful rare plants propagation program.[6] After creating an inventory of rare and state-listed plants throughout the city, workers propagated a number of species using local sources of seed and cuttings. These seedlings were then used to reintroduce rare plants and augment current threatened populations within the city.

In addition to those urban and suburban species that survive in remnant habitat patches, some species have learned to adapt and even thrive in buildings, city parks, rooftop gardens, and suburban backyards—often in ingenious ways. Peregrine falcons (*Falco peregrinus*), after being nearly extirpated from much of North America in the mid-twentieth century because of the use of the pesticide DDT, have made an impressive comeback aided by several groups of raptor specialists, including the Peregrine Fund. These highly efficient predators have now taken up residence in a number of cities, nesting on ledges high up on skyscrapers. In 2002, twenty-three peregrines were fledged from a dozen nests within New York City to the delight of birders (and the dismay of pigeons) throughout the metropolitan area.[7]

Local Production for Economic Development and Self-Sufficiency

Land-based industries, such as agriculture, forestry, and outdoor recreation, are important components of many local economies, even within major metropolitan areas. The American Farmland Trust estimates that 86 percent of the United States' produce and 63 percent of its dairy products are produced within urban-influenced areas.[8] The economic impact of these industries is not just in the jobs and direct revenue generated by farming and forestry but also in the supporting economy of processing facilities and related businesses. In some communities, the primary economic value of working lands is their scenic beauty, which can increase property values and attract tourist dollars. In these cases, private property owners contribute a significant public benefit by keeping their land undeveloped.

In today's globalizing economy, people often forget the benefits of local self-sufficiency, but to do so is a mistake. From an ecological standpoint, producing and consuming goods locally prevents the release of greenhouse gases as well as other environmental damage caused by transporting food, wood, and other products thousands of miles. Local forests and farms, many of them owned and managed by small landowners with a deep knowledge of their land, provide locally grown fruits, vegetables, and forest products that are often produced more

Figure 8-1. Local lands can provide useful resources, including firewood, lumber, and produce. The wood for this woodpile was cut and stacked by Brian Donahue, who has written extensively about the importance of supporting and using local forests and farms.

sustainably than agricultural or forest products from afar.[9] Yet, these lands are at risk: as development spreads outward from cities and into rural areas, the United States loses over a million acres (400,000 ha) of farmland each year, with much of this loss concentrated in especially productive regions, such as California's Central Valley.[10]

Producing and consuming local products from the land also makes us more aware of the impacts of our resource use decisions. When we use locally grown wood, we see the forests that it comes from and appreciate the effects that cutting this wood may have on the local ecosystems. But we may also understand that using wood from a rapidly growing second-growth forest near our home reduces the pressure to cut timber in more biodiverse old-growth forests across the continent or across the world (see Figure 8-1). While virtually all uses of natural resources affect the "global commons" of biodiversity, forests, oceans, or the atmosphere, humans can often reduce these impacts when they understand them more directly and see them locally.

The Power of Nature in Small Places

Many land use professionals strive to plan and design natural and built environments that not only meet basic human needs but also increase local "quality of life" by offering beauty, tranquility, and leisure opportunities. These goals are an increasingly large focus of citizens in inner cities and rural villages alike, who see natural areas as an important part of their hometowns. Here is the view of one citizen, the late Elizabeth McKinnon of Newton, Massachusetts, in an excerpt from a letter she wrote to city officials to persuade them to purchase a piece of forest:

> Recreation of the spirit for some can best be had by walking in the quiet woods; taking a picnic lunch to the pine grove on the hill and sitting with a friend or child on a thick bed of pine needles, unobserved; hearing birds and squirrels but no noises of the city; seeing a rabbit run across a clearing but no buildings, machines, or automobiles. Or by picking the purple and white violets on the banks of the brook; or by watching the ferns in spring grow from tight little curls to four-foot fronds in the swamp; or by traversing the network of narrow trails in the woods, made by how many generations of little boys playing Indians; or by picking as many different kinds of wildflowers as you can find to make a bouquet for your mother; or by coming across a colony of wild bleeding-hearts all in full bloom in June deep in the woods by the brook; or by watching a child, who when he was four was afraid of the woods, come running when he is seven to tell you about all the marvelous things he has seen in this small piece of wilderness that seems to him [as] rich and boundless as Yellowstone.[11]

The place McKinnon writes about is Cold Spring Park, a neighborhood park and nature area in Newton covering sixty-seven acres (27 ha). You may have a park like Cold Spring in your community: a place with some woods or grasslands, walking and jogging trails, soccer and baseball fields, and a couple of tennis and basketball courts. Biologically, Cold Spring is unremarkable; it contains a reasonable sample of local species—a local naturalist has recorded over 120 bird species in the park—but it is not a haven for native biodiversity, nor to our knowledge does it contain any rare or endangered species.

But if we consider the role it plays in the lives of children and adults living nearby, Cold Spring Park becomes very important indeed. Small places like this are the "nature" that most North Americans will experience during their formative years and throughout their adult lives (see Figure 8-2). Even for those lucky enough to visit a place like Yellowstone or the Grand Canyon, nothing replaces having easy access to nature near one's home, especially during childhood. Children who are able to explore tiny patches of woods or grassland or ponds in their neighborhoods develop a connection to the land and to the landscapes of their home region that will stay with them for their entire lives. They learn about the ebb and flow of nature and the cycles of life and death, and they understand that nature has an order and dynamic quite apart from that imposed by human care-

Figure 8-2. Small, local nature areas are often the main connection that children have with nature.

takers. They experience the sense of wonder and joy gained from watching birds, collecting autumn leaves, looking at insects under a hand lens, or simply inhaling the fresh smell of the forest in spring. They understand their place on the planet as members of just one of a vast diversity of species, each trying to survive in its own unique way.

Experiences such as these not only enrich our lives immeasurably but also help nurture generations of humans who care about protecting nature. Conservation biologist Frances Putz describes the impact that his neighborhood nature area had in steering him toward a life in conservation in an article entitled "A Breeding Ground for Conservation Biologists."[12] As a biologist, he acknowledges that his 2.5-acre (1 ha) patch of woods in suburban New Jersey has no real conservation importance—except that it helped turn him toward his career as a conservation biologist. The same can probably be said for almost every field biologist and conservationist: each one had a nearby piece of nature to explore in his or her childhood. On the other hand, those who grow up without so much as an empty, tree-covered lot to explore will probably miss a critical part of their personal development. Those who are cut off from nature have no understanding of nature's needs or of their own need for a healthy ecological surrounding. If people think that food comes from the supermarket, that wood comes from the lumberyard, and that animals live in zoos, what will they care about protecting wolverines and lynx in their natural habitat; cleaning up our estuaries; restoring our rivers, wetlands, and prairies; or protecting our forests? Will global climate change mean anything to them other than higher air conditioning bills and lower heating bills?

Some might ask whether the importance of nature in our communities is just a luxury for wealthy populations in developed nations, something to be considered once all our economic and social needs have been fulfilled. On the contrary, we would argue that access to nature is inseparable from human well-being. Madhav Gadgil, the dean of Indian ecologists, has stated that every child in every village in India should have a chance to experience a little wilderness—and that this should be a priority for the nation.[13] Dr. Gadgil knows very well the economic and social needs of his nation but believes passionately in the importance of nature for the healthy development of children, wealthy or poor.

Closer to home, in our own communities, nature offers a calming and centering influence in lives that are increasingly dominated by appointments, bills, cellular phones, and the trappings of a material culture—in other words, by stress. Psychologist Peter Kahn Jr., who researches how children and their parents view nature, quotes a parent from inner-city Houston: "It's a section of Alabama [Street] that I thought was so beautiful because of the trees, and they've cut down all the trees. And you know it hurts me every time I walk that way, and I hadn't realized that my son had paid attention to it, too."[14] For planners and designers, improving quality of life should be not just about providing better roads, better schools, and safer neighborhoods but also about keeping us connected to natural areas that refresh, enliven, and educate us.

Planning and Designing Local Open Spaces

Natural and seminatural lands in urban and suburban areas will almost always be multiple-use lands, providing some level of utility for plants and animals as well as for humans. Yet, how these lands are planned, designed, and managed can greatly affect their value for native biodiversity. Factors such as the size and shape of natural vegetation patches, structure of the vegetational communities, integration of water features, and management of succession and disturbance are critical, and all are typically within the purview of planners, designers, and developers. This section offers specific recommendations for how land use professionals can address these factors to improve the ecological compatibility of new and existing developments, public and private open spaces, and entire communities.

Working Lands

Working lands (Category 5 of the natural areas typology presented in Chapter 7) vary in terms of their habitat value from very little (e.g., monoculture farms) to moderate (e.g., some diversified farms and organic farms as well as production forests) to high (e.g., some ranchlands and lightly managed forests). In agricultural areas, retaining hedgerows, riparian corridors, and woodlots can greatly increase habitat for native species on the landscape; doing so is especially important for bird conservation because small patches of natural habitat may allow migratory species to traverse intensively farmed regions, such as the Midwest and the Great Plains.[15] Farmers can be encouraged to retain natural areas on their property through such initiatives as the U.S. Department of Agriculture's Conservation Reserve Program (which pays farmers not to cultivate sensitive lands) as well as educational and outreach efforts. It is important, however, that small habitat fragments and *stepping stones* in agricultural landscapes be coupled with larger habitat patches contained in formal nature reserves.

In working forests, the concepts of disturbance, succession, niches, and shifting mosaics presented in Chapters 4 through 6 can help inform ecologically based management. Retaining trees of many different ages as well as forest patches in different successional states will help increase habitat diversity on the site. In practice, this usually means using selective timber cuts (cuts that remove a portion of the trees at a time) or clear-cutting only small areas of the forest at a time. Rare vegetational communities and old-growth forests should not be cut at all.

Small Nature Areas and Local Parks

Planners and designers frequently create small nature areas in cities and suburbs through public purchase of land, incorporation of open space set-asides into new developments, and other means. The selection of such areas can benefit from a consideration of the "indispensable patterns for biological conservation" presented on page 114. One of these "indispensable patterns" is the protection of natural remnants in human-dominated areas that include—in order of priority—rare microhabitats, lands that provide valuable ecosystem services, and remnants of the former matrix habitat for generalist species and human enjoyment. Even in highly developed regions, opportunities often exist to set aside rare microhabitats, providing that planners have first identified these areas in municipal or county plans. The Blue River Glade, a small natural area of just eighteen acres (7 ha) in the heart of Kansas City, Missouri, illustrates this concept. This reserve is an excellent example of a limestone glade—a community type that is now rather rare in Missouri—and its proximity to urban neighborhoods allows local residents to participate in studying and restoring this special ecosystem.[16]

The design of small nature areas (Category 6) should follow the same general principles as for large reserves: maximize the area's size, interior habitat area, and connectivity to other natural areas while buffering the area from negative outside influences. Very small nature areas, such as those smaller than about five to ten acres (2 to 4 ha), will be mostly edge (see Figure 8-3). These areas will gen-

Figure 8-3. Small nature areas often experience extensive edge effects, as is the case for Hammond Woods in Newton, Massachusetts, where roads border and bisect the forest and where the pond has a large commercial development along an entire side.

erally not provide native habitat of the highest quality, but they can still protect important small habitats, such as vernal pools (seasonal water bodies that typically harbor a wide diversity of amphibians, insects, and other species). Regarding buffers, it is important to recognize that nature areas in cities or suburbs will often be subject to a variety of assaults, including fertilizer and pesticide runoff, human and domestic animal traffic, and noise and air pollution. However, these influences can often be reduced by establishing a low-intensity human land use, such as a park, playing fields, or low-density housing, between the nature area and the source of the heaviest impacts.

Nature reserves in cities and suburbs are often heavily used by humans, and indeed passive recreation is usually one of their primary purposes. However, if the site is large enough, planners and managers may be able to conserve its ecological value by "zoning" it into areas of different human use intensity. Many activities, such as picnic grounds and short interpretive trails, can be confined to portions of the site closest to roads and other sources of disturbance. This approach will keep other parts of the site relatively insulated from human foot traffic, which may help preserve populations of disturbance-sensitive animals as well as native understory plant species, such as orchids and ferns, while at the same time reducing invasion by exotic species. Land managers can further reduce impacts by restricting foot traffic to a few well-delineated trails and discouraging the formation of unoffical paths.[17]

Through creative and deliberate management, open spaces in urban and suburban areas whose primary purpose is not habitat conservation (Category 7 lands, such as municipal parks, golf courses, and school campuses) can also be transformed from biological deserts to valuable habitats. In many cases, a portion of the site that is not actively being used for recreation can be converted to a more natural area either through limited restoration work (e.g., planting trees and shrubs) or simply by allowing succession to progress. For example, at the Washington Elementary School in Berkeley, California, a 1.5-acre (0.6 ha) "environmental yard" was created by partially replacing an asphalt play yard with redwoods, meadows, small ponds, and a vegetable garden. The yard provides wildlife habitat and is used in the school's science education curriculum.[18]

Similarly, in Trumbull, Connecticut, the local land trust has initiated a "certified backyard habitats" program, which encourages landowners to plant their property with native species and wildlife-supporting plants. These backyard sanctuaries provide habitat for birds, mammals, and amphibians and offer some stepping stone linkages between community open spaces—all on private land that may otherwise be a monoculture of turfgrass dosed with toxic lawn chemicals.[19] Finally, as discussed above, parks and yards can also help buffer natural areas, especially if they are managed with minimal pesticide and fertilizer use. Specific landscaping guidelines to improve the habitat value of parks, yards, and other manicured landscapes are presented in the next section.

Ecological Landscape Design for Parks and Yards

It may not be an exaggeration to say that conventional landscape design is an environmental disaster. Turfgrass, which provides virtually no habitat value, covers an area in the United States about equal in size to the state of Pennsylvania—more land than is devoted to growing corn, wheat, or soybeans.[20] Lawns are also drenched with far more chemical pesticide per acre than farm fields, some of which ends up in streams and groundwater.[21] Furthermore, throughout the continent (not just in arid regions), watering of lawns and gardens is responsible for straining local water supplies and diverting water from aquatic habitats. Finally, many of the continent's most troublesome invasive exotic species are garden escapees, yet some of these species continue to be sold and planted.

Counteracting these environmentally damaging landscaping practices is a growing interest among some planners, designers, and landowners in designing small landscapes in a more ecologically sensitive manner. This approach has two principal components. First, native plants are used preferentially or exclusively in landscaping as a way of increasing populations of both the indigenous plants themselves and the various animals that depend on them. Second, the structure and placement of vegetation are deliberately planned to approximate natural vegetational communities of the area. Usually, this means designing multistrata landscapes that offer wildlife more resources and habitat niches than do simplified lawn and tree landscapes. Ecologists Margaret Livingston, William Shaw, and Lisa Harris suggest four factors pertaining to vegetation type and structure that are most important for enhancing the ecological value of a planted or heavily managed landscape, whether it be a backyard garden, a golf course, or the picnic grove at a county park:

1. *Total vegetative cover.* What percentage of the land surface is covered by plants as opposed to, say, buildings, pavement, or gravel?
2. *Native vegetation.* What percentage of the land surface is covered by native plant species?
3. *Escape cover vegetation.* What percentage of the land surface has vegetation with a shrub layer adequate to provide habitat for small mammals, reptiles, and ground-dwelling birds? This criterion can be measured based on the density of plant stems or leaf coverage per unit area and will vary depending on the habitat needs of animals in an area.
4. *Structural diversity.* How many layers of vegetation are present (e.g., herbs and grasses, shrubs, understory trees, midstory trees, and canopy trees)?[22]

Livingston, Shaw, and Harris suggest weighing the second and fourth factors twice as heavily because of their greater importance to wildlife. These criteria offer designers a semiquantitative method of comparing the habitat value of different landscaping alternatives. Similarly, planners could establish ecological landscaping guidelines as part of municipal or county development regulations, using these criteria as a way of measuring compliance.

Building on the framework presented above, Table 8-2 summarizes the ecological role of different types of vegetation within a landscape. When the goal of ecological landscaping on a given site is to provide habitat for a maximum diversity of native plants and animals, incorporating dense vegetation in all the different strata that would naturally occur on the site is a good strategy. Increasing a site's spatial heterogeneity (e.g., interspersing forest with meadow) will further augment habitat diversity but will also increase the amount of edge; thus, it may be a good option for small sites (e.g., less than five to ten acres, or two to four hectares) but not for larger ones. On the other hand, when the goal of ecological landscaping is to sustain populations of one or more rare species, the overriding concern should be to select vegetation that meets the needs of these species.

Table 8-2.
Role of Different Strata in Ecological Landscape Design

Vegetational Layer/Habitat Type	Habitat Functions and Values
Native grassland	High plant diversity; habitat for numerous insects, ground-nesting birds, and mammals.
Native shrubland or desert scrub	Often supports high diversity of birds, mammals, and reptiles.
Forest herb layer	In forest communities, many rare plant species are found in the herb layer. Replacing it with grass to create a park-like setting will eliminate this element of biodiversity.
Forest shrub layer	Cover and nesting areas for birds and mammals; food from fruit-bearing shrubs; insect habitat.
Forest midcanopy layer	Cover and nesting areas for birds and mammals; food from fruit-bearing trees; insect habitat.
Forest canopy (crown)	Conifers provide winter cover, while deciduous trees offer various types of food and nesting opportunities; including both can diversify habitat. Some species selectively use larger trees, which should be retained. Selecting species with varying flowering and fruiting cycles, as well as species that yield nuts, can also increase habitat value. In landscaped areas, maximizing the crown volumes of trees and shrubs is perhaps the most important single step to increase the number of species of breeding birds.[1]
Dead standing trees (snags)	Habitat for insects and cavity-nesting birds and mammals; food for insectivorous animals. If dead trees are not present or if it is not feasible to leave them standing, nest boxes can provide a partial substitute.[2]
Detritus	Dead wood and leaves contribute to soil formation and provide food and habitat for numerous decomposers and mammals. In dry areas, excessive detritus may increase the fire hazard.
Wetlands and water	The majority of vertebrate species in a region may depend on wetlands or water for part or all of their life cycle.

[1] R. M. DeGraff, "Urban Wildlife Habitat Research: Application to Landscape Design," in Lowell W. Adams and Daniel L. Leedy, eds., *Integrating Man and Nature in the Metropolitan Environment* (Columbia, MD: National Institute for Urban Wildlife, 1987).
[2] Lowell W. Adams, *Urban Wildlife Habitats* (Minneapolis: University of Minnesota Press, 1994), pp. 95–96.

Despite its numerous benefits, ecological landscape design has raised some concerns among designers and property owners that are worth addressing briefly. First, despite the concerns of some designers that natural vegetation is less attractive than planted exotic species, ecological landscaping, if well-designed, can be as aesthetically pleasing or more so than conventional landscaping. As landscape architecture professor Kenneth Lane has emphasized, an "ecological approach in landscape architectural design . . . need not negate visual design principles."[23] Second, although neighbors sometimes protest when a homeowner decides to plant native landscaping with a less well-tended look, courts have in some cases upheld the right of landowners to do so and rejected the right of municipalities to impose strict landscaping codes. Certifying one's property as a "backyard habitat" with a local or state conservation agency can improve legal standing.[24] Finally, in public parks, it is important to balance the benefits of dense vegetation with its possible security risks, although a recent study indicates that careful design can minimize this concern.[25]

Other Urban Habitats

While often overlooked as ecological features, stormwater management basins and constructed water features in new developments offer planners, designers, and developers an important opportunity to enhance plant and animal habitat. Many developments larger than a few tens of acres or hectares include such water features, either out of necessity or to provide occupants with a scenic and recreation amenity. To maximize habitat value, constructed ponds should have gently sloping banks and sides (a grade no steeper than one-to-ten is recommended) and contain shallow areas that will support emergent wetland vegetation.[26] Stormwater control structures that retain water, rather than just temporarily detaining it, can better support wetland and aquatic vegetation and thus offer better habitat. Shallow, marshy areas less than about three feet (1 m) deep provide better habitat for many wetland bird species than do deeper ponds.[27] Constructed water features can also have some deeper areas, which will provide even greater habitat diversity; some scientists have recommended maintaining a fifty-fifty ratio between marsh vegetation and open water for optimal habitat value.

Benefits and Costs of Interspersing Humans and Nature

For many land use professionals, safeguarding human health, safety, and welfare is the foremost objective of their work. Planners and designers are charged with ensuring that dwellings, neighborhoods, and communities are safe places to live, and most take this responsibility quite seriously. Throughout this book, we discuss some of the conflicts that can occur when human settlements are interwoven with forests, grasslands, and shrublands, yet we also point out the importance of providing easy access to nature for human communities. These lessons suggest that we should not pave over every acre but that neither should we be indiscriminate in siting development in natural settings. Instead, a nuanced understanding of the benefits and costs of interspersing humans and nature should inform the planning and design of human communities, an idea that we explore below using several examples.

The family of one of the authors lives beside a three-acre (1 ha) park that contains not much more than a Little League field, a small playground, and some open, grassy areas. The park's fauna is strictly limited to a selection of insects and occasional birds. No great ecological benefits accrue to the neighborhood from these three acres, and this is certainly not a place where children explore nature. On the other hand, this heavily managed and disrupted ecosystem creates no great ecological costs either.

Three blocks away, the sixty-seven acres (27 ha) of Cold Spring Park provide a wider range of benefits: neighbors walk or run along the park's trails, schoolchildren explore its woods, and its wetlands supply ecosystem services such as flood control. The park includes a well-developed fauna of insects, birds, and midsize mammals, such as raccoons, skunks, and opossums. There are no resident populations of large-bodied creatures or "megafauna," although residents occasionally report seeing deer, coyote, or wild turkeys in and around the forest. Cold Spring Park does not have an intact ecology, but it does provide significant educational and recreational as well as some ecological benefits to its human neighbors.

In 2000, this swampy park became the locus of an ecological problem. West Nile virus began appearing here in crows, which died in significant numbers throughout the neighborhood. Mosquitoes in the genus *Culex* transmit the virus from birds to humans, and although humans are just incidental hosts for this virus, it can be deadly in our species (see Figure 8-4). The standing waters and swampy areas of Cold Spring—which offer excellent breeding sites for mosquitoes—were implicated in harboring malaria in the early twentieth century and now facilitate the spread of West Nile, another exotic disease. Had the swamp been drained to make way for a school (as has been proposed several times), West Nile virus most likely would not have colonized Cold Spring Park, but neither would the park now provide the ecological and educational benefits that it does.

More extensive seminatural areas in suburban and exurban communities can provide even greater ecological benefits to their human neighbors—ranging from watershed protection to food and fiber production to scenic enjoyment—but the range of ecological threats from physical and biological sources may also be greater. Lyme disease provides an interesting case study of the relationship between land use and human health threats. Endemic to the U.S. Northeast and

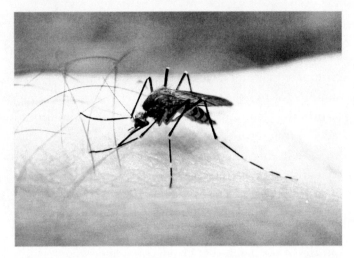

Figure 8-4. The mosquito-borne West Nile virus was first recorded in the United States and Canada in 1999. Since then, it has caused several human deaths and prompted the creation of seasonal mosquito control programs in cities throughout North America.

upper Midwest, Lyme disease is a potentially debilitating ailment caused by a spirochete bacterium (*Borrelia burgdorferi*) transmitted by deer ticks. Deer ticks rely on both small animal hosts (such as mice or birds) and large mammal hosts (such as deer or humans) to complete their life cycle, but the primary "reservoir" of the pathogenic bacterium is white-footed mice (*Peromyscus leucopus*).[28] By building houses in suburban and exurban areas, humans not only create ideal habitat for deer and mice but also insert themselves directly into prime Lyme disease breeding grounds. As it turns out, though, suburban areas appear to harbor many more infected deer tick nymphs than do exurban and rural areas. In places where humans have heavily fragmented the landscape with roads and housing, many species of small mammals have become locally extinct, allowing populations of the human-tolerant and bacterium-harboring white-footed mouse to explode.[29] Thus, we have a situation where preserving the biodiversity of local ecosystems tends to reduce the risk of human disease while sprawling and ecologically incompatible development patterns have led to documented increases in Lyme disease in humans.[30]

Fire probably represents the greatest abiotic threat to humans living close to natural ecosystems. As the Pine, Colorado, example in Chapter 1 illustrates, several factors can increase wildfire danger to human communities: proximity to fire-prone ecosystems, a history of fire suppression in these ecosystems, and architectural and site designs that increase vulnerability to fires. In fire-prone ecosystems, maintaining regular, naturally occurring, low-intensity blazes can help reduce fuel buildup so that massive crown fires are rare. With a natural fire regime, the risk to human life and property might be greatly lessened—but even then, should we be building homes deep inside fire-prone forests? Conversely,

Box 8-1
Goals to Consider When Interspersing Human and Ecological Communities

- *Protect the local natural environment.* Some regions no longer have large expanses of native habitats, so the role of biodiversity protection falls to the networks of smaller reserves and undeveloped lands that most regions do possess.
- *Realize economic value from local lands.* Land-based industries, such as agriculture, forestry, and outdoor recreation, are important components of many local economies. Given the critical role these lands play, land use professionals must carefully consider these lands in their plans.
- *Realize noneconomic value from local lands.* Land use professionals strive to increase local quality of life by planning and designing natural and built environments that not only meet basic human needs but also provide beauty, leisure, and opportunities for spiritual renewal.
- *Safeguard human health and safety.* Nature will always contain a variety of threats to human health and safety from fires, floods, storms, and pestilence. Careful planning of the interfaces between the built and natural environments can help prevent or lessen some of these problems.

even brush-choked forests would not be a threat to life and property if humans' homes were safely isolated from the fire-prone forests.

While we have offered several examples of how "unhealthy" or out-of-balance ecosystems can threaten the health and safety of nearby residents, it is worth noting that certain aspects of healthy ecosystems can also cause problems for humans. The populations of large mammals around Pine, Colorado, are quite healthy: elk and mule deer are plentiful, as are black bear and mountain lions. These last two predators can occasionally threaten humans. Although the risk is low, during the past decade, several people have died in mountain lion attacks in California and Colorado, and a degree of caution is warranted. Thus, while we advocate land use choices that maintain healthy, intact ecosystems, humans must recognize that even healthy ecosystems may contain some sources of danger.

We conclude this chapter by reviewing the factors (as shown in Box 8-1) that planners should consider when determining whether, how, and to what extent to intersperse humans and nature in communities and regions.

Do the benefits of interweaving human and ecological communities outweigh the costs? Or, are there ways to interweave humans and nature safely, so that we can reap the benefits with minimal risk from physical threats, such as fires and

Box 8-2
Guidelines for Interspersing Humans and Nature

- *Whenever possible, keep natural systems intact.* In general, healthy ecological communities are good not only for the organisms living in them but also for neighboring human communities. Conversely, communities that are ecologically unbalanced as a result of the removal of key native species, the introduction of exotic species, or the suppression of natural disturbance processes may present a significant human health or safety hazard.
- *Whenever possible, buffer human settlements from natural systems.* Even in healthy ecosystems, some biotic or abiotic elements may spill over the boundaries between human and natural communities. Wolves, mountain lions, deer, and bison wander out of reservations; beavers drastically change the landscapes where they live; birds and mosquitoes fly over human-created boundaries; and fires and floodwaters stop for no human demarcations. Conversely, humans, pets, and other human-generated effects cross into natural communities. As a result, in most regions, we will need to maintain buffers that protect nature from us and us from nature.
- *When it is not possible to maintain intact natural systems, consider the need for active management to reduce threats to human settlements.* If we do not have healthy, balanced, and buffered ecosystems, we may need to adjust the way our local ecosystems operate so that they do not harm us. For example, we may need to develop preventive fire regimes, clear brush, or manage populations of animals such as deer so that they do not create health problems for neighboring human communities.

floods, and biological threats, such as Lyme disease and West Nile virus? The principles shown in Box 8-2 may help lead us in that direction.

In this and the previous chapter, we have discussed natural and semi-natural areas of various types; in the next chapter, we will discuss how damaged lands can be restored and how natural and semi-natural lands can be managed for long-term ecological health.

9

Restoration and Management

Recall for a moment the imaginary transcontinental flight that we took at the beginning of Chapter 6. Viewing North America from the air quickly reveals that humans have changed the land dramatically across most of the continent; in fact, some regions have few or no remaining large blocks of intact habitat. Furthermore, the land is dotted, if not blanketed, with sites in various states of degradation, from intensively used agricultural lands to mining sites to urban brownfields. Many conservationists who once wrote off such human-influenced landscapes as lost causes now recognize the importance of trying to create healthier ecosystems from those that have been overused or abused. The process of improving and maintaining the health of ecosystems is the subject of this chapter.

Just as there is no simple dichotomy between pristine and damaged ecosystems, there is no single process that turns a damaged area into one that is again ecologically intact. Conservationists have proposed various terms to describe the improvement of sites, but we will use just two: *restoration* and *reclamation*. *Restoration* means returning an ecosystem to its original condition or state, while *reclamation* focuses on the remediation of heavily damaged sites so that they can serve some useful purpose even if they are not brought all the way back to their original condition (see Figure 9-1). To illustrate these concepts, we present case studies of two sites that lie at very different points on the continuum: the copper mines of Butte, Montana, and the grasslands of Prairie Crossing, in Grayslake, Illinois.

Figure 9-1. Ecosystems range in condition from pristine to heavily damaged. The processes of reclamation and restoration move ecosystems toward the pristine end of the continuum.

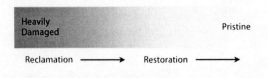

Reclaiming Land after Mining in Butte, Montana

In Butte, Montana, underground and open-pit copper mines have disrupted much of the landscape. When we say "in Butte," we do not mean *near* Butte or *in the general region of* Butte; these mines are right in the city (see Figure 9-2). Here, at the largest Superfund cleanup site in the United States, ecological restoration efforts are focused not on creating a close approximation of a pristine native habitat but on creating more livable neighborhoods in a city that has been ravaged by the effects of mining for more than a century.[1] Several distinct processes have led to Butte's environmental problems, and each requires its own responses to return the landscape to a healthier state.

Butte and mining have been synonymous since the late 1800s. Gold was discovered there in 1864, and silver soon after, but the really serious money came from one of the most base of metals: copper. Marcus Daly discovered copper here in 1882, and by 1884, 300 copper mines were operating on The Hill, as Butte is often called.[2] At least a few of Butte's underground mines continued to operate until 1975, but a drastic change in technology to open-pit mining took place in 1955 when the Berkeley Pit opened. The Pit, like the underground mines, was in the city—but in this case, the Pit destroyed the city one neighborhood at a time to get at the copper ore below. By 1982, when mining in the Pit was finally shut down, the hole in the ground measured 1 mile by 1.5 miles (1.6 by 2.4 km), and it was over a quarter-mile (0.4 km) deep.[3]

The different types of mines created different environmental problems. The old underground mines, some of which went down nearly a mile (1.6 km), brought up huge amounts of ore full of various heavy metals. While most of the ore went by train to a nearby smelter, a great deal of material stayed in and around Butte, polluting the ground with these metals. The Pit, however, was another story. When mining ceased in 1982, workers shut off the giant pumps that had kept the Pit and adjoining mine shafts free of water. Groundwater began seeping into the Pit and surface water ran in as well, adding about 6 million gallons (22 million L) per day to the Pit and causing the water level to rise approximately two feet (0.6 m) per month.[4] However, the liquid flowing into the Pit is not really water—at least, it is nothing you could use for drinking or washing. Because the surrounding rock contains sulfur compounds, the liquid is really a

Figure 9-2. In Butte, Montana, copper mining has taken place for over a century. Here, a headframe, which stood over the top of a mine shaft, still stands in a Butte neighborhood.

sulfuric acid solution full of heavy metals. Hydrologists have calculated that when the acid in the Pit reaches a level of 5,410 feet (1,650 m) above sea level, it will begin to flow outward and contaminate the underground aquifer. This situation, unlike the issue of contaminated tailings from older mines, is continually getting worse and is expected to reach a critical state in about 2020, when the Pit's acidic water begins its migration outward.

In short, Butte has two major problems that need to be addressed: the heavy metals of the mine tailings that lie on the ground near the old underground mines and the metals and acid of the water in the Berkeley Pit. The challenge for restorationists working in Butte is twofold: first, to sharply reduce the threat to human and ecological health of toxic compounds in the soil and water, and, second, to return the formerly mined areas to land that is once again viable—either for natural vegetation or for limited human use.

Restoring Grasslands in Grayslake, Illinois

In Grayslake, Illinois, an hour's train ride northwest of Chicago, a group of neighbors in 1987 purchased a 677-acre (274 ha) tract of farmland that had been slated for a massive development. Instead of the 2,400 condominium units originally planned, this group proposed a smaller development called Prairie Crossing, which would showcase emerging principles of ecologically based planning and design. A major component of this plan was to transform large portions of the site—which at the time consisted of soybean fields—into restored prairies, wetlands, wet prairies, and savannas.[5]

In the reclamation of mine sites in Butte, any reasonable use of the land would be a large improvement over the existing barren piles of tailings. At Prairie Crossing, however, the developers and ecologists restoring the site had specific targets in mind for their restoration activities. They wanted to re-create high-quality examples of the type of prairie and savanna ecosystems that existed in northeastern Illinois before it became so heavily agricultural. To do so, they needed to address several challenges inherent in converting a heavily managed ecosystem into one containing the native species, structure, and processes formerly present on the site. First, decades of intensive farming had altered the soil profile and introduced chemical fertilizers, pesticides, and herbicides, creating a hostile environment for many native species. Second, because viable seeds for most prairie species were no longer present in the soil, the restorers needed to find sources of seeds or seedlings from other locations and successfully establish them in the restoration area. Finally, healthy prairies are highly dependent on frequent fires, but the restored grasslands at Prairie Crossing would be situated in the midst of a 362-house development, raising obvious management issues. To address these challenges, the Prairie Crossing developers needed ecological information that could guide the restoration efforts, they needed access to native plant species, and they needed expertise to implement the project.

The Restoration Process

As the examples of Butte and Prairie Crossing illustrate, restoration and reclamation efforts span a wide range of goals, scales, and contexts. However, several common themes run through most restoration projects, and a common sequence of steps is often used to advance such projects. In this subsection, we focus on the process of restoration rather than on its detailed mechanics. The information provided here is intended to help planners and designers assess when and how restoration might play a part in their projects, understand and critique restoration plans and designs that are presented to them, and work with restoration ecologists or engineers with whom they may collaborate on projects.

Ecologists Richard Hobbs and David Norton have developed a five-step methodology for guiding restoration projects, which we use here to structure our discussion. The process consists of the following stages: (1) identifying and addressing the processes leading to degradation in the first place, (2) defining restoration goals, (3) developing strategies, (4) implementing these strategies, and (5) monitoring the restoration and assessing success.[6]

Step 1: Identify and Address Processes Leading to Degradation

As the descriptions of mining in Butte and agriculture at Prairie Crossing demonstrate, the causes of ecological degradation are many and varied—but in all cases, restorationists must determine *why* a site has become degraded. If one does not properly recognize and address both the initial causes of degradation and any later problems that might have occurred, it is unlikely that restoration efforts will be successful. In both settings described above, the causes of degradation were obvious. Sometimes, however, the causes of ecological degradation are harder to determine; all we can see at first are the effects, and we must find the source so we can act. Restorationists may have to perform ecological detective work, such as trying to find the pollution source that is causing a lake to eutrophy (to become oversupplied with nutrients, a condition that can eventually lead to a loss of oxygen).

Although the original causes of degradation in Butte (the continual dumping of heavy metal–laden material on the surface) stopped once underground mining stopped, the area required significant cleanup. In areas where mine tailings were piled on the ground, restorationists had to remove the noxious material or cover it; in either case, they would have to bring in new topsoil and plant appropriate vegetation. At Prairie Crossing, initial soil testing revealed that years of agricultural practices had led to elevated nutrient levels, while certain non-native weeds associated with farms were abundant.

In some cases, the source of degradation is not an added component—such as toxic mine tailings or exotic species—but, rather, something missing from the ecosystem. This was the case in Prairie Crossing, where native grassland species and fire—a critical ecosystem process—were both missing from the landscape. Those restoring the site had to find seed sources and incorporate fire back into the ecosystem, without which it would be impossible to recover a prairie or savanna landscape. Thus, causes of degradation can include both "missing pieces" (e.g., species, ecological processes, or soils) and "unwelcome additions" (e.g., excess nutrients, pollutants, or unwanted species), and restorationists should look for both.

Step 2: Define Realistic Goals and Measures of Success

Goal setting is a critical stage in any restoration project—and one that can be exceedingly contentious. Perhaps the single most important word in the title above is the adjective realistic. However, what is "realistic" for one group of restorationists may be far beyond another group's wildest dreams—and since restoration requires money, time, and effort, goal setting will have an immense impact on the overall price, time sequence, and likelihood of a project's success. If, in an attempt to be realistic, one initially sets low goals, these expectations may put an upper limit on how effective the restoration can be. On the other hand, overly ambitious goals can lead to a project that spreads its resources too thin, resulting in less success than might have been achieved with more realistic goals.

The physical, chemical, and biological properties of an ecosystem represent three separate, though interrelated, sets of possible goals for reclamation and restoration. Physical properties include soils, topography, hydrology, and other environmental conditions. Chemical properties include measures of ecosystem functioning, such as carbon uptake by plants and nutrient cycling. Biological properties include the types, abundances, and distribution of species present as well as their interactions. These sets of properties are closely interconnected and can be generally thought of as a ladder: it is usually impossible to restore the biological or chemical properties of an ecosystem as long as the physical environment remains heavily degraded. Thus, restoration projects often begin with physical manipulations, such as smoothing out mining trenches or reestablishing natural hydrologic flows to a wetland. When setting goals, restorationists need to consider how and to what extent they will address all three sets of characteristics.

Butte and Prairie Crossing offer two very different examples of the relative emphasis that restorationists might place on physical, chemical, and biological restoration goals in different situations. In Butte, several factors influenced the development of the reclamation and restoration plan for the old mine sites. First was the sheer size of the problem. The mine sites cover several square miles, most of which contain heavy metal–laden soils. In addition, the giant, open Berkeley Pit is almost two square miles (5 square km), and surrounding areas are also damaged. Second, while the toxic metals found in these soils posed a threat to human and environmental health, the threat was not of the highest magnitude, since these metals are far less toxic than, say, mercury or dioxin. Third, the mine yards were virtually devoid of vegetation and their soils mostly could not support plant growth. Finally, the sheer volume of soils—1.6 million cubic yards (1.3 million cubic meters)—and the problem of disposal made it impracticable simply to remove them.[7] With these considerations in mind, it became clear that the project's principal goal should be to reduce to safe levels the amount of heavy metals reaching the people of Butte and the surrounding environment rather than to create a perfectly clean area. This "waste in place" approach could not have been considered if the project goal was to reestablish a pristine ecosystem.

At Prairie Crossing, the overall vision of the developers and their consulting ecologist Steven Apfelbaum, of Applied Ecological Services, was to restore many

Figure 9-3. Restored prairie at Prairie Crossing on land that used to be soybean fields. (Photo courtesy of Steven Apfelbaum.)

of the native prairie, savanna, and wetland communities that had been present prior to the early 1800s, but the specific restoration goal was much more nuanced (see Figures 9-3 through 9-5). First, Apfelbaum and his colleagues had to use clues such as nearby prairie remnants and historical records to determine what kinds of plant communities once inhabited the area. After they had a sense of the historical plant communities, they needed to decide whether the site could still sup-

Figure 9-4. Some homeowners in Prairie Crossing have elected to plant their yards with native prairie species. (Photo courtesy of Steven Apfelbaum.)

Figure 9-5. Restored wetlands at Prairie Crossing not only create habitat for native species but also contribute to the development's natural stormwater management system, which uses native wetland and upland vegetation to filter stormwater. (Photo courtesy of Steven Apfelbaum.)

port these communities or whether it had changed too much in the intervening years. Based on observed gradients in environmental conditions (mainly soil and moisture), they created a "plant species palette" for different parts of the site that reflected preexisting conditions as well as a realistic assessment of current land suitability. Finally, the restorationists considered whether to try to introduce the full range of native plants and animals that once existed at the site or a more limited suite of species. They determined that not only would it be cost prohibitive to introduce all species initially but that it may also be futile, since some species colonize a prairie only after it has existed for decades. In addition, because Prairie Crossing is part of the 3,000-acre (1,200 ha) Liberty Prairie Reserve and is located near the Des Plaines River habitat corridor, it was deemed unnecessary to introduce animals that could disperse to the site from nearby natural areas.[8]

The example of Prairie Crossing illustrates not only that it is not always possible or desirable to re-create exactly the historical ecological conditions on a site, but also that sound alternatives providing much of the structure, function, and biodiversity of the original ecosystem can often be formulated if adequate ecological research and planning is conducted. Regardless of the form the goals take, restorationists must make sure to specify their goals clearly ahead of time to give themselves a benchmark by which to measure their efforts.

Steps 3 and 4: Develop and Implement the Restoration Plan

Developing and then implementing a restoration plan are technically two separate steps, but because they are based on the same concepts, we discuss them together here. Since the 1980s, the field of restoration ecology has expanded greatly as conservationists have recognized the need to restore damaged ecosystems and as laws have been enacted to require such restoration. Early on, practitioners mostly improvised, generating new approaches and technologies with each new project. Now, however, a growing body of knowledge about restoration techniques exists, and land use professionals have hundreds of experts whom they can consult as well as numerous off-the-shelf restoration "products" they can incorporate into projects. Much effort has gone into developing restoration methods for specific ecosystem types—rivers, estuaries, grasslands, forests—and a wide variety of technical and semitechnical books are available on the subject.[9] Table 9-1 presents a range of restoration techniques that may be appropriate in projects with different challenges, goals, and constraints.

The restoration efforts at Butte and Prairie Crossing illustrate how restorationists combine different types of interventions to achieve a particular set of goals. For example, the restoration plan for Butte called for initial actions to improve the physical environment, such as moving especially highly contaminated soils to sites where they are less likely to affect the city's people and ecosystems, building concrete ditches to channel polluted stormwater into sedimentation ponds and away from Silver Bow Creek, and recontouring contaminated areas to reduce erosion and runoff before covering them with crushed limestone and eighteen inches (46 cm) of topsoil. Once these extensive physical alterations were complete, the biological restoration—which consisted of seeding with native plant species—was relatively straightforward (see Figure 9-6).

At Prairie Crossing, relatively few alterations to the site's physical and chemical properties were required, although restorationists needed to address the elevated nutrient levels that had resulted from years of agricultural fertilizer use. To do this, they planted cover crops that rapidly absorbed many of the nutrients, creating a lower nutrient environment suitable for the prairie species. Most of the interventions at Prairie Crossing were targeted toward changing the site's species composition. In a few locations where infestations of farm weeds would have impeded the establishment of prairie species, herbicides were used to reduce competition from the non-native weeds. In most areas, however, prairie plants were simply introduced and allowed to grow. Given the relatively large area being restored, seeding was chosen over seedling planting as the method for reintroducing the prairie plant species.

Table 9-1.

Examples of Restoration Techniques to Meet Different Restoration Goals

Ecosystem Component Being Restored	Restoration Goal	Sample Intervention Techniques
Physical properties	Remove toxic contaminants in soils	Mechanically remove soil Implement bioremediation (the use of plants or microbes that absorb or break down toxins)
	Reestablish aspects of natural slope and topography	Mechanically move earth Stabilize slopes using "geotextiles" or soil-stabilizing plant species
	Reestablish natural soil profile	Import topsoil or organic matter Plant fast-growing species to add organic matter
	Reestablish natural stream channel and bank structure	Mechanically remove dams or channelization structures Place woody debris in stream channel and bank using machines or human power
Chemical properties	Reestablish natural nutrient regime (on land)	Plant fast-growing species to absorb excess nutrients, then harvest them to remove nutrients from the site Plant nitrogen-fixing species or use manure or fertilizers to add nutrients
	Reestablish natural nutrient regime (in water)	Harvest lake weeds Dredge nutrient-rich sediments
	Improve riparian nutrient and sediment filtering properties	Plant various species with deep roots and ground-covering foliage Alter hydrology to create oxygen-rich or oxygen-poor soil zones
Biological properties	Reintroduce native plant species	Seed by machine or hand Plant seedlings or nursery specimens
	Reintroduce native animal species	Move animals from other populations Introduce animals from captive breeding programs
	Reintroduce soil biota to improve functioning	Inoculate soil with native soil insects, bacteria, and fungi
	Maintain or establish a particular successional state	Conduct prescribed burning Cut or mow vegetation
	Eliminate invasive exotic species	Conduct prescribed burning Physically remove exotic species using machines or human labor Apply herbicides or pesticides Introduce biological control agents, such as predatory insects, bacteria, or viruses

Figure 9-6. Reclamation efforts in Butte have transformed old mine tailings sites from bare, metal-laden earth, as seen on the right, to sites covered with native grasses, as on the left.

Step 5: Monitor the Restoration and Assess Success

The monitoring process should begin at the start of a restoration project with the collection of baseline ecological data that will allow for valid comparisons later. Once restoration actions have been implemented, it is essential to continue monitoring the site and assessing progress so that restorationists know whether their goals are being met and whether they need to adjust their plan of action. In Butte, for instance, the restoration plan called for revegetated areas to have at least 35 percent of the ground covered by an agreed-upon list of native plant species (see Figure 9-7). Specific goals such as this make it easier to assess the success of a restoration project and reduce the risk of disagreements between restorationists and regulators.

In many cases, it may take years or even decades for the natural process of succession to change a restoration site from newly reclaimed or newly planted land into the desired ecological community. Ideally, monitoring should continue during this period to assess the project's ultimate success. On sites where such long-term monitoring has taken place, the findings often attest to the ability of natural systems to heal themselves over time once negative human impacts are removed and limited restoration work is undertaken. For example, the 264-acre (107 ha) Tifft Nature Preserve in Buffalo, New York, was a municipal and

Figure 9-7. According to the reclamation plan, revegetated areas in Butte must have at least 35 percent of the ground covered by an agreed-upon list of native plant species.

industrial waste site as recently as 1972. Under pressure from local citizens, the city adopted a restoration and management plan in 1975 and replanted portions of the site with grasses, shrubs, and trees. By the late 1980s, succession had resulted in vegetational communities that provided habitat for 175 bird species, mammals including fox and beaver, and numerous reptiles, amphibians, fish, and invertebrates.[10]

Land Management

Almost everywhere we look, humans are managing land—a homeowner managing his quarter-acre yard for grass and flowers, a farmer managing her fields for corn or tomatoes, or a provincial park superintendent managing her park for recreation and wildlife habitat. Conservationists usually manage land to improve or maintain its habitat value for desired native species and to introduce, promote, or maintain various natural ecological processes and functions. Planners, designers, and developers may have numerous occasions to manage land or contribute to land management decisions. For example, they may be involved in preparing a master plan for a public park, establishing the terms by which common open space in a subdivision will be used and maintained, or formulating a plan or regulatory program to guard against such natural hazards as fires and floods. In this section, we focus primarily on managing land for biodiversity and other ecological values, but it is worth remembering that land management almost always has implications for both humans and ecosystems and that humans can benefit significantly from ecologically based land management efforts. For example, riparian management to preserve streamside habitat also helps recharge aquifers and protect humans from floods. Similarly, allowing fire-maintained ecosystems to experience fire on a regular basis can reduce the risk of catastrophic, property-destroying crown fires.

In the past few decades, recognition has increased among conservationists that nature reserves will not necessarily serve their intended function simply because they have been protected from human interference; instead, they must be managed. For one thing, all reserves—and especially small and midsize ones—are connected to the world beyond their boundaries and are vulnerable to human influences ranging from greenhouse gas emissions (a global influence) to fire suppression (often a national policy) to the activities of hunters and hikers (a local influence). But more fundamentally, as discussed in Chapter 4, succession and disturbance change an ecosystem's physical and biological characteristics over time. Unless a nature reserve is large enough to contain a shifting mosaic of all successional stages, succession and disturbance may mean that the conservation targets one set out to protect will disappear in a few decades while other conservation assets might appear. Large reserves have fewer management issues related to both outside influences and succession and disturbance because nature has more latitude to "run its course," but even in North America's largest reserves, a certain amount of "ecological babysitting" is still practiced.[11] Land management challenges may be even greater outside of nature reserves, where ecological goals must be reconciled with human demands on the land.

Managing Succession and Disturbance

Many restoration and management activities are an attempt to accelerate or prevent succession or to introduce or suppress disturbance. Thus, for any site that one is attempting to manage, it is important to consider disturbance and successional processes by asking the questions shown in Box 9-1.

MAINTAINING NATURAL DISTURBANCE PROCESSES

Allowing natural disturbance processes to follow their course with minimal human interference is usually the best way to ensure that organisms and ecosystems continue to experience the types and frequency of disturbance that they

Box 9-1
Understanding Ecological Change When Making Land Management Decisions

- Is the site's current successional state consistent with the management objectives? If not, is active intervention needed?
- If left alone, will the site change significantly over time as it undergoes succession? Are these successional changes compatible with the management objectives, or do they need to be actively manipulated?
- Is the site subject to large-scale disturbances, such as fires and floods? Have humans interfered either by suppressing natural disturbances or by introducing non-natural ones? If the ecology of the site requires regular disturbance, does the disturbance process need to be managed by humans in any way?

need to survive and regenerate. However, in many cases, the context of the study area is such that some natural disturbances would threaten human health or safety. In situations where natural disturbance processes cannot be allowed free rein, land managers may either have to temper their impacts or introduce them under carefully controlled conditions.

In fire- and flood-prone ecosystems, the tendency over much of the last century was to prevent disturbance wherever possible—to put out every fire and build ever-higher levees and dams. But we are now learning that efforts to eliminate all disturbance may be counterproductive over time: in other words, when we prevent small disturbances, we increase the risk of large, catastrophic ones. For example, when small fires are not allowed to burn off undergrowth, conditions begin to favor huge, destructive fires. Land managers can reduce this risk by setting prescribed burns to mimic the cleaning actions of small natural fires.

Similarly, when we build levees to confine rivers instead of leaving the river access to functioning wetlands that can absorb flood waters, we create conditions that can lead to catastrophic floods, such as the Mississippi River floods of 1993. Conversely, allowing small floods to occur along the length of a river may reduce the risk of a single large flood. As these examples illustrate, the ecologically minded planner or designer should think like a student of t'ai ch'i: know where your opponent might attack with the greatest force and, instead of resisting, fade back and allow the opponent's energy to be spent bit by bit.

MIMICKING NATURAL DISTURBANCE PROCESSES

When it is not feasible to allow natural disturbance processes free rein, land use professionals can use a variety of tools to mimic natural disturbances in a

Figure 9-8. Restored prairie in northeastern Illinois is maintained using prescribed burns to minic the wildfires that once burned grasslands in the region. Professional fire technicians oversee the burns to ensure that nearby structures are not damaged.

way that helps to maintain and restore native ecosystems. For example, in many flood-prone areas, the timing and intensity of floods have been altered by the thousands of large and small dams across North America; because of these dams, fully natural flood events no longer occur on most rivers. Managers can try to mimic the natural patterns of flooding required by aquatic and floodplain organisms by manipulating water releases. However, this strategy can rarely fully re-create the flow pattern of an undamned river.

Fire is another disturbance process that may need to be carefully managed, especially in settings where heavy loads of fuel have accumulated. Managers may need to set fires under carefully controlled situations to decrease the fuel load and to make sure fire is applied where it is needed (see Figure 9-8). In managing sand barrens communities on Martha's Vineyard off the coast of Massachusetts, for example, ecologists use fire and clearing (tree and shrub cutting) to change forests to more open ecosystem types, such as savannas, shrublands, and grasslands. Once lands have become more open, ecologists mow, use grazing animals, and set prescribed fires to maintain these open areas.[12] Each of these management methods mimics the effects of the Native Americans who helped shape the open nature of the Martha's Vineyard landscape by setting fires and girdling trees. These open areas are necessary for the survival of rare community types, such as grasslands, heathlands, and scrub oak–heath shrublands. They also support several rare plant species, such as the sandplain gerardia, Nantucket shadbush, and bushy rockrose, as well as numerous rare moth species.[13]

Mowing programs are critical to managing succession in urban and suburban landscapes and can be readily manipulated by park managers, homeowners, and groundskeepers. Whereas on Martha's Vineyard ecologists used mowing to arrest succession, in manicured, human-dominated landscapes, mowing frequency can be reduced to allow native grasslands to grow. Rather than mowing grassy areas once a week, these areas could be cut once every one to three years—often enough to prevent trees and shrubs from establishing but infrequent enough to provide habitat for numerous plant, insect, bird, and mammal species. Ideally, only a portion of the grassland should be mowed each year, and mowing should be timed to avoid periods of nesting and peak usage by birds.[14] Such a program could be (and has been in many places) readily implemented in road margins, back yards, and appropriate portions of public parks, schoolyards, golf courses, and other grassy areas to improve habitat value and reduce maintenance costs. These three examples of flood management, fire management, and mowing illustrate just a few of the many ways land managers can help maintain and restore native ecosystems by learning to mimic natural disturbance regimes.

Managing Invasive Exotic Species

The introduction of invasive exotic species is a special type of disturbance with the power to change an ecosystem considerably. Invasives such as *Melaleuca*, Eurasian milfoil, and the gypsy moth can take over huge swaths of native habitat, displacing native plants and disrupting the feeding preferences of native animals. Whenever possible, the best management strategy is to prevent the arrival of invasives. Second best is a combination of educated vigilance and rapid, all-out response. If caught early enough, the invasion can sometimes be completely repelled, as occurred when the African snail (*Achatina fulica*) was eradicated from southern Florida seven years after a boy brought three snails to Miami.[15] All too often, however, exotic species become well established before they can be found and wiped out. The goal at that point shifts from eradication to delay, containment, and obstruction. Methods such as mowing, burning, or targeted pesticide application can help keep these species at least partially in check. And, occasionally, a biological control agent—a parasite or an insect herbivore that specializes on an invasive plant—can be found in the invasive species' homeland and imported. While these importations of control agents are sometimes quite successful, they can also backfire if the agent is not as specialized as it originally appeared to be and begins to feed on native species.

Managing Land within Developments

The management of habitat and other unbuilt land within development projects is an important but often neglected component of ecologically based design.

It is usually best to establish management guidelines at the time land is developed, especially if the development contains land set aside for conservation. A common approach for managing open space in housing developments is to designate a homeowners' association as the managing authority, but this authority should be exercised within an ecological framework agreed upon when the development is approved. A separate consideration arises when buildings and neighborhoods have been designed to reduce human exposure to natural hazards such as wildfire. Ongoing management may be required to keep these safeguards in place, and, given the public safety aspect of such defenses, it may be best not to leave these management responsibilities to individual property owners.

10

Ecologically Based Planning and Design Techniques

Let's return for a moment to Exponentia, our beleaguered community with typical post-1950s, North American development patterns (see Chapter 3). Although Exponentia has a comprehensive plan, zoning ordinances, and even detailed site design standards, the resulting development looks remarkably unplanned. Houses, condominiums, shopping centers, and office parks are separated into single-use pods linked by wide, habitat-fragmenting roads. There is certainly some greenery on the landscape, but aside from a few parks, most of it is leftover scraps of unbuildable land or token landscaped "open space" within developments. What few natural habitats remain are accessible only to salamanders with driver's licenses. Looking east toward the mountains, development is sparser but still regular enough to break up any large blocks of natural land.

Focusing in on individual developments, we see a landscape that has been clear-cut, regraded, and replanted with turfgrass and exotic plant species—a landscape where natural water flows have been rerouted to underground pipes and stormwater detention ponds. These developments are the product of standards and regulations—dimensional requirements, road widths, pipe diameters, curb types, and turning radii for fire trucks—that are exceedingly detailed yet give little regard to the natural environment. We wish that Exponentia were a straw man, a grotesque exaggeration of reality, but in fact this picture should resonate with residents in almost every part of the United States and Canada.

The recent "smart growth" movement is an attempt to address the environmental, social, economic, and quality of life problems associated with growth patterns such as those in Exponentia. Impetus from land use professionals, environmentalists, community activists, politicians, and some developers has prompted major changes in how planning and development occur in some jurisdictions. If nothing else, the smart growth movement has increased public awareness of the costs of poorly planned growth, with articles on sprawl appearing in such popular publications as *USA Today, Newsweek,* and many metropolitan newspapers. Yet progress has been spotty, with improvements in some areas offset by stasis or even regression in others. For example, local and state funding for land conservation has increased, but so, too, have vehicle miles traveled per capita and land consumption per capita, two key indicators of sprawl.[1]

As we discuss in the Introduction, this book focuses primarily on two important aspects of smart growth: (1) addressing the effect of human activities on ecological integrity and biodiversity, and (2) safeguarding humans and their property with regard to the ecological context. In this chapter, we examine some of the more promising smart growth tools and techniques (both established and cutting-edge) available to planners, designers, and developers from the standpoint of these two goals. We begin the chapter by discussing the processes by which ecological data can be incorporated into plans. The next three subsections describe effective planning and design techniques for protecting biodiversity and ecological integrity at three different scales, beginning at the landscape scale (counties and regions), then moving to the sublandscape scale (cities, towns, and counties) and to the habitat scale (lots and sites). You may be familiar with cluster development from the perspective of a planner or developer, but how does it look from the perspective of a turtle? Scientific studies can help answer this type of question, informing the work of land use professionals with reliable information about how better to design for biological conservation.

The final subsection reviews practices for enhancing human health, safety, and welfare in the ecological context. Although we purposely keep discussion of each technique brief and centered on ecology, this ecological focus does not imply that other planning goals—such as meeting society's housing, transportation, and economic needs—are unimportant. The planner's and designer's role is to integrate all of these goals into a cohesive whole—and we hope to advance this process by elucidating one such goal.

Using Ecological Data

In Chapter 7 and again in the planning exercise in Chapter 11, we discuss the types of ecological data that planners and designers should seek to obtain for their site or study area—for example, what species and habitats are present, what types of natural and human disturbances affect the area, and what conditions occur beyond the study area boundaries. Once ecological information has been collected, planners and designers face the challenge of incorporating it into planning decisions where other factors come into play.

A common technique for integrating multiple factors in land use planning is *land suitability analysis* using overlay maps. This approach, which has been in use for at least ninety years, is probably best explained in Ian McHarg's landmark book, *Design with Nature,* which marked the birth of modern environmental planning.[2] In this process, maps of individual environmental factors (e.g., vegetation, slopes, soils, hydrology, and floodplains) are overlaid to evaluate the capability of land to accommodate different uses, including conservation, agriculture, low-density development, or high-density development (see Figure 10-1). Human factors—such as infrastructure availability, transit service, and household income—while not strictly related to the capability of the land, can also be added to integrate additional goals into the planning analysis. The advent of geographic information systems has simplified the process of land suitability analysis and allowed more sophisticated modeling and weighing of different factors, but, overall, the technique has changed little since McHarg's presentation in *Design with Nature.*

One of the most important places to use ecological data is in the preparation of municipal and county master plans, comprehensive plans, and other long-term planning documents. Many states already require such plans to include a chapter on natural resources or environmental protection, and local and regional ecology should be featured prominently in such a chapter, if not given its own chapter in the plan. This part of the plan should contain an analysis and maps of ecological communities and native species in the jurisdiction, their ecological context, threats to ecological resources, and goals and strategies for protecting local biodiversity and ecosystem functions. This information can also inform the other chapters of the comprehensive plan, including land use, transportation, open space, and public facilities. Color Plate 8 offers an example from East Bethel, Minnesota, showing how ecological information can be mapped and analyzed to guide an open space planning process.

Landscape Scale (Counties and Regions)

The landscape scale is usually the best scale at which to begin thinking about the conservation of species and ecosystems. As discussed in Chapter 6, landscapes are repeating *mosaics* of ecosystems and land uses on the order of tens to perhaps a hundred miles or kilometers across; examples might include metropolitan Atlanta or Cape Breton Island in Nova Scotia. The landscape scale most often corresponds with the jurisdiction of counties, metropolitan or regional governments, or, sometimes, small states and provinces—almost all of which are involved in

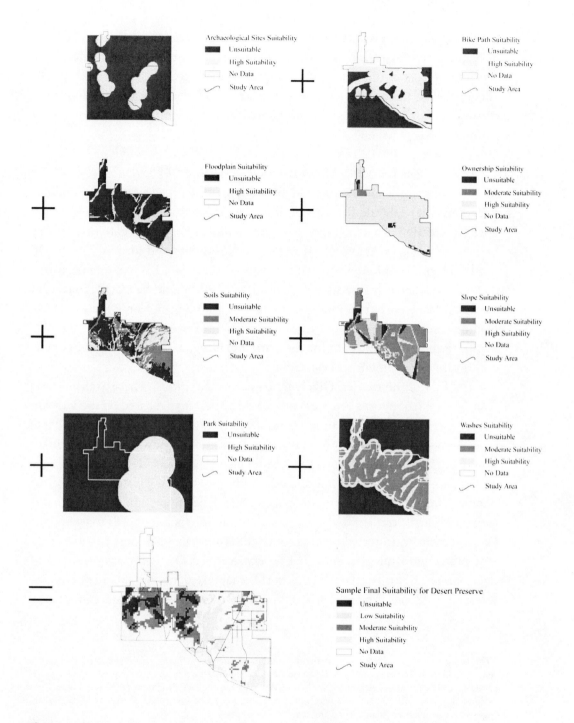

Figure 10-1. During the process of *land suitability analysis,* illustrated here, data on different land characteristics are overlaid to identify the best locations for conservation, agriculture, urban development, and other land uses. This type of analysis is a central component of ecologically based planning and design. (Graphic courtesy of Frederick Steiner.)

land use planning. A worthy conservation goal at the landscape scale would be to implement the "aggregate-with-outliers" model (see page 115), in which large contiguous patches of natural or seminatural lands are set aside for such values as core habitat and headwater stream protection. Similarly, large patches of agricultural and urban lands can be designated so as to gain the benefits of aggregating these land uses.

Landscape Conservation and Development Plan

Planning at the landscape scale must address the broadest possible land use question: where should humans build, farm, or ranch, and where should they not? The creation of a *landscape conservation and development plan* (LCDP) can help answer this question in a simple, easy-to-understand format. The LCDP need only consist of four elements: core habitat, secondary habitat, intensive production areas, and urban areas (see Figure 10-2).* Although the LCDP is our term for a plan that blends traditions of conservation planning and large-scale land use planning, such planning is not without precedent. For example, Color Plate 9 is a long-term, large-scale plan for the Portland, Oregon, area that describes general future development and conservation patterns.

The first of the four LCDP elements is *core habitat.*** These are the landscape's system of nature reserves and should be designated based on the location of rare species and habitats, intact natural systems, and lands providing valuable ecosystem services, such as groundwater recharge and headwater stream protection. Landscape ecology principles should also inform the designation of core habitats to create a system that includes hubs (areas with considerable interior habitat), linkages (corridors or stepping stones, depending on the species of concern), and small "outlier" reserves. Not all of the core habitat needs to be in public ownership or protected through outright acquisition; planners can use other land protection strategies, including *purchase of development rights, transfer of development rights* (explained later in this chapter), donation of land or land interests, and various types of *conservation easements.* These techniques may allow

---

* This typology is a variation on the tripartite classification of core habitat, buffer area, and matrix, which some conservation biologists have suggested for conservation planning. However, intensive production areas, such as row crop agriculture and plantation forestry, merit a separate category since they are neither buffer areas (because they offer little habitat value) nor urban areas. Intensive production areas also tend to be an important focus of planners working in rural and semirural landscapes.

** The concept of "core habitat" presented here is different from what many conservation biologists mean when they discuss "core reserves": very large reserves, tens to hundreds of miles or kilometers across, that are off-limits to almost all human activities. While core reserves may be achievable in some areas, they are rarely feasible in the context of planning and design work. Therefore, we focus instead on smaller, more varied core habitats, which are essential to biodiversity conservation and are feasible in almost every jurisdiction, at the scale where planners and designers tend to work.

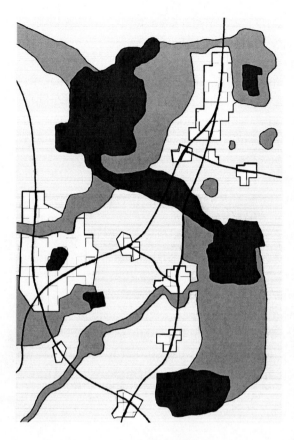

Core Habitat

Secondary Habitat

Intensive Production Area

Urban Areas

Major Road

Figure 10-2. The landscape conservation and development plan is a generalized landscape-scale planning map showing the proposed location of core habitats, secondary habitats, intensive production areas (agriculture and forestry), and urban areas. Ecological analysis, landscape ecology principles, and the goals of the region's residents and leaders should all inform the creation of this long-term plan.

for a low level of continued human activity on the land as long as it is compatible with the local ecology.

The *secondary habitat* can be thought of as buffer areas that surround the core habitat. These buffers provide the following ecological values:

- Increasing the quality of interior habitat in the core areas by reducing external impacts to these areas
- Increasing the amount of habitat available to species that can tolerate low to moderate levels of human activity
- Designating large areas that will have near-normal ecosystem functioning (e.g., groundwater recharge).

From a planning perspective, secondary habitat consists of those land uses that generate very modest ecological impacts, disturbing only a small portion of the land in a manner that has no long-term negative effects. For example, low-intensity forestry, very low-density development, and many types of passive (nature-based) recreation could provide secondary habitat, as could low-intensity agriculture that provides significant habitat value.

Intensive production areas include heavily managed agricultural lands and tree plantations. These areas usually provide little habitat value but are important to planners for other reasons, including creating jobs and income, providing locally produced food and fiber, and limiting suburban sprawl by putting rural lands to an economically productive use. Finally, *urban areas* are shorthand for all places where built land has become the landscape matrix. Thus, urban areas would also include most suburbs and would encompass a wide range of residential and nonresidential land uses.

As the previous explanation suggests, the LCDP is essentially a broad-scale land suitability analysis identifying how intensively each part of the landscape should be used. Because it is based more on innate characteristics of the land than on transient human considerations, the plan can afford to look far into the future—twenty-five to fifty years—to envision land configurations (e.g., a restored riparian belt or a new satellite settlement) that may not be immediately achievable. As such, it is a larger-scale and longer-term framework within which more detailed local and short-term plans may be developed, leading ultimately to such implementation mechanisms as zoning maps and ordinances. The LCDP is intentionally abstracted from implementing regulations so that it can illustrate a bold vision (connected habitats, contained cities) without first resolving all of the politics of how it will be implemented. We move now to two specific techniques— urban growth boundaries and transfer of development rights—by which a landscape scale plan could be implemented.

Urban Growth Boundaries and Infrastructure Target Areas

Urban growth boundaries (UGBs) curb sprawl by targeting growth into pre- existing cities and immediately adjacent areas. A UGB is essentially a line on the map within which development is encouraged and outside of which development is prohibited or strongly discouraged. The best-known example of a UGB in North America is in Portland, Oregon. Within Portland's UGB, public funds are invested in infrastructure (including light-rail transit) to support moderate to high development densities. Land uses outside the boundary are generally limited to agriculture, conservation, and very low-density development. The Portland UGB is reviewed and expanded from time to time to ensure that it always includes enough land for twenty years of projected growth; thus, it is intended not as a tool for preventing growth but as a means for directing it to specific areas.

If used properly, UGBs can be an effective instrument for achieving the desirable aggregate-with-outliers pattern at the landscape scale (see Figure 6-9). To achieve this goal, the UGB should be drawn to exclude lands of high ecological value—for example, the core habitat areas in the LCDP—while including areas with suitable location, soils, and topography to support dense development.

However, since land outside the UGB is not prohibited from human use (for example, much of the land south of Portland is intensively farmed), the use of a UGB does not eliminate the need for providing additional protection for core habitat areas.

A related tool, *targeted infrastructure investment*, directs public infrastructure spending into those areas deemed most appropriate for new growth or redevelopment. For example, Maryland's Priority Funding Areas Act encourages cities and towns to identify where the state should focus its investments in roads, sewers, and other facilities and programs that support development.[3] Informed by local ecologically based planning, Maryland municipalities can use this program to strengthen existing human communities while avoiding implicit public subsidies to development in ecologically sensitive areas. Other jurisdictions have taken steps to address phenomena such as "school sprawl," in which a new school is sited at the periphery of the community and therefore encourages further spread-out development on farmland and native habitat. Targeted infrastructure investment can work equally well on the state, county, and local levels. For example, the city of Gloucester, Massachusetts, has designated "sewer service areas," which will bring sewer lines to places where they are needed to solve preexisting wastewater disposal problems but without extending them to nearby undeveloped areas, where they would allow houses to be built on rocky ledges draining directly to sensitive salt marshes. Local infrastructure service areas, such as the one in Gloucester, can help save tax dollars as well as native habitat.

Transfer of Development Rights

Transfer of development rights (TDR) is another planning tool used to aggregate undeveloped lands at the landscape scale. Most TDR programs designate two areas: a development rights *sending area,* where the jurisdiction wants to discourage development, and a *receiving area,* where higher density development is deemed to be desirable. TDR allows landowners in the sending area to sell the rights to develop their land to landowners or developers in the receiving area, thus transferring those rights from one site to the other (see Figure 10-3). As a result of the transfer, the land in the sending area is permanently protected from development, while additional development can be built in the receiving area. Long-standing TDR programs, such as those in Montgomery County, Maryland, and the Pinelands of southern New Jersey, have protected thousands of acres of farmland and native habitat at little cost to the public while still providing economic return to the owners of the protected land.

Several kinds of TDR programs exist, each with its own advantages and disadvantages.[4] For protecting biodiversity and ecological integrity, the most important consideration is to designate sending areas to correspond with high-

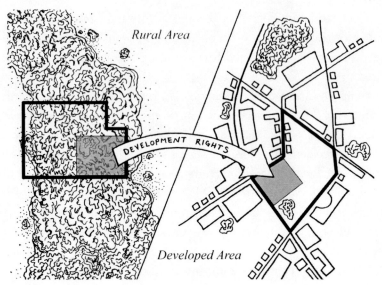

Figure 10-3. Transfer of development rights (TDR) typically allows additional development to occur in and near existing settlements in exchange for protecting rural lands from development. Planners can use this tool to create large ecologically intact areas of natural habitat. The heavy black outlines in the diagram show the boundaries of the TDR sending area (at left) and the TDR receiving area (at right).

quality core and secondary habitat areas. For legal reasons, most TDR programs do not prohibit development in the sending area, although they may discourage it by reducing the allowed density of development. Given the essentially voluntary nature of most TDR programs, the successful programs are those that establish incentives to make it more profitable for landowners in the sending area to sell their development rights than to build on the property itself. To promote biological conservation goals, incentives could be offered on a "sliding scale" so that the most valuable tracts of habitat within the sending area are worth the greatest number of development credits if their owners participate in the TDR program. Even with good incentives in place, however, TDR cannot always be counted on to protect any particular parcel. Thus, if the study area contains unique or especially valuable conservation targets, it may be wise to supplement TDR with other land protection strategies, such as outright acquisition.

Sublandscape Scale (Cities, Towns, and Counties)

We define the sublandscape scale as groups of land uses and ecosystems within an area roughly several miles or kilometers across. Examples would include the entire jurisdiction of many North American cities, towns, and townships; portions of counties; and watersheds of third- or fourth-order streams. Whereas the overall conservation vision should be established at the landscape scale so as to plan for large patches, persistent populations, and functioning ecosystem processes, the sublandscape scale is especially relevant to planners since this is the level at which many regulatory and administrative tools are implemented. Two important conservation goals for planners working at the sublandscape scale are (1) to implement the LCDP by directing land use at the local level,* and (2) to influence the sequence of land transformation (which areas are developed first). Four approaches for reaching these goals are discussed below.

Conventional Zoning

Conventional zoning is often referred to as *Euclidian zoning* after the landmark 1926 U.S. Supreme Court case *Village of Euclid (Ohio) v. Ambler Realty Co.*, which established its constitutionality as a permissible exercise of local governments' police power. This approach, which remains planners' principal tool for directing development, involves dividing a jurisdiction into various zoning districts, each of which allows different types of land uses and has different requirements for lot dimensions and other development characteristics. The districts are usually delineated on a zoning map, and the accompanying requirements for each district are described in a zoning ordinance, code, or bylaw.

From the standpoint of ecology, Euclidian zoning can be either positive or negative. The fundamental concept of zoning a jurisdiction based on the suitability of the land in each area to accommodate different human uses is basically the same approach used in ecologically based planning. The problem is that zoning maps are often based less on the land's *environmental* suitability than on its *economic* or *transportation* suitability, historical precedent, or even political expediency. For example, countless jurisdictions have chosen to locate their industrial districts along rivers and in floodplains, creating a host of ecological problems as well as planning dilemmas for communities whose residents now want public access to their waterfronts.

A deeper problem of relying exclusively on Euclidian zoning to protect biodiversity and ecological integrity is the great difficulty of designating zones that exclude development completely. This restriction in the use of zoning is based on federal laws and judicial precedent in the United States and, to a lesser extent, in Canada that generally prohibit the government from "taking" property without

---

* The idealized planning process presented here involves close cooperation between different levels of government to prepare a broad-brush LCDP at the county, regional, or state level (with local input) and then implement it primarily at the municipal or county level (or both). In reality, this level of cooperation does not always exist—either for logistical reasons (e.g., not enough planning resources) or for political ones—but this should not derail the basic approach advocated here. For example, in the absence of an LCDP prepared at the county, regional, or state level, local governments can still place their planning and zoning activities in a larger ecological framework by looking outside the boundaries of their jurisdictions.

duly compensating the owner. In the United States, zoning that denies essentially all economic uses of a piece of property has been deemed an illegal "regulatory taking."[5]

Aware of this legal constraint, many planners have turned to *large lot zoning* to discourage development or at least reduce its density in areas that are less environmentally suitable for development. Residential or "rural residential" zoning districts in suburban and exurban areas commonly require a minimum lot size of two, three, or five acres (0.8, 1.2, or 2 ha) for a single-family house, and in some rural parts of the U.S. Midwest and West, the minimum lot size is ten, twenty, or even forty acres (4, 8, or 16 ha). Large lot zoning has certainly resulted in lower housing densities, but it is no longer much of an impediment to development: because of a number of sociological factors—including the growing willingness to commute long distances, the rise of telecommuting, the growing numbers of retirees and second-home owners, and an increased emphasis on quality of life in choosing a house—plenty of people want to live on large lots in more remote locations.

In Chapter 6, we pointed out that large lot zoning almost always hurts native species and ecosystems because it spreads human influence over a wide area, removing much of the land's ecological value without using it efficiently for human purposes. A much better approach is to aggregate most human settlement in designated areas, ideally those areas of lower ecological value or uniqueness, using such tools as transfer of development rights and conservation subdivision design (see below). Nevertheless, because large lot zoning is and probably will continue to be widely used, we explore in Box 10-1 what types of conservation values may be provided on lots of different sizes. We also offer suggestions for how low-density housing development might be modified to reduce its negative impact on native biodiversity.

"Greenprinting"

As we discussed in Chapters 3 and 6, development guided by conventional zoning controls usually proceeds along an unfortunate trajectory. First, natural lands are perforated, dissected, and fragmented with houses and businesses, which are usually built on those sites that are flat, well-drained, and have good soils. Then, as additional waves of development occur, built areas merge together until the remaining natural lands have been reduced to small, isolated patches with greatly reduced ecological value. These scraps of natural land are usually inadequate for maintaining natural ecological processes as well as terrestrial and aquatic habitat for many native species, and the result is a heavily degraded local environment.

One alternative to this depressing sequence is to prepare a *greenprint*—a map identifying potential conservation areas, such as wetlands, steep slopes, rare species habitat, and rare ecological communities—very early in the development of a community. Then, as growth arrives, it can be directed to less sensitive lands. Over time, as the community nears buildout, a protected, interconnected conservation network will take shape within the matrix of developed lands. This approach is very similar to the landscape conservation and development plan discussed above, but it applies at a finer scale. Whereas the LCDP identifies large patches for core habitat, secondary habitat, production lands, and urban areas, the community greenprint recognizes that within each of these large patches is a finer-scaled mosaic of ecologically valuable as well as less valuable areas. With the greenprint in hand as guidance, the planner can work to protect sensitive lands through a variety of means. For example:

- The most important lands could be targeted for protection through outright purchase or conservation easements.
- The next most important lands could be the target of environmental protection laws (see below) or could be protected using transfer of development rights.
- The remaining greenprint lands should be considered during site planning. Various site planning guidelines (see below) can encourage or require developers to steer clear of these areas as they design and develop individual sites.

Environmental Protection Zoning

The term *environmental protection zoning* refers to zoning districts, overlay zones,* and other regulations that prohibit or restrict development in environmentally sensitive areas. These designations can apply to a wide range of areas, including wetlands, floodplains, stream corridors, steep slopes, ridgelines, viewsheds, and plant and wildlife habitat. They can be enacted at all jurisdictional levels, from federal wetland protection laws in the United States to various provisions at the state/provincial, county, and local levels. Endangered species laws are somewhat different from zoning-based environmental protections in the sense that they do not ordinarily delineate on a map those areas that are subject to land use restrictions; instead, the jurisdiction areas are defined according to the habitat needs

---

* An overlay zone is a mapped zoning designation that stipulates an additional layer of land use control beyond that provided by the base zoning district. For example, a lot adjacent to a river might be in a residential *base zone* as well as a floodplain protection *overlay zone*. The base zone may limit land uses on the lot to single-family houses, while the overlay zone may require any new buildings to have a finished-floor elevation above the 100-year flood elevation.

Box 10-1

Large Lot Zoning: Can It Provide Any Ecological Benefits?

While it is clear that large lot zoning is ecologically detrimental in many respects, it is worth exploring whether, and under what circumstances, this zoning approach may offer some ecological value. Like many questions in ecology, the answer to the question "Can large lot zoning provide any ecological benefits?" is "It depends." However, we can develop some useful guidelines by answering this question in the context of several different conservation goals.

Conservation Issue	Considerations[1]	Guidance on Minimum Lot Size and Other Design Factors[2]
Can large lots provide habitat for generalist animal species?	Some human-tolerant mammals and birds can survive in suburban areas. Gardens that contain native plant species offer insect and bird habitat.	Lots of *1 acre (0.4 ha) or less* may suffice as long as vegetation is properly managed (see pages 161–64).
Can large lots protect stream water quality and natural hydrology?	Physical and biological stream characteristics begin to degrade when impervious surface in the watershed reaches 7 to 10 percent.[3]	House lots of *at least 2 acres (0.8 ha)* usually result in impervious coverage below 10 percent. To prevent pollution, site design should protect riparian buffers, minimize turfgrass, and properly manage stormwater.
Can large lots provide habitat for reptiles, amphibians, and mammals with small home ranges?	Some such species can survive on patches of 1.5 acres (0.6 ha) as long as adequate water features are included.	Lots of *at least 4 acres (about 2 ha)* where water features are protected may offer habitat value. Corridors to nearby native habitats may improve this value.
Can large lots protect native plant communities and rare animals with small home ranges?	Viable populations of many plants can persist on 12-acre (5 ha) habitat patches buffered at least 100 feet (30 m) from buildings, yards, and roads to minimize edge effects. Such patches can also sustain populations of some small animals.	Houses centered in lots of *15 acres (6 ha)* each will have habitat patches of 12 acres between them. Corridors to adjacent habitats may improve long-term population viability.
Can large lots protect populations of forest interior birds, human-sensitive grassland birds, and midsized carnivores?	Patches of 60 acres (25 ha) can support many area-sensitive bird species as well as predators such as foxes. However, human influences may still limit biodiversity.[4]	Houses centered in lots of *50 acres (20 ha)* each will have habitat patches of 60 acres between them. Corridors to adjacent habitats may improve long-term population viability.

Can large lots protect populations of large-bodied, wide-ranging mammals?	Animals such as black bears and elk are very sensitive to road density.	Large lot zoning is not suitable to protect these species because of their very large space requirements and high sensitivity to human activities.

In each instance cited above, the desired conservation goal can be met only if the house is situated appropriately on the lot such that the most sensitive habitats are located as far from human influences as possible. The guidelines in the table also assume that the entire lot will remain natural habitat with the exception of the house, a small yard, and a driveway. The size of the disturbance patch created by development on a lot is very important: if small, it may not introduce all of the disturbance processes into the nearby natural areas.

In addition, the table assumes that the entire landscape in question is to be developed with house lots of the indicated size. Even with very large lots, this pattern of evenly distributed, low-density development (and the roads needed to access it) will perforate and fragment the landscape to a large degree, significantly curtailing its overall habitat value. However, habitat provided on large lots may become more valuable to native species if it is linked into a larger complex of habitat in nearby conservation areas. These considerations indicate that large lot zoning can offer much more ecological value if it is used in combination with such other conservation tools as land acquisition, riparian zone protection, and low-impact development (see below). Using this approach, zones of low-density housing development can be used to buffer core habitat areas from more intensive human land uses. They may also offer limited habitat value in their own right.

In what is essentially a twist on large lot zoning, some jurisdictions have established protective zones for farming, forestry, or habitat lands that combine large minimum lot sizes with other policies to discourage subdivision and development of the land. For example, a model Agriculture and Forest Protection District proposed for Minnesota would allow no more than one division of land (i.e., one subdivided lot) for each forty acres. Newly created house lots would need to be between one and two acres (0.4 and 0.8 ha), thus preserving the remaining thirty-eight to thirty-nine acres (15 to 16 ha) for farm/forestry uses. Subdivided farm/forest parcels would need to be at least twenty-five acres (10 ha), thus retaining the "large patch" benefits of these rural land uses.[5] Similar approaches can be used to steer development away from sensitive habitats.

NOTES

1. Information is derived from the following sources except where noted: Lowell W. Adams and Louise E. Dove, *Wildlife Reserves and Corridors in the Urban Environment* (Columbia, MD: National Institute for Urban Wildlife, 1989) and references cited therein; several papers in Lowell W. Adams and Daniel L. Leedy, eds., *Wildlife Conservation in Metropolitan Environments* (Columbia, MD: National Institute for Urban Wildlife, 1991); Eric A. Odell, David M. Theobald, and Richard L. Knight, "Incorporating Ecology into Land Use Planning: The Songbirds' Case for Clustered Development," *Journal of the American Planning Association* 69, no. 1 (2003): 72–82.

2. For the third, fourth, and fifth rows of the table (4-acre, 15-acre, and 50-acre lots), minimum lot size is determined by calculating the smallest square lot that, when tiled in sequence with other equally sized square lots, will contain a circular habitat patch of the indicated size plus a 100-foot (30 m) buffer in the undeveloped space between houses on adjacent lots, assuming that the houses are situated in the center of the lot and that each house plus its surrounding structures extends 50 feet (15 m) from the center of its lot. It should be noted that smaller lots could contain a habitat patch of the indicated size if houses were situated closer to the edge of the lot.

3. C. L. Arnold and C. J. Gibbons, "Impervious Surface: The Emergence of a Key Urban Environmental Indicator," *Journal of the American Planning Association* 62 (1996): 243–58.

4. Jeremy D. Maestas, Richard L. Knight, and Wendell C. Gilgert, "Biodiversity across a Rural Land-Use Gradient," *Journal of American Planning Association* 17, no. 5 (2003): 1425–34.

5. Minnesota Environmental Quality Board and Biko Associates Inc., *From Policy to Reality: Model Ordinances for Sustainable Development* (2000), http://server.admin.state.mn.us/resource.html?Id=1927 (accessed August 2, 2003).

of listed species as identified through field studies, vegetation mapping, and similar methods.

Environmental protection zoning has undoubtedly contributed to the protection of native species and habitats, even when this was not its primary intended purpose. For example, floodplain protection zones are usually established to prevent property damage but often have the effect of preserving a riparian buffer that filters pollutants, shades the stream, and provides a habitat corridor for species movement. In addition to environmental protection zoning that offers "incidental" habitat benefits, many jurisdictions have enacted specific habitat protection ordinances. For example, the town of Falmouth, Massachusetts, has defined a Wildlife Overlay District, within which any proposed development must take steps to protect identified habitat for deer, fox, coyote, ground-nesting birds, reptiles, amphibians, and state-listed threatened and endangered species. The town may require developers of land within the district to set aside wildlife corridors that are contiguous with corridors on adjacent sites, cluster development to minimize its overall footprint, avoid the use of wildlife-restrictive fencing, and retain indigenous vegetation.

PROTECTING FRESHWATER ECOSYSTEMS

In Chapter 6, we presented a range of human threats to freshwater ecosystems and their biodiversity. Addressing these threats requires two sets of steps. First, watershedwide efforts are needed to limit the effects of human land uses, such as chemical, thermal, and nutrient pollution, as well as erosion (these approaches are discussed in the next section, "Habitat Scale"). Second, adequate buffers of natural vegetation must be maintained alongside water bodies. Both steps are critical: without watershed management, pollutants will quickly exceed the capacity of buffers to absorb them (and may pollute the groundwater); without vegetated buffers, such critical functions as bank stabilization and stream shading will be lost.

Planners often ask how wide a riparian buffer of natural vegetation must be for it to perform the desired ecological functions. Again, this depends on the function in question. Even a narrow vegetated corridor (e.g., twenty-five feet, or eight meters, wide) is valuable for shading the stream, contributing detritus, stabilizing the bank, and providing habitat for animals that live in or near the bank. However, other functions—such as trapping sediment and pollutants, absorbing or eliminating excess nutrients, and providing riparian habitat and movement corridors for many vertebrate species—generally require greater width. Riparian corridors function as filters in several ways:

- Fine particles and organic matter in the soil absorb pollutants.
- Plants incorporate nutrients into their tissues.

- Vegetation and leaf litter slow the flow of water and sediment from uplands to the stream.
- Under certain conditions, bacteria consume biologically available nitrogen and release it to the atmosphere as nitrogen gas.

All of these functions are enhanced by dense vegetation, a well-developed soil organic layer, silty or loamy soils (as opposed to sandy or clayish soils), minimal human disturbance, and flat topography. Riparian corridors lacking these characteristics will need to be wider to provide the same filtration function. Similarly, a wider corridor is needed when the surrounding watershed is steep, experiences high rainfall or many heavy storms, or has high rates of erosion or pollution from urban land uses, agriculture, or clear-cutting.

These factors suggest that the width of naturally vegetated riparian corridors should be determined case by case. However, this approach is not practical for most planners and designers and may also run afoul of legal requirements for regulatory consistency. A more realistic approach is to define a default width requirement, which may then be reduced, if necessary, based on site-specific evidence. Several studies have recommended a minimum buffer width of 100 feet (30 m), assuming the factors identified above are favorable.[6] Doubling this width would increase the corridors' value for wildlife movement and improve filtration functions, especially where conditions within the buffer or the watershed are less than optimal.[7]

Recently, many jurisdictions have adopted or recommended riparian protection laws based on these scientific findings. For example, Massachusetts restricts development within 200 feet (60 m) of perennial streams outside urban cores; Clark County, Washington, requires county review and habitat protection measures for projects proposed within 150 to 250 feet (46 to 76 m) of streams, depending on their size; and the Connecticut Department of Environmental Protection recommends a 100-foot (30 m) buffer along perennial streams and a 50-foot (15 m) buffer along intermittent streams.[8]

Development Phasing

Development phasing has historically been used as a tool to prevent rapid bursts of growth that exceed a community's ability to provide the new roads, schools, and public safety services demanded by a new development. One form of development phasing consists of *growth rate limitations* that either (1) cap the number of building permits that may be issued in a jurisdiction within a given time frame or (2) require developments over a certain size to be phased in over several years. Under the first approach, for example, a municipality might set a townwide maximum of 200 building permits per year, while under the second approach, it might limit the construction of a major new housing development to no more than 25 percent of the total units per year. Another type of develop-ment phasing links development approvals to infrastructure availability through such techniques as concurrency requirements or adequate facilities ordinances. These provisions require that infrastructure such as roads and sewers be in place before development can proceed at a given location. If a developer wants to build in a location that lacks adequate infrastructure, he can either fund the infrastruc-ture himself or wait until publicly funded infrastructure is extended to the site.

By thinking spatially, planners can use development phasing as a tool to af-fect the sequence and speed at which native habitat is transformed to built land. In Chapter 6, we presented a land transformation sequence that retains large patches of natural vegetation on the landscape for as long possible while weav-ing corridors and small reserves into the built portion of the landscape (see Fig-ure 6-10). Fortunately, this land transformation model is consistent with many of the teachings of good planning practice, which recommend aggregating built areas in order to attain efficiencies of land use, transportation, and infrastructure while enhancing the social and economic synergies of tight-knit communities. A development phasing policy to promote ecologically optimal land transforma-tion might include the following provisions:

- An adequate facilities ordinance matched with an infrastructure plan that targets new roads, water and sewer lines, and public facilities to less ecologi-cally sensitive areas aggregated together and in close proximity to preexist-ing settlements
- A growth rate limitation ordinance that establishes a maximum citywide (or countywide) annual building permit cap as well as an ecologically based "point system" that gives preference in the issuance of the permits to proj-ects that (1) are close to existing settled or degraded lands versus large blocks of native habitat, (2) have low impacts related to habitat destruction and fragmentation, and (3) provide ecological benefits, such as habitat restoration or improved watershed management

Habitat Scale (Sites and Lots)

The habitat scale offers the widest range of challenges and opportunities for de-signers such as engineers and landscape architects. This, too, is where develop-ers can have the greatest influence. While often maligned as environmental villains, developers have a critical role to play in protecting ecological integrity. First, they control the land (subject to regulatory constraints) and, with it, the power to protect, conserve, and restore. The rise of flexible development regula-tions makes it increasingly possible to do so while still profiting handsomely. Perhaps even more importantly, developers and their allies in the marketing industry strongly influence consumer preference for real estate products. Conventional wisdom in real estate marketing is often at odds with ecological design—for example, the notion that home buyers prefer large private yards to protected open space, or exotic landscaping to native species. But these "preferences" are in large part a creation of marketing efforts to sell the product that developers have historically built.

Ecologically minded developers can redirect this marketing energy to promote more harmonious forms of development. This point is illustrated by the example of Village Homes, a green development in Davis, California, that includes a natural vegetation stormwater management system, edible landscaping, and other eco-innovations. When the first units were placed on the market in the late 1970s, some realtors refused to show them since they did not fit the standard model; now, Village Homes is among the most desirable addresses in Davis, and its units sell faster and for more money than comparable houses in other developments.[9]

For designers and developers, three principles may help with planning a site in a way that protects its conservation values while providing access to nature for future human occupants. Throughout this book, we have emphasized the importance of understanding and designing land with regard to its ecological context. Thus, a first principle for ecologically based site-scale planning involves designing each small piece of the landscape in a way that essentially implements larger-scale ecological plans, such as the LCDP and the sublandscape-scale greenprint. Zoning regulations may mandate consistency with these plans, and designers can use them to help understand the potential contribution of their site to landscape-scale conservation goals.

Second, when opportunities exist to integrate small patches of nature into site plans, designers should consider not only how humans can benefit from such amenities as walking trails or bird-watching areas but also how these small patches can simultaneously advance conservation goals, such as protecting unique microhabitats or stepping stones. As we discussed in Chapter 8, there are few parts of the landscape that we can afford to dismiss as ecologically unimportant; even urban parks can provide ecological benefits if properly designed.

Third, recalling the concept of ecological health discussed in Chapter 6, site designs should strive to use land in such a way that it does not become permanently degraded or impair the integrity of off-site ecosystems through such impacts as pollution or fragmentation. The following three specific design techniques illustrate how these principles can be applied at the habitat scale.*

* Although all of these techniques are applied at the scale of sites or lots, they tend to be enabled or mandated by laws enacted at the municipal or county level.

Reducing Development's Footprint

Limiting the amount of land occupied by human activities is probably the best way to protect ecological values at the habitat scale. Techniques such as *conservation subdivision* design (also known as cluster development or open space residential development) set aside undeveloped land by essentially shifting development from one part of the site to another. Instead of spreading houses evenly across the site using "cookie cutter" geometry, developers may group them together on smaller lots, ideally on the least environmentally sensitive lands. The remainder of the site is then reserved as undeveloped land, typically with a conservation restriction to prevent its future development (see Color Plate 10). Planned unit developments (PUDs) take a similar approach, except that the development is usually a mixture of housing and nonhousing uses and is built at a higher density. Finally, many jurisdictions require a portion of any development site or newly created lot to be reserved as "open space." While this type of requirement is common, in many cases the open space is merely lawn or planted non-native shrubs that offer little habitat value.

The ecological value of conservation subdivisions, PUDs, and on-site open space varies from substantial to none. To maximize ecological value, the designer can plan the site around key natural features rather than identify the open space as everything that is left over after all the buildings and roads have been situated. In his books *Conservation Design for Subdivisions* and *Growing Greener*, planner Randall Arendt recommends a four-step site planning process whereby natural site features—such as wetlands, floodplains, steep slopes, scenic vistas, and unique vegetation—are first mapped and overlaid to identify those portions of the site that are the highest priority for protection. Arendt suggests that this resource mapping and prioritizing process be based in part on a site walk with the landowner, the developer, a landscape architect, and the municipal or county planner reviewing the project; to this list, we would also add an ecologist or wildlife biologist. Using the base map, the designer then delineates open space areas and development envelopes. Buildings and roads are added next, and lot lines are drawn in at the very end.[10] This design process is almost the reverse of the conventional cookie cutter approach, in which designing a subdivision is essentially a geometry exercise carried out with little regard for features of the land.

The site analysis phase—the first step of the four-step process—is the best opportunity to incorporate the lessons of ecology into site planning. Looking beyond the site itself is essential for identifying the most important portion(s) of the site for conservation; for example, an opportunity may exist to site the open space so as to abut an existing reserve, create or extend a corridor, or protect a rare microhabitat located on the site. Several data sources can inform this context analysis, including the greenprint (if available) as well as other local ecological maps or data layers that show land cover, rare species habitat, and protected land in the surrounding area. Other important factors to consider include the following:

- How the site layout can maximize interior habitat versus edge
- What species or communities should be targeted for conservation on the site given its size and limitations
- What flows (people, animals, wind, chemicals) will influence the open space and how levels of each one can be optimized through layout of the natural areas

It is worth noting the tension (frequently unacknowledged) among the different goals often pursued for open space within conservation subdivisions and other developments. For example, aesthetic considerations may favor the protection of highly visible open space, such as farmland, vegetated buffers near the road, or woods close to each house.[11] In contrast, landscape ecology principles might favor a design that clusters development closer to the road, leaving the backlands as unfragmented natural habitat (see Figure 10-4). This is not to say that a community should always protect the intact native habitat instead of, say, farmland, a scenic vista, or even a soccer field. However, planners and designers should be aware of the tradeoffs involved, and, if they choose not to maximize ecological integrity, make that choice because of a conscious decision to pursue a different goal.

A common and valid critique of conservation subdivisions and similar site-scale clustering techniques is that they do not really solve the problem of sprawl—

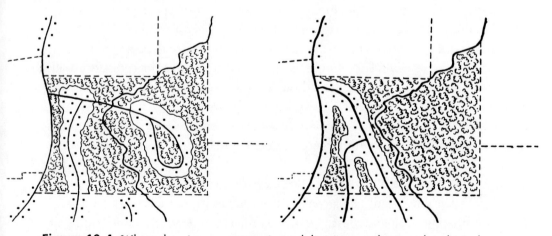

Figure 10-4. When planning a conservation subdivision, aesthetic and ecological goals sometimes conflict. An aesthetic focus might lead to design (a), where the frontage on the major road is left undeveloped and each house is located adjacent to ample open space. An ecologically focused plan (b) could provide more interior habitat and additional buffering of forested lands to the east (right) of the site by clustering all the houses closer to the road. Both site plans contain the same number of houses.

Figure 10-5. Requirements for wide roads, shallow grades, and long sight distances translate into the need to destroy and regrade large amounts of native habitat.

low-density development spilling into rural areas. In landscape ecology terms, clustering aggregates land uses at the site scale, but not at the landscape scale, where it matters most. This critique points to a few recommendations for planners. First, open space protected through clustering should fit into a citywide or countywide greenprint or similar ecological framework to help conserve ecological values at a larger scale. Second, when considering whether to require a minimum percentage of a development site to remain as open space, planners should weigh the value of the open space against the possible ecological benefits of more concentrated development (which might ultimately reduce the demand for additional land conversion). For example, large front, side, and rear lot setbacks usually provide little ecological benefit (although they may offer some human benefit) and can contribute to sprawl. Finally, for a very large site—perhaps a few thousand acres or more—clustering and PUDs can be an effective technique for securing natural habitats with large-patch benefits.

Ecologically Based Site Development Practices

Whether one is building a conservation subdivision, a city park, or a shopping center, the ecological outcome of the project can be vastly improved by incorporating sensitive design features (see Figures 10-5 and 10-6). Unfortunately, most of these features are at odds with conventional development practices. Table 10-1 compares conventional and ecologically sensitive approaches to several aspects of site design. Many of the sensitive development practices can actually yield substantial savings to developers by reducing expensive site preparation

Figure 10-6. This photo illustrates some of the principles of sensitive site design, including the use of narrower roads and the retention of native vegetation. The development shown in the photo contains 33 dwelling units on 64 acres (an overall density of about one unit per two acres), yet 86% of the site was retained as undeveloped woodlands and meadow.

costs, such as earth moving and roadway construction. Planners can facilitate the use of these practices by ensuring that local development regulations do not preclude such approaches (by, for example, mandating excessively wide roads). Some jurisdictions also have regulations that proactively encourage or require the use of sensitive development practices.

Environmental Review

In many jurisdictions, state/provincial and local environmental review is required for major development projects. On the local level, environmental review may be part of subdivision review or site plan review or may be required in conjunction with the issuance of a special permit (a conditional use permit). These reviews almost always consider engineering factors, such as stormwater runoff and grading, but ecological considerations are often lacking. Even where the law requires an evaluation of the project's habitat or wildlife impacts, the analysis provided is often cursory, biased, or ill informed. By not requiring (or not enforcing the requirement for) meaningful ecological assessment as part of local environmental review, planners miss out on a prime opportunity to promote conservation within development projects. An ecological assessment requirement based on the considerations in this book might call for the information shown in Box 10-2.

Regarding the last point in Box 10-2, one way to view an ecosystem is as a package of values and services: species diversity, genetic diversity, nutrient cycling, hydrological functioning, and so on. A worthy goal for land use proposals is to retain—if not increase—the total value of this package through a strategy of "minimize, mitigate, compensate." First, minimize losses by avoiding impacts

Table 10-1.

Overview of Ecologically Sensitive Site Development Practices

Conventional Practice	Sensitive Practices	Relevant Ecological Factors
Land Clearing and Grading		
Much of the site is clear-cut to facilitate earth moving and to "max out" development potential. On sites with topographic relief, extensive regrading often occurs; engineers may try to "balance" cut-and-fill slopes.	Cluster development to reduce the amount of clearing and grading required. Provide smaller lawns in favor of more natural vegetation. Site buildings and roads to *minimize* the need for cut and fill.	Earth moving disrupts the soil profile and kills much of the soil biota; stockpiling topsoil for later respreading worsens these effects.[1] Even if native vegetation is replanted in cleared and graded areas (and it rarely is), it may take decades to approximate a natural community.
Impervious Surface		
Many jurisdictions require developers to build wide roads and overly large parking lots, creating unnecessary impervious surfaces.	Clustered subdivisions may require 40 percent less roadway than conventional designs. Narrower roads offer several ecological benefits. Parking requirements should reflect actual daily usage; permeable pavements can be used for overflow parking areas. Taller buildings and the use of parking structures can reduce total impervious area.	In urban and suburban areas, the amount of impervious surface in a watershed is usually the most important factor influencing the health of freshwater ecosystems. Excess impervious surface indicates ecological as well as economic waste: less pavement means more land available for native habitat.
Stormwater Management		
Curbs, gutters, storm drains, and underground pipes collect stormwater and transport it to a centralized discharge point or detention/retention pond.	Design stormwater management systems that mimic natural ones by treating and infiltrating water on-site (rather than piping it away), using natural vegetated systems for treatment and infiltration, and integrating stormwater management with landscape design.[2]	Systems that allow stormwater to infiltrate into the ground (as opposed to running off through gutters or pipes) increase base stream flow while reducing flooding. Ecologically based systems are also often better at trapping and neutralizing pollutants in stormwater and can be more aesthetically pleasing.

Construction-Period Impacts

Earth moving operations result in large patches and piles of bare earth, which are very susceptible to erosion.

Prior to construction, delineate a no-disturb zone on a plan and in the field. Phase construction to limit the extent of bare soil at any time, especially during rainy periods. Stabilize bare slopes with mulch or plants right away. Use perimeter protections to minimize silt runoff leaving the site.

Erosion from construction sites is roughly 2,000 times that from forested land and 200 times that from urban land.[3] This silt can end up in streams, smothering their biota. Heavy machinery can damage plant roots, compact soil, and kill its resident organisms, leading to the death of trees and a reduction in the soil's ability to sustain native plants.

Road Design

Wide roads based on traffic engineering standards destroy native vegetation and increase impervious surface. Requirements for shallow grades, wide turning radii, and long sight distances translate into a need for more clearing and regrading. They also encourage cars to speed.

In many cases, requirements for road width, grade, turning radius, sight distance, and graded shoulders could be reduced without sacrificing safety.

Research on the mortality and habitat fragmentation effects of roads indicate that wider roads, higher vehicle speeds, and paved roads (versus unpaved) all increase detrimental effects on native fauna. Wide roadsides planted with non-native grasses tend to worsen these effects.

Landscaping

Commercial and residential properties are landscaped with turfgrass and ornamental garden species (many of them non-native) that offer little habitat value.

Use native plant species predominantly or exclusively in landscaped areas. Where possible, mimic the structure of natural vegetational communities of the area and introduce several layers of vegetation (such as herbs, shrubs, and trees) to increase habitat diversity.

Conventional landscaped areas are a major contributor to the spread of invasive species, overuse of local water supplies, and runoff of fertilizers and pesticides. Ecologically based landscapes can provide habitat for numerous native species while reducing or eliminating off-site impacts.

---

[1] Lowell W. Adams, *Urban Wildlife Habitats* (Minneapolis: University of Minnesota Press, 1994).

[2] The "low impact development" approach to stormwater management was initiated in several communities in the Chesapeake Bay watershed to improve water quality and create stormwater systems that mimic natural processes. More information is available from the Low Impact Development Center (http://www.lowimpactdevelopment.org) and the U.S Environmental Protection Agency's Office of Water (http://www.epa.gov/nps/lid), with additional resources at http://www.lid-stormwater.net.

[3] James G. MacBroom, *The River Book* (Hartford: Connecticut Department of Environmental Protection, 1998).

Box 10-2
Sample Requirements for Ecological Analysis as Part of Environmental Review

- A map showing the site's land cover or vegetation types, ecological attributes such as unique habitats or rare species occurences, and surrounding context. This requirement creates an information loop in which site-specific studies (conducted by developers and others) are incorporated into citywide or countywide maps, which are in turn consulted to help plan for future site-specific projects.
- A map and calculation of the acreage in each habitat type on the site both before and after development. This "accounting" approach makes clear both the degree of the habitat impacts and the extent to which the development will affect high-quality versus lower-quality habitats.
- Identification of any rare or threatened species on the site; the habitats, conditions, and resources they require; and the measures proposed to avoid impacts to these species.
- Discussion of how the proposed development will affect off-site ecosystems—for example, by diminishing or enhancing habitat connectivity or by changing the rate of nutrient runoff.
- Discussion of proposals to mitigate losses to the site's ecological integrity through ecological restoration, land protection, or other efforts.

in the first place. Next, mitigate any losses through designed solutions, such as replanted vegetation or constructed wetlands for treating polluted runoff. Finally, compensate for loss in one value with improvement in another—for example, by restoring an area of degraded land. To be sure, various "eco-assets" are not interchangeable or fully separable from one another. Yet, if a site is to be modified for human use, tradeoffs must inevitably be made. Although it is difficult to truly replicate a natural habitat, a "no net loss" approach is a major improvement over conventional practice that often fails to identify, much less address, the loss of ecological values.

Up to this point in the chapter, we have focused on approaches to protecting native species and ecosystems in developed or developing landscapes. We now turn again to the second of the major themes of this book: safeguarding human communities from natural hazards.

Protecting Human Safety in the Ecological Context

In 1993, flood waters ripped through the midwestern United States, breaching more than a 1,000 levees, damaging 70,000 buildings, and killing fifty people.[12]

Figure 10-7. Land in Chesterfield, Missouri, that was under ten feet (3 m) of water during the floods of 1993 is now the site of 7 million square feet (650,000 square m) of new commercial space.

Near the confluence of the Mississippi and Missouri rivers in Chesterfield, Missouri, the Smoke House market, a local landmark identifiable by the giant pig on its sign, wallowed in more than ten feet (3 m) of muddy water. Luckily, at the time, the market had few close neighbors; much of the surrounding land was farm fields. Ten years later, this floodplain is home to the largest strip retail center in the United States—part of 7 million square feet (650,000 square m) of new commercial development here (see Figure 10-7). In pursuit of tax revenue and jobs, local and state officials not only allowed extensive development in the Missouri River floodplain but also used public funds to subsidize a bigger levee and a new highway interchange to make this development possible. Nor is this an isolated example: at least ten major development projects are under way within a short drive of Chesterfield, many of them publicly subsidized. These projects are slated to urbanize 14,000 acres (5,600 ha) of agricultural floodplain, most of which was underwater in 1993.[13] While new levees offer some protection to these developments (at least until the next massive flood hits), they will also worsen flooding in other areas and raise the overall level of the rivers, reducing the effectiveness of all downstream levees.

Thirty miles away in Arnold, Missouri, the community responded to the 1993 floods in a very different way, purchasing 85 residences, 2 businesses, and 143 mobile home pads in flood-prone areas. Two years later, when another massive flood hit the region, many of the flood-prone lands in Arnold were already vacant, and there was little need for evacuations, sandbagging, or disaster relief.[14] What can we learn from these two examples?

First, developing in hazard-prone areas sets the stage for extremely damaging and expensive natural disasters. For example, in the 1990s alone, the United States experienced property losses totaling $30 billion from Hurricane Andrew in 1992, $16 billion from the Mississippi and Missouri river floods of 1993, $20 billion from the 1994 Northridge Earthquake, and billions more from other disasters.[15] Time and again, structural defenses, such as levees and seawalls, have provided a false sense of security. According to natural hazard expert Raymond Burby, "because people do not understand that structural protection has limits . . . structures have been found to actually induce development in hazardous areas and to increase, not decrease, the likelihood that when a large flood or hurricane does occur, losses truly will be catastrophic."[16]

Unfortunately, despite such catastrophic losses, many local governments have failed to incorporate meaningful natural hazard planning into their land use programs, even when adequate information exists. For example, a 2001 study of earthquake planning in Southern California revealed that, following a major earthquake in the region in 1971, much better seismic data have become available and building codes have improved to protect structures against earthquakes. However, this information generally has not influenced planning, zoning, and land use decisions.[17] It appears that many local governments essentially ignore the threat of natural hazards until they actually happen, at which point there may be a brief window of opportunity for action before other issues again take precedence.

Historically, people have used flood-prone areas because of their economic value for agriculture, transportation, and other uses. Other hazard-prone areas lure people with their own attractions, such as beautiful views from steep hillsides or the sense of natural seclusion afforded by being nestled deep within a (fire-susceptible) forest. To be sure, planners and developers must weigh the economic benefits of human activities in hazard-prone areas against their costs. However, those who say the free market should determine whether development occurs in hazard-prone areas are disingenuous when they argue for freedom from government involvement. In fact, taxpayers subsidize development in hazard zones several times over: first, to provide protective structures, infrastructure, and public safety services to allow the development to occur there; next, to subsidize rebuilding of public and private property when losses do occur; and, finally, to shoulder indirect costs as hazard protection in one area often shifts the danger to another location or sets the stage for an even more catastrophic event later. With these issues in mind, it is impossible to justify unrestricted development in hazard-prone areas by any but the narrowest of views.

The endeavor of protecting humans and their property from the ecological context can be summarized in two words: *location* and *design*. Influencing location is more commonly the role of the regulator, whereas engineers, architects, landscape architects, and developers play an important role in design. The location of hazard-prone areas is commonly identified using topographic, seismic, soils, vegetation, and weather pattern maps. Planners can then avoid or limit development in high-risk areas through such measures as the following:

- Refusing to subsidize development in hazard-prone areas (as Chesterfield did) and instead using public funds to buy land, development rights, or buildings in these areas (as Arnold did)
- Zoning to prohibit development in the most hazard-prone areas or to at least limit development to those uses that are less susceptible to serious loss
- Educating the public about natural hazard risks or requiring hazard disclosure statements for prospective property buyers

Assuming that development will occur at a particular hazard-prone location, careful design can reduce exposure to the hazard while maximizing defensibility (i.e., the ability to protect the development once a hazard materializes). Design approaches include building placement, landscape design, building materials, and orientation. The following discussion presents some of the key locational and design factors that can help protect humans from natural hazards. While many of these techniques may seem obvious, it is remarkable how often they are ignored. As in Chapter 4, the discussion is organized by the four Greek elements of nature: earth, air, fire, and water.

Earth

Earthquakes and landslides are probably the two most important types of earth hazards for natural hazard planning. Seismic maps can help identify fault lines and earthquake-prone areas with considerable (though not exact) detail. Soils prone to liquefaction—a rearrangement of the soil grains caused by vibration and resulting in the loss of soils' weight-bearing structure—can be identified on soil maps, and development can be discouraged in these hazardous areas through zoning or other regulations. Designers can incorporate various structural and architectural features to help buildings withstand seismic activity and safeguard their inhabitants; many of these are already part of building codes in earthquake-prone areas such as California.

Slope and soil type are two important factors affecting the probability of ground failure at any given site. The city of Huntsville, Alabama, recently learned the perils of ignoring such factors after a landslide tore a 700-foot (200 m) long swath down Monte Sano Mountain, shortly before the other side of the mountain was to be developed. The city's response to this environmental wake-up call was to revise its zoning ordinance concerning building on steep slopes through-out the city.[18] When building does occur in landslide-prone areas, engineering solutions, such as regrading and the construction of retaining walls, can be used to stabilize the ground, but these often come at the cost of considerable distur-bance to natural habitat.

Air

Most hurricane-related deaths and property damage result from storm surges, but high winds and flying debris can also be very destructive.[19] Identify-ing areas most prone to coastal storms and storm surges is relatively straight-forward, and zoning tools can be used to reduce or prohibit development in areas subject to the highest storm surges. Setting structures back from the shoreline (above the maximum flood height for coastal surges) and keeping them off of natural dunes can also allow beaches and dunes to absorb the energy from storm surges while minimizing erosion losses. These practices may limit development in desirable (and profitable) beachside locations, but the virtual certainty of storm damage in some locations should compel planners to steer development away from these areas anyway. With other types of storms such as tornadoes, it is dif-ficult or impossible to delineate narrow zones of especially high hazard. In these cases, planners and designers must turn to design rather than locational solutions to reduce the risk of property damage and loss of life. In all areas subject to major storms, structures should be built to withstand high winds, while windows and doors should be designed to protect inhabitants from flying debris.

Fire

As discussed earlier, wildfire is a danger wherever humans have inserted themselves into fire-prone ecosystems. The hazard is even more acute when decades of fire suppression by humans have increased fuel loads to the point where they can sustain massive crown fires. While this hazard can be avoided by not building in fire-prone areas, such a solution is probably unrealistic in some places given that fast-growing regions such as Southern California and metro-politan Denver and Salt Lake City all contain many dry, fire-prone ecosystems. When development does occur in such areas, designers should consider creating buffers around the development that are less prone to fire. For example, roads, sports fields, irrigated landscaped areas, and natural or manmade water bodies can all act as fire buffers between a development and a nearby fire-prone ecosys-tem. Another approach is to conduct manual fuel removal or periodic prescribed burns under controlled conditions on lands near the development. Once excess dead plant material and other fuel has been removed, these buffer areas are less likely to sustain a major crown fire that could spread to the development. Finally, since wildfire moves especially rapidly up slopes and gullies, developers in fire-prone regions should avoid building on steep slopes and in canyons.

Once a development location has been selected, site design is critically important to protect structures against wildfire. The goal is to create "defensible space" around every structure that slows the spread of wildfire and facilitates fire-fighting activities. For instance, the Wildfire Mitigation Program in Boulder County, Colorado, recommends a three-zone system of defensible space around every structure in a fire-prone area.[20] In the innermost zone surrounding the building, fuel loads are sharply reduced and clear space is provided for firefighters to work. The first three to five feet (1 to 1.5 m) should be cleared of all vegetation, while the next six to eight feet (2 to 2.5 m) should consist of a low, fire-resistant ground cover such as grass. In the "transition zone"—which extends 75 to 125 feet (20 to 40 m) from the structure—vegetation should be modified to remove low plants and "ladder fuels," which allow fire to leap from the ground to tree crowns or roofs. Thus, shrubs and small trees should be removed, larger trees stripped of their lower branches, and trees widely separated so that their crowns do not touch. Homeowners also need to pay careful attention to other fuel sources near their house, such as woodpiles, sheds, and outdoor furniture.

Finally, beyond the transition zone, additional forest management using some of the practices discussed above may be required to safeguard the development. Some of these design recommendations clash with considerations presented elsewhere in the book—for example, to retain multiple strata of native vegetation. These conflicts illustrate the tradeoffs that must sometimes be made when humans live in potentially hazardous, disturbance-prone environments. They also suggest an ecological as well as human safety imperative not to build in such areas.

Many architectural design approaches to reducing wildfire hazard appear obvious but are often overlooked. In fire-prone areas, such building materials as brick and stone are preferable to wood or vinyl (which is toxic when burned). Because roofs are usually most vulnerable to fire, fire-resistant roof coverings should be used and attic space should be sealed so that sparks and embers cannot enter. Windows and glass doors are also vulnerable; these can be protected by using heat-reflective glass and fire-resistant shutters and by providing additional defensible space around them. Other appurtenances, such as balconies, chimneys, fencing, and utility poles, must also be carefully sited and designed to minimize vulnerabilities to the building.[21]

Water

Of all the natural disasters, flooding results in the greatest property losses in the United States.[22] Floodplains have been mapped for most parts of the United

States and many parts of Canada, although actual flood zones are prone to change over time as a result of changing conditions in the watershed—especially increased development. Nevertheless, the existence of these maps makes it easy for planners to regulate development in flood zones by adopting overlay zoning designations that correspond to the federal or provincial flood maps. Within these zones, development can be either prohibited outright or required to be elevated above the maximum expected flood height. Some jurisdictions also require the provision of compensatory flood storage (e.g., constructed wetlands) to make up for any development that does occur in a floodplain.

This chapter has highlighted several planning tools and design techniques that can help land use professional create ecologically compatible developments, communities, and entire landscapes. The purpose here was not to present an exhaustive list of all such tools but, rather, to give some specific examples of how planners, designers, and developers can apply an understanding of ecological processes to their work. The final chapter of the book is an interactive planning and design exercise that offers the reader an opportunity to practice doing just this.

11

Principles in Practice

Gestalt is a German word meaning "a unified whole . . . that cannot be derived from the summation of its component parts."[1] This word could describe the challenge facing planners and designers who seek to incorporate the lessons of ecology into their work. As we hope this book has indicated, ecologically based planning cannot be reduced to a recipe: there are few definitive answers and many uncertainties; solutions must be site specific yet context sensitive; and planners and designers must balance ecological factors against a plan's other, often competing, objectives. From designers of the land, the world demands integrated, ecologically based solutions.

For planners in the mid-twentieth century, the term *gestalt* connoted the practice of classifying land and deriving solutions from intuitive "gut feelings." This "gestalt method" of planning, which relies heavily on individual judgment, has largely been replaced by more empirical planning processes, in which factual data, public input, and a clear decision-making methodology ideally lead to more rational planning solutions.[2] This more systematic approach is essential for ecologically based planning: because so many ecological factors are relevant to planning and development activities, it is important to be clear about which of these factors are being addressed, how, and why. Intuition and intelligent synthesis are still important, but they follow and build upon ecological analysis. Therefore, let us begin by reviewing the key ecological lessons of this book (as shown in Box 11-1) before moving on to the planning exercise.

Box 11-1
What We Can Learn by Listening to Ecology

- Ecosystems usually behave according to certain general patterns, but chance plays a large role, too. Ecological communities and ecosystems are exceedingly complex, and our understanding of them is incomplete.
- The context and history of a site or study area play critical roles in determining its ecological form and function.
- Native species and ecosystems are important to protect for several reasons. They provide valuable, if not irreplaceable, ecosystem services and other economic benefits, and they offer humans aesthetic and spiritual nourishment.
- Long-term ecological integrity depends on the sum of four factors: the integrity of the physical environment, the integrity of native biota, the size and configuration of habitats within the landscape, and the context of the landscape.
- Planning must proceed based on the best ecological knowledge available at the time, recognizing that it may be a combination of well-known facts and working hypotheses.
- To ensure human health, safety, and welfare, planners and developers must know their ecological neighborhood—both biotic and abiotic.
- Nature reserves and open spaces can serve many different purposes for humans as well as native species. People should be clear about their goals before they plan or design these areas.
- Many planning and design techniques currently in practice—and others waiting to be developed and perfected—can help planners and designers apply the lessons of ecology to their work.

The planning exercise is divided into two parts corresponding to two different scales: (1) the site scale, at which developers, engineers, landscape architects, and development review officials typically work, and (2) the municipal or county scale, at which many planners work. The exercise is set in a hypothetical county in the southern Appalachian region of the southeastern United States. Although the places depicted in the exercise do not actually exist (and any similarities to a real site, town, or county are purely accidental), the details of the species and ecosystems profiled are accurate. The exercise incorporates a multitude of real ecological planning issues that currently face communities throughout North America: a sprawling suburban metropolis, development at the gateway to a recreational area, an expanding road network threatening to fragment natural ecosystems, agricultural production adjacent to sensitive waterways, and a patchwork of managed and unmanaged forests in public and private ownership. As you work through the exercise, think about the similarities between this hypothetical landscape and the one where you reside.

Part 1: Residential Development at the Site Scale

The Situation

Your firm has been hired to design a new residential development on a 128-acre (52 ha) site in the western foothills of the Jigsaw Mountains.* The developer (your client) envisions the project as providing a mix of single-family and small-scale multifamily housing in a bucolic setting close to the recreational amenities of the nearby national forest. He hopes to market the units to commuters from the nearby metropolis (about twenty miles or thirty kilometers, to the west), early retirees, or even second-home owners who want to "get away from it all" in a peaceful location.

Having just finished reading this book, you want to begin applying the lessons of ecologically based design to your work. As the lead designer on the project, you explain the basic principles of this approach to your client. You emphasize the importance of safeguarding the development's future inhabitants from natural hazards and also point out that effort spent at the outset to protect natural resources on the site could shorten the project's permitting timeline, given the county's recent emphasis on resource protection as spelled out in its new comprehensive plan. In addition, you explain to your client the ways in which ecologically sensitive development practices can reduce construction costs. These arguments make sense to the developer, and he likes the idea of doing the right thing ecologically. He also sees a promising new marketing angle for his development if he can depict it as "at one with nature."

Part 1A: Asking the Right Questions

At the start of the job, you are given a typical existing conditions plan prepared by a surveyor and showing the property boundaries, roads, and contour lines (see Figure 11-1). Although development plans are often prepared based primarily on this minimal amount of information about the site, clearly more must be known to inform ecologically based design. What questions would you need to ask before planning the site? *Please take a few minutes and write these questions down before proceeding to the next step of the exercise.*

Solution to Part 1A

Ecological due diligence requires you to look well beyond the boundaries of the site, as well as forward and backward in time, to anticipate the natural processes of disturbance and succession affecting the site. Doing so will help fulfill

---

* If the "hat" you wear in real life is that of a developer, planning or zoning board member, development review official, or citizen, working through this exercise from the perspective of a designer will give you a better idea of what you should expect from a good ecologically based site plan.

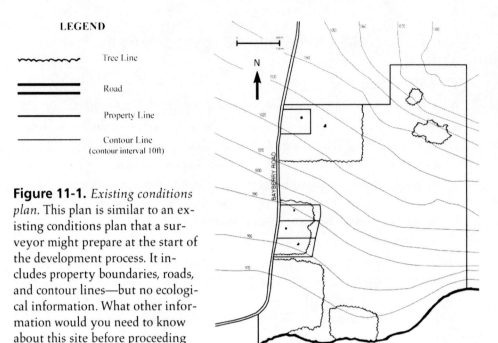

LEGEND

〜〜〜〜〜〜〜   Tree Line

━━━━━━━   Road

━━━━━━━   Property Line

──────   Contour Line
(contour interval 10ft)

Figure 11-1. *Existing conditions plan.* This plan is similar to an existing conditions plan that a surveyor might prepare at the start of the development process. It includes property boundaries, roads, and contour lines—but no ecological information. What other information would you need to know about this site before proceeding with ecologically based design?

one of your primary responsibilities as a site planner: to safeguard the health, safety, and welfare of the site's future human inhabitants in relation to their ecological context. In addition, to protect and restore native species and habitats, you will need to obtain information on the site's biological diversity, its ecology, and its conservation status, which should be depicted in map form whenever appropriate. (Sources and approaches for gathering such information are discussed in Chapters 2 and 7 and in Appendix B.)

Asking and answering the following questions will provide a good basis to proceed with ecologically based design. *The brief answers to these questions provided below and shown on the site ecology map (Color Plate 11) and the ecological context map (Color Plate 12) should be used to inform the second part of the site planning exercise.*

What disturbance processes affect the site?
Answering this question requires looking beyond the site's boundaries and also forward and backward in time. You learn that forest fires regularly occur in the national forest and the private timber lands to the north and east of the site. Some areas are managed with prescribed burning of underbrush to enhance wildlife habitat or timber production, while other areas have dangerously high fuel loads as a result of decades of fire suppression by humans. You also infer from seeing

many downed trees during your site walk that soil instability and windthrow of large trees is a common occurrence on the steeper parts of the site. In the spirit of due diligence, you consider other disturbance processes, such as flooding and hurricanes, but find that these processes are unlikely to occur on the site.

What ecosystems are present?

This question can be answered by using aerial photographs or satellite images combined with field surveys to identify the ecosystems on the site. On this site, the riparian zone includes an agricultural ecosystem (farm fields plus hedgerows) as well as a mature bottomland hardwood forest. The northeastern half of the site is a young oak-pine forest that was clear-cut about twenty years ago. Within this forest matrix is an outcropping of limestone where a distinct glade ecosystem has formed, harboring a diverse community of grasses, wildflowers, and animals adapted to live in hotter, drier conditions and in thin, rocky soils. The perennial stream creates a fifth distinct ecosystem at the edge of the site (see Color Plate 11).

What important native species are present, including rare, keystone, umbrella, and dominant species? For these species, are the local populations viable or not? Are they isolated, part of a larger population, or part of a metapopulation?

You hire an ecologist to help answer this question, who identifies several important species on the site. As it turns out, the population of the federally listed endangered Indiana bat (*Myotis sodalis*), which hibernates in the cave within the state forest just south of the site, also requires nearby riparian and hillside forest for roosting and foraging. The bat roosts in dead and dying trees where the bark has begun to peel away from the trunk—trees that are typically found in mature hardwood forests such as the one on the site.[3] The hardwood forest is also home to several species of Plethodontid salamanders, lungless amphibians that breathe through their skin. The Plethodontids also require mature forest with some moist areas and woody debris. The limestone glade harbors several rare flowering plants and mosses that live only in this unique environment. Finally, the stream at the southern edge of the site—like most intact stream ecosystems in the Southeast—harbors a great diversity of mollusks and fish, many of them endemic to a relatively small region. As heavily managed landscapes, the farmland and the oak-pine forest provide habitat for many generalist species that are found throughout the county but no species of particular interest for biodiversity conservation. (It is beyond the scope of this planning exercise to answer the population questions, but in a real planning project, this would be an important next step.)

What is the site's ecological context in space and time?
Key aspects of context include disturbance and succession, adjacent land uses, protected areas, landscape connectivity, and abiotic flows, such as water and nutrients. We have already discussed fire, soil instability, and windthrow as important physical disturbances within the site's forest ecosystems. However, biological agents also cause disturbance. A variety of insect and fungal infestations—including the southern pine beetle, gypsy moth, and anthracnose fungus—have affected large areas of nearby forest and might at some time spread to the site. Successional changes in the forests of this region generally follow the patterns described in Chapter 4. Following a clear-cut or major natural disturbance, drier south-facing slopes such as those on the site would tend to sprout various shade-intolerant deciduous species as well as pines, such as shortleaf pine and loblolly pine. Absent human or natural disturbances, such as fire, herbicide spraying, or thinning to promote stands of pure pine, the forest would tend to mature into an oak-pine forest, such as that found on the eastern half of the site. In moister areas, such as the southern portion of the site, succession leads toward an oak-hickory forest.

Other important aspects of the site's context are shown in Color Plate 12. This map indicates that the site is contiguous with large patches of undeveloped land to the north, east, and south, although some of these lands are heavily managed for timber harvesting. To the west is a patchwork landscape of forest, agriculture, and encroaching suburban development. Flows of silt and herbicides from upstream logging practices sometimes degrade water quality in the stream as it passes the site, while agrichemicals flowing into the stream from the site and nearby ones to the west influence water quality farther downstream.

What is the current condition of the ecosystems at the site?
At least four factors should be considered when answering this question: invasive species, missing species, chemical pollution and nutrient loading, and fragmentation. In terms of invasive species, kudzu vine is a problem in the hardwood forest, while planted shrubs—such as multiflora rose and bush honeysuckles—have spread from the farm's hedgerows into the surrounding woods. The most important missing species in the forest ecosystems are top predators, such as the gray and red wolves that once lived here. In their absence, populations of white-tailed deer and other herbivores have proliferated, affecting species composition in the forests and even threatening the survival of some herbaceous woodland plants.

Turning to chemical pollution and nutrient loading, you learn that such land use practices as logging and herbicide applications for forestry occasionally contribute silt and pollutants to the stream as it passes the site but that, overall, the stream ecosystem is in fairly good condition. Acid rain is an additional pollution threat—in this case, one that originates in cities and at smokestacks hundreds of miles or kilometers to the west. Finally, the effect of fragmentation on the ecosystem's condition must be considered. On the one hand, the site is contiguous with large areas of undeveloped forest to the east; on the other hand, much of this forest is actively logged, which reduces its value as core interior habitat.

How are human activities likely to change or influence the site's ecology in the future?

To answer this question, you must look beyond the site to consider both local influences (such as growth and development patterns) and regional and global influences (such as global climate change). On a local level, you examine the county's zoning map, review growth trends and projections in the county, and compare a current land use map with a historical one from twenty years ago. This information reveals that suburban and exurban growth are beginning to spread eastward toward the site, that agricultural land is gradually being converted to either forest or developed land uses, and that some protected land exists north and directly south of the site but none to the west. Scientific models predict that global climate change over the next century may make the southeastern United States considerably warmer, with average temperatures rising by 5°F to 9°F (3°C to 5°C) and the summertime heat index (a measure of heat discomfort that includes temperature and humidity) increasing by at least 10°F (6°C) and as much as 25°F (14°C). The models disagree about whether the Southeast will become wetter or drier but agree that heavy rains are likely to occur more frequently. One model predicts that drier conditions in the Southeast could change the predominant vegetative cover from forest to savanna.[4]

What might the site have looked like in earlier times, and what are the opportunities for restoration?

Remnant patches of old-growth vegetation nearby as well as ecological studies can provide a window through which to observe past ecosystems. Prior to the 1800s, forests blanketed the area, with hardwoods (including the now almost defunct American chestnut) being the dominant vegetation type. Regular disturbances were caused not only by natural events but also by Native Americans' use of fire. Over time, the forests on the site, if undisturbed, would acquire old-growth characteristics, such as numerous old trees, snags (standing dead trees), and a diverse forest floor community. There may also be opportunities to restore the connectivity of the local forests.

What other human factors affect how this site can or should be developed?
Obviously, designers must not neglect those human factors that are normally
considered when planning for development, such as zoning, transportation access, water and wastewater infrastructure, public facilities and services, and market considerations. However, since there are already many good planning texts
that cover these topics (and since they are a standard part of designers' educational training), we will not discuss them here, except as they relate to this ecologically based planning exercise.

Part 1B: Preparing the Plan

Now that you have a basic understanding of the site's ecological form, function, and context, you can proceed with preparing an ecologically based site plan.
As mentioned above, the developer wants to build a residential development offering a variety of housing types in a country setting that will appeal to commuters, early retirees, and possibly second-home owners. The zoning for the site
offers two different development options:

1. A conventional "rural residential" layout that allows single-family houses
   on 50,000 square foot (1.15-acre or 0.46 ha) lots, and
2. A Planned Residential Development option that allows the same total number of units as the first option, but in a mix of single-family and/or multi-
   family dwellings (up to four units per building) built on lots as small as
   10,000 sq. ft. Under this second option, the development must provide open
   space as well as community or recreational amenities.

Given these zoning options, your client's wishes, and your knowledge about the
site's ecology, how would you plan this site for development? Try sketching out
a site plan showing the location of buildings, roads, and undeveloped areas. (To
do so, you might want to use tracing paper or an enlarged photocopy of the existing conditions plan or the site ecology map.) Beyond the information shown
on your site plan, what other considerations should go into the planning of this
development?

Solution to Part 1B

Three different site planning approaches are illustrated in Figure 11-2, Color
Plate 13, and Color Plate 14, respectively. The conventional subdivision plan in
Figure 11-2 is designed in accordance the first zoning option (single-family
houses on 50,000 square foot lots). This design ignores most of the principles
discussed in this book, and will result in an environment that is poorer for humans and native species. For example, although the oak/pine forest to the north
and east of the site is fire-prone, the plan provides no fire buffer, thus threatening the safety and property of future inhabitants. In addition, despite the site's

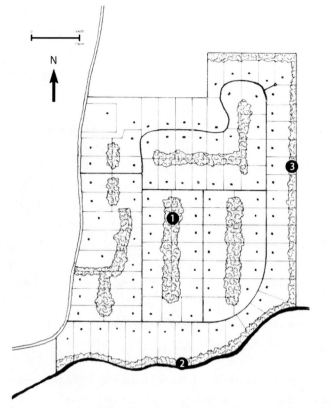

Figure 11-2. *Conventional subdivision plan.* This plan illustrates how development might proceed under the "rural residential" zoning option, absent any attempt to implement the concepts of ecologically based planning presented in this book. As is typical in conventional subdivisions, the entire site has been divided into individual house lots, and any residual patches of native vegetation (1) are so small that they offer little habitat value. Even though local laws mandate a fifty-foot (15 m) riparian buffer (2), this buffer may not be wide enough to provide a viable habitat corridor or filter out pollutants before they reach the stream. Residents may also be at risk from wildfire, because the houses on the east (3) abut an expanse of oak-pine forest, yet no protective buffering has been provided. Finally, this development provides no natural areas for its residents to use.

scenic, natural context, the plan provides no place for future residents to enjoy nature.

From an ecological standpoint, this plan's greatest drawback is its almost complete conversion of native habitat to houses, roads, and lawns. As a result, most native species associated with the glade, hardwood forest, and oak/pine forest habitats will disappear. The loss of mature hardwood forest on the site may even threaten the survival of the bat population that roosts nearby. Although a few small residual patches of trees are shown on the plan, these will probably support only generalist species that can survive in close proximity to humans.

The other two designs—the "rural cluster" plan shown in Color Plate 13 and the "village cluster" layout illustrated in Color Plate 14—both follow the second zoning option (single- and multi-family housing on small lots surrounded by open space). These plans both incorporate three elements for sound ecologically based planning for this site:

1. *Choosing a development pattern that does not take up too much space:* The Planned Residential Development (PRD) zoning option is far more conducive to ecologically based design than the conventional rural residential approach shown in Figure 11-2. Whereas the conventional design blankets the entire site with individual house lots and roads, the PRD option allows development to be concentrated on the most environmentally suitable portions of the site while setting aside undeveloped land for native species and ecosystems. Designers seeking to harmonize development with the natural environment (and planners trying to encourage such development) should make use of flexible zoning tools such as PRDs, conservation subdivisions (cluster developments), and transfer of development rights.

2. *Protecting human health, safety, and welfare in relation to the ecological context:* The greatest natural threat to this development will be forest fire, which is a regular occurrence in the surrounding oak/pine and pine plantation forests. To protect human lives and property, therefore, both of the ecologically based site plans buffer the dwellings from the surrounding oak/pine forests by design features such as community gardens, roads, a sports field, and a "town green." A buffer is less important to the south because the native oak/hickory forest is less fire-prone.

3. *Protecting the site's important species, habitats, and ecosystems:* As discussed above, the portions of the site that are most important for the protection of biodiversity include the limestone glade in the northeast (which sustains an assemblage of rare plant species), the hardwood forest near the stream (which provides food and shelter for the Indiana bat and the Plethodontid salamanders), and the stream itself (which contains rare mollusks and fishes). To safeguard these ecosystems, development on the site should steer clear of the important terrestrial habitats as well as a buffer area along the stream. In addition, land use patterns should minimize the potential for silt, chemicals, or untreated runoff to enter the stream.

Within these three basic parameters, there are many good ways to lay out the roads, houses, and open space on the site, two of which are shown in Color Plate 13 and Color Plate 14. From an ecological standpoint, the rural cluster plan (Color Plate 13) has several advantages. First, it maintains a wide stream buffer of at least 600 feet (180 m), which is ample to filter surface runoff before it reaches the stream, provide a wildlife movement corridor containing interior forest habitat, and create some distance between the houses and the nearby state forest, which is home to bear and coyote.

Second, it proposes retiring the farm fields adjacent to the stream and restoring them to native hardwood forest. These fields are now the only "missing link" in a continuous corridor of riparian forest to the east and west of the site. (Also, retiring these fields will reduce fertilizer and pesticide pollution to the stream.) Third, the plan preserves a wide forested corridor between the stream and the uplands to the northeast of the site, which will help provide connectivity between forest patches even if some of the surrounding lands are developed or converted to low-habitat-value pine plantations in the future.

Finally, the plan retains some of the existing agricultural land on the site, while also introducing community gardens where residents can grow fruits and vegetables. As discussed in Chapter 8, local food production is an important aspect of sustainability; the site plan therefore seeks to balance the protection of native habitat and the protection of productive agricultural land.

The village cluster plan (Color Plate 14) clusters the development even more tightly and concentrates it on the previously disturbed agricultural lands. Compared to the rural cluster plan, it results in less habitat alteration and intrudes less into the contiguous block of forest habitat that extends eastward from the site. The higher density design results in more of a "neighborhood" feel, with many of the houses clustered around common open spaces. However, none of the dwellings is more than a two- or three-minute walk from the natural forest that has been preserved on the eastern two-thirds of the site.

Both the rural cluster and village cluster site plans raise some interesting restoration and management challenges. For example, in the rural cluster plan there are a few possible ways to restore the farmland in the southwest corner of the site to riparian forest. One solution is simply to abandon the farming activities and allow succession to run its course; at the other extreme, one could plant seedlings of desired tree species. Given cost constraints and the proximity of existing hardwood riparian forest ecosystems east and west of the restoration site, a relatively "hands-off" approach might be the most feasible. However, initial active management will be needed to make sure that invasive species do not take over and that the site is sufficiently stabilized so that topsoil does not erode into the stream.

As the designer, you may also need to work with the developer and local planning officials to design a long-term management framework for the conservation and agricultural lands on the site. Who will own these lands and determine how they are managed? Should a management plan be drafted now, as part of the planning process? Who will pay for managing the land and taking care of any problems that arise? What role (if any) will future residents of the development play in managing these lands? The discussion on land management in Chapter 9 addresses some of these questions.

Part 2: Planning for Growth by Listening to Ecology

In Chapter 6, we suggested that the *landscape* is the most effective scale at which to plan for the conservation of biodiversity. A much smaller focus area is too small to consider important ecosystem processes and flows or to plan for the long-term viability of populations of many wide-ranging species. A larger focus area can sometimes help in understanding and protecting biodiversity but is inconsistent with how human land use decisions are usually made—at the local or county level—and thus may be less effective, unless the large-scale vision can be reflected in smaller-scale plans. The scale of a landscape is typically tens of miles or kilometers across or, in terms of human boundaries, roughly the size of a county, a few counties, or part of a state or province. Depending on the subdivision of local governments where you live, most planning may actually occur at the sublandscape scale (miles or kilometers across). This is consistent with the appropriate scale for biodiversity planning as long as the sublandscape scale plans are carefully situated within their landscape context.

From the preceding discussion, it is clear that municipal, county, and regional planners should be on the front lines of human efforts to conserve biodiversity. This part of the planning exercise offers a chance to apply the lessons of this book from the perspective of these planners. Since it is not practical to use a landscape-scale study area of hundreds or thousands of square miles or kilometers for the planning exercise, a smaller area of roughly fifty square miles (130 square km) is used. It may help to think of this scale in terms of the local government jurisdictions where you live. For example, a plan at this scale could be a comprehensive plan for a town, township, small city, or portion of a county or a region.

The Situation

As a staff planner in a public-sector planning agency, you have been asked to prepare a land use plan for an area of roughly fifty square miles (130 square km, or 32,000 acres). The plan should reflect a long-term (twenty- to thirty-year) vision for the future and will serve as the basis for your jurisdiction's official zoning map as well as for decisions related to public facility and infrastructure investment, land and resource conservation, and other policies. Since the mission of your planning agency (as well as your professional responsibility as a planner)[5] includes the protection of natural resources, such as native species and habitats, you decide to prepare the plan using the ecological planning approach presented in this book.

Part 2A: Asking the Right Questions

As you begin working on the plan, you have access to the various data sources that planners typically use—local and regional census data, state economic statistics, and various geographic data layers, including transportation networks, land use, rivers and streams, and tax maps (property boundary maps) available through your agency's geographic information system (GIS) department. What additional geographic data layers and other information would you need to prepare an ecologically based plan for the study area? What questions would you need to ask before preparing the plan? *Please write down these answers before proceeding to the next step.*

Solution to Part 2A

One good way to depict ecological information at a municipal or county scale is to prepare a set of annotated maps that show basic environmental data plus text or graphic annotations that explain major ecological functions, processes, or flows. Depending on the complexity of the ecosystems in your study area and the amount and type of data available to you, this effort could consist of a dozen or more maps or as few as three. Below, we present what we consider to be the three indispensable maps and corresponding sets of questions to ask about your study area. *These questions, answers, and maps should be used to inform the second part of the community-scale portion of the planning exercise.*

1. LOCAL ECOLOGY.

This map and analysis describe the local vegetational communities and ecosystems, ecosystem processes, and species of conservation interest (see Color Plate 15). The base map should depict vegetational communities in as much detail as possible, as well as surface water features and major human corridors that fragment the landscape, such as roads. In addition, the map should identify the protection and management status of natural lands within the study area to help indicate their current and likely future ecological integrity. Thus, the local ecology map includes ecosystem delineations and functions as well as human delineations of the landscape. This map and the accompanying analysis should answer the following questions.

What ecosystems and vegetational communities are present?
The eight land cover categories shown in Color Plate 15 provide a first approximation of the different ecosystem types in the study area. The three forest

types—deciduous, mixed, and conifer—range from lightly to heavily managed. For example, most of the hardwood forest is lightly managed, with occasional use for timber harvesting, hunting, or recreation, while many of the evergreen forests are heavily managed commercial pine plantations. Each of the forest ecosystems contains an ever-changing mosaic of vegetational communities regulated by natural disturbance, human disturbance, and succession. There are also some small but distinct vegetational communities created by their soil or microclimate, such as riparian floodplain forests, limestone glades, and hillside seeps. These smaller ecosystems may not show up on a sub-landscape scale map but are still important to identify because they may be especially rich repositories of biodiversity. Human-dominated ecosystems in the study area include agricultural areas and developed land.

What species of conservation interest are present?

As discussed in Chapter 5, species of conservation interest are often rare species, keystone species, or umbrella species. Several rare species in this landscape are discussed on page 221, including the Indiana bat, Plethodontid salamanders, freshwater mollusks and fishes, and grasses and flowering plants within the limestone glades. Two umbrella species are worth noting. At the eastern edge of the study area and extending into the national forest beyond, the black bear (*Ursus americanus*) is considered an umbrella species because of its requirement for large and predominantly roadless habitat areas (generally more than 5,000 acres, or 2,000 hectares), a variety of forest types to meet seasonal foraging needs, and some late-successional forests with large snags and cavities for denning.[6] Brook trout (*Salvelinus fontinalis*), which live in the southern of the two rivers shown on the map, require cool, well-oxygenated streams with gravelly bottoms and a pool/riffle structure. Thus, they are not just an umbrella species for other sensitive freshwater species but also an indicator of overall watershed health. One keystone species (actually a group of species) in the hardwood and mixed forests are the oaks (*Quercus* species), which provide an important food source (acorns) for numerous bird and mammal species.

For the species of conservation interest, are the local populations viable or not? Are they isolated, part of a larger population, or part of a metapopulation?

Answers to these questions may not be readily available to planners or even to ecologists. Nevertheless, clues can be found by examining the distribution and abundance of species of conservation interest both within and outside the study area. For example, knowing from a field guide that Plethodontid salamanders require moist hardwood forest and disperse only tens of meters during their lifetimes, you could infer that the salamanders within your study area are divided into a number of subpopulations, each somewhat isolated from the others by the intervening matrix of unsuitable pine plantation or dry oak-pine forest. With additional information about the typical area of the salamanders' home range or population density, you may also be able to estimate which patches of hardwood forest are capable of sustaining viable populations of these amphibians in the long term. Similarly, knowing that the home range of black bears is roughly eleven to fifteen square miles (28 to 40 square km), you could infer that the bears found in the study area are part of a population whose range extends well into the national forest. Forest managers may be able to tell you whether the bear population is increasing, holding steady, or decreasing,

What is the current condition of the ecosystems of this landscape?
As discussed earlier in this chapter, some of the major factors affecting ecosystem condition include invasive species, missing species, chemical pollution and nutrient loading, and fragmentation. The amount and persistence of fragmentation are especially important to consider at the landscape and sublandscape scales when planning for future development and conservation. For example, the western part of the study area is beginning to be fragmented by essentially permanent developed land uses. While native vegetation in the central and eastern portions is fragmented by agriculture and pine plantations, these land uses are probably both less persistent and less incompatible with native ecosystems than urban development is. In addition, some of the former farms in the central portion of the study area have been abandoned and are beginning to revert to forest. Minimizing fragmentation by considering these and other factors should be an important aspect of the planning outcome.

Where are the most important habitats in the study area?
This question can be answered in a few different ways depending on the available data. The first choice is to delineate critical habitats based on preexisting data, if it is available (see Chapter 7 and Appendix B). If this is not possible, one could estimate the most important habitats based on information on the species of conservation interest (e.g., habitat requirements) plus landscape ecology principles. These considerations would lead you to conclude that the most important habitats in your study area include riparian forests and floodplains, limestone glades and other rare microhabitats, unmanaged or lightly managed forests contiguous with the protected areas, and hardwood forests within one mile of the Indiana bat roosting cave in the southern nature reserve. These areas are delineated as orange circles on Color Plate 15.

How well protected is the study area's native biodiversity?
Answering this question requires looking at the relationship between ecological boundaries and human boundaries. As shown on Color Plate 15, the study area

contains relatively little land that is protected from development, and some of it—the national forest—is not managed primarily for conservation. The two reserves that are managed for conservation do contain critical habitat, but other ecologically important lands in the study area are not protected. In addition to the protection status of these lands, other conservation opportunities and threats should be examined. For example, proposed roads, sewer extensions, or market pressures could all constitute conservation threats, while zoning laws or lack of market demand could provide some level of protection (albeit usually temporary or incomplete).

2. LANDSCAPE-SCALE ECOLOGY.

Looking beyond the boundaries of the study area to the landscape scale allows us to consider broader land patterns and flows as well as processes that occur over longer time frames. At this scale it is helpful to map the same base data suggested for the local scale—land use or land cover, surface water, roads, protected areas, and critical habitat areas—although this may be done at a coarser scale (see Color Plate 16). This analysis should also consider other factors from outside the study area that impinge on conservation and land use planning within the study area, as presented in the following questions.

Are there critical habitat areas nearby? If so, are they linked to natural areas within the study area?
As shown in Color Plate 16, several large natural areas are situated north, south, and east of the study area, which are currently linked to natural lands in the study area and have the potential to remain so in the future. These linkages appear important for maintaining black bear habitat as well as genetic flow between the population of Indiana bat in the study area and nearby populations just outside the area. In addition to linkages, such barriers as large rivers, highways, cities, or large monoculture farms in the surrounding landscape should be noted because these could negatively affect conservation efforts within the study area. Finally, it helps to examine the landscape context of the two major river corridors that traverse the study area: the river in the northern part of the study area has several dams and a major reservoir downstream of the study area, while the river in the southern part of the study area is free-flowing. This information might help prioritize riparian conservation efforts within the study area.

What other outside human and natural forces are likely to impinge on the study area in the future?
Relevant outside forces will vary from place to place but could include influences such as: (1) a major tree pest or disease in the next county or state that is likely to spread to the study area; (2) regional development pressures that are likely

to affect the study area; (3) state/provincial or national policy decisions or major infrastructure projects such as road construction that may encourage new development; and (4) global climate change.*

3. LOCAL NATURAL HAZARDS.

To accomplish their mission of protecting human health, safety, and welfare, planners must document and guard against an array of natural hazards. This information can be mapped using a combination of preexisting data sets (e.g., 100-year floodplains as delineated on U.S. Federal Emergency Management Agency flood insurance rate maps in the United States or floodplains mapped through the Flood Damage Reduction Program in Canada) and estimates of areas most threatened by hazards such as fires, landslides, and violent storms. For hazards that have not yet been mapped, planners can create estimated hazard zone maps by using data layers on the factors that contribute to the hazard, such as land cover type, slopes, and soils. For example, you might know from past experience that landslides occur most often on soil type X in areas exceeding 30 percent slope, or that Ponderosa pine forests that have not burned within the past twenty years are most susceptible to destructive wildfires. Color Plate 17 is an example of a natural hazards map for the study area showing the areas most susceptible to four different hazards: flooding, wildfire, landslides, and large predators.

Again, these three maps and sets of questions provide what we consider to be a minimum level of information necessary to proceed with ecologically based planning. They are a supplement to—not a replacement for—traditional planning analysis.

Part 2B: Preparing the Plan

The American Institute of Certified Planners' Code of Ethics and Professional Conduct states that "a planner must pay special attention to the interrelatedness of decisions." In other words, planners almost never plan for just a single objective. So it is with biological conservation, which must share space at the planner's table with economic development, affordable housing, efficient transportation, and myriad other goals. The political realities of property rights, local resistance to change, and the agendas of elected and appointed officials add another challenge, as any practicing planner can attest. They also impel planners to search for solutions that find common ground among these often competing objectives and stakeholders.

---

* In some regions, such as coastal or boreal areas, where there are generally agreed upon predictions of the effects of global climate change, this should be an important part of the analysis. In areas where the likely effects of climate change are less well established, your analysis might ask more generic questions, such as "if species need to migrate north to adapt to a warming climate, are there enough viable north-south corridors or stepping stones in or near the study area for these species to use?"

To make the planning exercise more realistic, let's add some basic parameters or assumptions about the other planning goals and constraints that must be incorporated into the plan:

1. The plan must accommodate a projected population increase in the study area from 12,000 at present to 18,000 in twenty years.
2. Community goals necessitate that the plan identify solutions to increase the amount of affordable housing and bring in new commerce and industry to provide jobs and property tax revenue.
3. Funds will be available from local and state sources to protect about 4 percent of the study area's land as open space over the next ten years.
4. Local voters and politicians generally oppose policies that are perceived as denying or sharply curtailing individual property rights.

Keeping in mind these parameters and the ecological information presented above, what would your land use plan look like? As you prepare your solution to this section of the planning exercise, focus on two aspects of the plan: (1) create a generalized future land use map showing areas designated for different types of conservation and development (to do this, you might want to use tracing paper or an enlarged photocopy of the local ecology map), and (2) formulate any additional policies that you think are necessary to guide future land use. *Please prepare the map and additional policies before proceeding to the solution.*

Solution to Part 2B

As most planners know, many valid ways of solving a land use question often exist, each of which balances multiple considerations in a slightly different way. Thus, the solution presented below and in Color Plate 18 is intended not as the single "best" solution but as a good solution that illustrates many of the principles of ecologically based planning.

When creating a land use plan, the order in which different land uses are delineated can strongly influence the final planning outcome. Until recently, for example, planners have generally paid the most attention to where housing, commerce, and industry should be located; as a result, extensive areas of prime farm soils and biologically important river valleys have been paved over when less productive or environmentally sensitive sites might have done just as well or almost as well. Ecologically based planning operates according to a different paradigm that optimizes the fulfillment of human as well as ecological needs on the landscape by prioritizing the use of limited land resources. In other words, since conservation lands are some of the least interchangeable of the various competing land uses (i.e., a species can be conserved most easily in the places where it lives, and an ecosystem can be conserved only by protecting the land where it exists), it makes sense to select and designate these areas first. Similarly, prime farm soils should generally be reserved for agriculture, even though they may also be good building sites. Once these "fixed" land uses have been designated, the planner can then apportion the remaining land among such uses as housing, industry, recreation, and second-priority conservation and agricultural areas. Here are some of the considerations that were used in delineating these various land uses as shown on Color Plate 18:

- *Conservation areas.* The most critical conservation lands should receive the highest levels of protection (such as outright acquisition) and are shown in a medium green on Color Plate 18. These lands include the areas designated as "critical habitat" on Color Plate 15 and other lands of high biodiversity value, such as riparian forests, forest near the bat cave, and ridgetop forest in the central part of the study area. Small conservation areas are also designated in each of the two larger communities so that residents there will have easy access to nature areas. Finally, a stretch of floodplain just east of the northern of the two town centers was selected for conservation in order to preclude inappropriate floodplain development and help protect water quality in the downstream reservoir shown in Color Plate 16.

  Although land acquisition funds are limited (and, thus, only 4 percent of the study area is designated for acquisition), other land protection strategies, such as transfer of development rights (TDR), can be used to guide development away from biologically important areas. As discussed in Chapter 10, TDR allows landowners to transfer development rights from "sending areas," where development is not desired (shown in light green) to "receiving areas," which are well suited to accommodate development (shown in brown). Land is thus conserved through a real estate transaction without the need for publicly funded land acquisition and without denying property rights to landowners in the TDR sending area. As shown in Color Plate 18, TDR could be used to help conserve "buffer" lands around existing protected areas and to steer development away from environmentally sensitive ridgeline and headwater forests. The TDR sending area also includes two large blocks of prime farmland, where excellent agricultural soils (and flooding issues) make the land especially suitable for agriculture but unsuitable for development. Thus, in the parlance of the landscape conservation and development plan discussed in Chapter 10, TDR is used to protect secondary habitat areas and intensive production lands. The TDR sending and receiving areas are also delineated so as to aggregate natural lands, agricultural lands, and urban lands in order to reduce habitat fragmentation, maintain a "critical mass" of farms in certain areas, and attain the efficiencies inherent in tighter-knit development patterns.

- *Other rural lands.* These areas, shown in pale yellow on Color Plate 18, are also intended for secondary habitat and intensive production but represent lower priority examples of each than the lands designated for acquisition or as TDR sending areas. Accordingly, residential development is not actively discouraged in the other rural lands as it is in the TDR sending areas. Since these lands make up the largest part of the study area, effective policies to guide any development that occurs here are especially important. The minimum lot size for residential development is a key consideration and should be based on the factors shown in Box 10-1. The other rural lands would be an excellent location to allow and encourage conservation subdivision design and to implement a greenprinting approach. These policies could help reduce the footprint of new development and ensure that buildings and roads are placed on the least environmentally sensitive portions of the site. An areawide greenprint could also create secondary conservation corridors and additional buffers around the more highly protected conservation lands.

- *Targeted development areas.* Areas designated for future higher-density development are shown in brown on Color Plate 18. These are also the TDR receiving areas—places where a developer could build at higher density in exchange for purchasing the development rights from land in the TDR sending area (thereby protecting that land). As shown on the map, most of the areas designated for higher-density development are adjacent to settlements, which means that existing infrastructure, such as roads, sewage treatment facilities, and fire stations, can serve this development.

While there is obvious appeal to directing new development into and adjacent to existing settlements, this type of development may not satisfy all market niches. One of the reasons people move to the study area is to enjoy the natural setting, recreation opportunities, and proximity to the national forest. Thus, two large development tracts are designated on land that is currently rural but that does not contain critical conservation features. These areas could be developed with condominiums, a golf course, a resort, or another type of complex that would help the community meet its housing and economic goals by promoting development in suitable locations. Finally, it is worth noting that in an actual land use plan, the areas designated for future higher-density development would probably be further subdivided into different types of residential and commercial zones—a step that we omit here for the sake of simplicity.

To implement ecologically based planning, the map-based land use plan should be supplemented by additional policies to guide future development and conservation. Transportation and road construction policies are a critical but often-overlooked opportunity to meld ecological and human needs. Since roads fragment habitat and often bring with them new development (which further fragments habitat), an appropriate aspect of local transportation policy may be to designate certain areas to be roadless. A roadless policy would prevent public funds from being used in a way that actively promotes the fragmentation of important habitats. For example, building a north-south road over the ridge in the center part of the study area (in the vicinity of the 1 on the map) might improve circulation, but from what we know about the local ecology, this would be an especially bad place to build a road. Thus, the ridgeline in the central part of the study area and the TDR sending area in the southeast corner could be designated as locations ineligible to receive public funding for new road construction.

Several of the other ecologically based planning approaches discussed in Chapter 10 would also be appropriate for use in the study area. Environmental protection zoning in the form of overlay zones could be used to restrict development in some of the hazard areas shown on Color Plate 17, such as floodplains and erosion-prone steep slopes. Requirements for ecologically sensitive development practices and the use of native species in landscaping and site design would help reduce the negative effects of developed lands on native species. Finally, for fire-prone sections of the study area, policies could be established that safeguard new developments from wildfire through the use of fire buffers, less-combustible building materials, or other design features.

Afterword

The resiliency of North America's landscapes stands out wherever one looks across the continent. On abandoned farm fields and pastures, trees return with surprising rapidity and vigor once farming ceases, forests grow again where they were once cut down, and wooden buildings disintegrate and gradually blend into the natural landscape. In the places where people have farmed, logged, or lived in modest numbers, ecosystems can often recover on their own or with a little help from humans.

But today's cities, towns, and suburbs—with their paved roads, parking lots, and concrete buildings—function very differently from farms and working forests. Soils that have been paved over no longer support plant growth; sunlight heats the pavement and rooftops, creating new local weather patterns while sustaining only the hardiest of plants; and water flows off the urban landscape into the channels we create, neither recharging aquifers nor providing habitat. Because they change ecosystems so profoundly, our cities and towns will not release their grip on the land as gently as did the dirt roads and wooden buildings of centuries past. Furthermore, by driving habitats, populations, and even entire species into oblivion, modern land use patterns often eliminate the very building blocks needed for ecosystems to recover in the future.

The decisions that we make today—where we build roads and structures, whether we divide or connect habitats, how we manage fires and flooding in ecosystems—will change the landscape far into the future. If we are not careful about our decisions, we will leave our children and grandchildren a degraded continent of cramped landscapes and unhealthy ecosystems. As the landscape changes, our understanding of the natural world will change as well. Psychologist Peter Kahn describes how each generation grows up assuming that the natural environment of their childhood was healthy and largely pristine.[1] But during the course of every generation, in the years between childhood and adulthood, human influence over the natural world spreads and deepens, and the next generation's children grow up in a world with less ecological integrity than the one in which their parents grew up. This new generation also assumes the landscapes of their childhood to be healthy, so that, over time, our society's understanding and expectation of what constitutes a healthy ecosystem progressively decline.

What kinds of landscapes will we bequeath to our children—and what will we enable them to bequeath to their children? Can we maintain healthy and biologically rich native ecosystems and restore degraded ones, or will we allow our landscape legacy to be poorer than the one we inherited? By incorporating insights from ecology and conservation into land use decisions, today's planners, designers, developers, and engaged citizens can help create a North American landscape that supports both healthy human communities and healthy ecological communities.

Appendix A: Current Status of Biodiversity in North America

Every continent has its own wonderful biological diversity, and North America is no exception. Our continent has certainly undergone many changes at the hands of humans, but even today, large portions of the landscape still remain in natural or seminatural conditions and small gems of nature can be found in every corner of the continent. This appendix describes some of the patterns of biological diversity that exist in North America and some of the continent's special ecological places.

Patterns of Diversity across North America

The broadest pattern of biodiversity is the distribution of *biomes,* or major ecosystem types, across the continent (see Figure A-1). As can be seen on the map, biomes in the United States are generally distributed as a series of bands that run from north-south, while biomes in Canada tend to be oriented west-east.

Biomes are determined by a combination of factors, primarily temperature and precipitation, with soil type and history playing secondary roles. In northern Canada and Alaska, the effects of severe cold most of the year, a short growing season, and little precipitation combine to create the treeless tundra that stretches around the world in circumpolar regions. According to some classification schemes, tundra regions never experience a month in which the average temperature exceeds 50°F (10°C).[1] To the south of the tundra stand the great boreal forests that also circle the globe, stretching across northern Europe and Siberia as well as North America. Here, although the climate is still quite dry, the warmest month or few months average higher than 50°F, enabling coniferous trees to grow.[2]

Farther south, interactions between the prevailing westerly weather patterns and the continent's major north-south mountain ranges help to create the great north-south

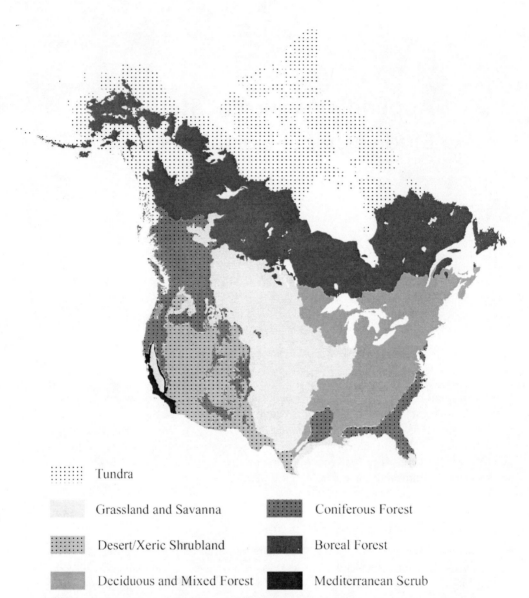

Tundra

Grassland and Savanna

Coniferous Forest

Desert/Xeric Shrubland

Boreal Forest

Deciduous and Mixed Forest

Mediterranean Scrub

Figure A-1. Ecologists classify the landscape according to ecological units known as biomes. This map shows the distribution of biomes in North America. (Modified from Taylor H. Ricketts et al., *Terrestrial Ecoregions of North America: A Conservation Assessment* [Washington, DC: Island Press, 1999].)

bands of wet forests, dry shrubands, moister grasslands and savannas, and moist forests that cover the landscape from west to east. Warm, moist air sweeps in from the Pacific Ocean over the coastal mountains and, as it rises and cools, deposits its moisture along the western edge of the continent. East of the major mountain ranges, the now-dry winds do not deposit enough rain and snow to support forests, except at the highest elevations, and desert, shrubland, or grassland conditions prevail. It is only in the eastern portion

Figure A-2. A single biome can contain several ecoregions, each of which may contain habitats and ecosystems of highly contrasting character, such as the montane forests and meadows seen in this photograph.

of the United States and Canada, where moisture from the Gulf of Mexico streams north and then east, that deciduous forests can grow.[3]

A biome map offers only a coarse description of what the landscape actually looks like. Each biome, such as tundra or coniferous forest, contains multiple *ecoregions*—relatively large areas of land consisting of a distinct assemblage of natural communities that is united by common environmental conditions, species, and disturbance processes.[4] At still finer levels, one finds different types of ecosystems nestled within each ecoregion. Various types of wetlands, distinct types of forest or grassland, and a variety of other ecosystems exist in each ecoregion and biome, adding to the diversity of species within each (see Figure A-2).

Traditionally, conservationists have used political boundaries as the basis for most of their analyses, describing the number of bird species in Ontario, for example, or salamander species in North Carolina. Even today, this scheme makes sense for historical reasons. Records have traditionally been kept state by state or province by province, and there is great value in being able to compare recently collected data with historical data. But ecologists and conservationists now recognize that political boundaries can be arbitrary and ecologically misleading. Instead, it makes sense to create ecologically distinct regions that have internal consistency and are recognizably different from neighboring regions. Accordingly, conservation groups across North America including the World Wildlife Fund and The Nature Conservancy have recently started mapping ecoregions, and both organizations have begun using ecoregions as the basis for their North American conservation efforts.

Highlights of North American Biodiversity

North America contains some of the world's greatest biodiversity treasures, and it is worth reviewing these briefly to emphasize how important a role North Americans have to play in protecting global biodiversity. Furthermore, globally and regionally significant biodiversity is not limited to just a few parts of the continent: every single region and biome in North America contains important species and ecosystems. The following information is taken from three sources: The Nature Conservancy's *Precious Heritage*, the World Wildlife Fund's *Terrestrial Ecoregions of North America*, and the U.S. Geological Survey's *Status and Trends of the Nation's Biological Resources.*[5]

Alaska and Northern Canada

Some of the world's largest expanses of intact forest are found across northern Canada and Alaska. These great forests and the nearby tundra include some of the best examples of intact large predator–large herbivore relationships, featuring large caribou herds, polar and grizzly bears, and wolves. The migrations of the caribou herds, which may cover more than 600 miles (1,000 km), are one of the outstanding biological phenomena on the planet, and some of the world's most fertile bird breeding grounds stretch across the tundra of the far north. The coastal regions across the north are home to some of the highest concentrations of large marine mammals.

West Coast of the United States and Southern Canada

The West Coast of the continent is home to a wide variety of plant species and ecosystem types. The world's finest temperate rainforests stretch along the coasts of British Columbia, Washington, Oregon, and California. Redwoods (*Sequoia sempervirens*), which may reach 330 feet (100 m) in height and are the tallest trees on Earth, inhabit some of these forests along with other giants, such as the Douglas-fir (*Pseudotsuga menziesii*) and Sitka spruce (*Picea sitchensis*). California is also home to one of the five Mediterranean climate zones in the world and is a globally important center of plant diversity.

Western United States

The Chihuahuan and Sonoran deserts of the Southwest contain tremendous plant and animal diversity, while the Yellowstone region is a relatively intact, large ecosystem. The isolation of the "sky islands" in the American Southwest—mountain ranges separated by expanses of desert—have led to great evolutionary diversification, especially among smaller animals and plants that do not disperse easily.

Central United States and South-Central Canada

This region was once one of the largest grasslands in the world, although today it is mostly covered by corn and soybean fields in the east and wheat fields in the west. Still, in the upper Midwest, the prairie pothole region serves as an important migratory stopover point for many species of migrating waterfowl, as does the Platte River for some half-million sandhill cranes (*Grus canadensis*)—one of the greatest migration spectacles anywhere on Earth.

Eastern United States and Canada

The forests of the southeastern United States are quite diverse, harboring a wide variety of tree species and other vascular plants. These forests also contain large numbers of land snail and amphibian species, and the freshwaters of the Southeast still harbor the most diverse freshwater mollusk fauna in the world. The eastern portion of the continent, moreover, is the site of surprisingly large expanses of regenerating forest that have regrown over the past century, since the abandonment of the majority of the region's farms.

Numbers of Species

The United States and Canada both contain a large number of native species. Although each nation has about 7 percent of the world's land area, the United States contains far more species. Given the relative locations of the two countries, this difference is to be expected, for in temperate regions the number of species generally increases as one travels from the polar regions toward the tropics.

Different groups of organisms display different distributional patterns. For instance, among mammals, reptiles, and butterflies, the southwestern United States has the highest species diversity of any region in the two countries. In contrast, trees, other vascular plants, amphibians, land snails, freshwater fishes, freshwater mussels, and crayfish all have their highest number of species in the southeastern United States. In fact, the Southeast is the richest region in the world for freshwater mussels and crayfishes, and the United States has more species in these groups (and freshwater snails) than does any other nation.[6] The United States also contains more species of conifers and freshwater fishes than might be expected given the size of its landmass. Not all groups display pronounced north-south gradients in species richness: in the western part of the continent, many bird and tree species are found even relatively far north in Canada.

Patterns of Endemism across North America

The distribution of *endemic species,* or species that are restricted to a single geographic area, is another important facet of biodiversity. Endemism can occur at any geographic scale; a species (or subspecies or genus) can be endemic to a single meadow, a state, an ecoregion, a nation, or a continent.

Since so many of the species in North America are widely distributed, relatively few species are endemic to a single ecoregion.[7] Certain regions, however, do have higher levels of endemism than others, and these areas tend to be in the southern part of the United States. Mammals, for instance, have their highest levels of endemism throughout the South, and especially along the West Coast. Butterfly and reptile endemism is highest in the Southwest, reaching its peak in the Chihuahuan Desert. None of these groups, however, have more than seven endemic species in a single ecoregion.

In contrast, amphibian and land snail endemism is highest in the Appalachians, with a high level of snail endemism in Hawaii. Freshwater fish, crayfish, and mussels have their highest levels of endemism in the southeastern United States, with many other mussel species endemic to the Ohio River watershed. Furthermore, endemic species from these groups are far more numerous than those from the mammals, butterflies, and reptiles. The Appalachian/Blue Ridge forest ecoregion has 21 endemic amphibian species and 122 endemic land snails, and the Tennessee-Cumberland aquatic ecoregion is home to 67 endemic fish species, 40 crayfish, and 20 freshwater mussels.

Tree endemism is especially high in the southeastern United States, the Chihuahuan Desert, and Hawaii, with the southeastern conifer forest ecoregion having twenty-six endemic tree species. Endemism in other vascular plants is high in both the Southeast and the mountainous Southwest, with more than 200 endemic vascular plant species in both the southeastern conifer forest ecoregion and the Colorado Plateau shrublands ecoregion. Hawaii is extraordinarily high in endemic plant species, with its four ecoregions each having at least 100 endemic species and two having more than 400 each. Regions with high levels of endemism—such as the southeastern and southwestern United States and Hawaii—are of particular importance globally for conserving biodiversity.

Current Status and Future Trends

While North America contains some true treasures of biodiversity, the current outlook for biodiversity conservation on the continent is bleak and growing worse in many ways. Although humans have been influencing North America's landscape for millennia, the pace, amount, and permanence of human changes to the landscape since European settlers arrived here is truly stunning. Most conservationists agree that the greatest threats to biodiversity in North America today are the loss of native habitat and the introduction of exotic species. Overhunting and pollution threaten biodiversity as well, although not as seriously as habitat loss and exotic species. Global warming may become one of this century's greatest threats, although it is not yet clear how great an impact it will have on the world's biodiversity. Counteracting these threats is the fact that many native ecosystems are capable of significant recovery if left alone or given some help by restoration ecologists.

In this section, we discuss trends in the status of biodiversity across the United States and Canada, paying special attention to the loss of habitats and the appearance of invasive exotic species.[8]

Tallgrass Prairie
More than 96 percent of the tallgrass prairie in North America has been lost. Tallgrass prairie once covered nearly 167 million acres (68 million ha), an area the size of Texas, but today little more than 5 million acres (2 million ha) remains, an area the size of Massachusetts. The situation is far worse in several states and provinces: Illinois, Indiana, Iowa, North Dakota, Wisconsin, and Manitoba have all lost more than 99.9 percent of their tallgrass prairie. Corn and soybean fields now cover nearly all of the land where this ecosystem once existed.[9]

Wetlands
The coterminous United States contained more than 220 million acres (89 million ha) of wetlands in 1780. Two centuries later, more than half of these wetlands were gone. Florida and Texas have each lost more than 7.5 million acres (3 million ha) of wetlands, an area the size of Maryland. In addition, seven states—California, Illinois, Indiana, Iowa, Kentucky, Missouri, and Ohio—have each lost more than 80 percent of their original wetlands.[10]

Old-Growth Forests in the United States
According to an extensive literature review led by conservation biologist Reed Noss, 85 to 90 percent of the original primary (virgin) forest in the entire United States was destroyed by the early 1990s. In the forty-eight contiguous states, however, the situation is worse: approximately 95 to 98 percent of the virgin forest was destroyed by 1990, in-

cluding 99 percent of the eastern deciduous primary forest.[11] In the eastern United States, however, ecologists are discovering many previously unrecognized—albeit small— patches of old-growth forests.[12]

Old-Growth Forests in Canada

According to the report by Noss and his colleagues, various researchers had estimated the loss of Canadian old-growth forests at 48 to 60 percent as of about 1990.[13] However, since then, there has been extensive industrial-scale logging of Canada's coastal rain-forests and boreal forests for timber and pulp, so that figure likely has increased.

Intact Habitat

While some regions of the continent retain large blocks of relatively intact habitat, others have suffered significant degradation, including some that have virtually no in-tact habitat remaining. The World Wildlife Fund team defined intact habitat as "relatively undisturbed areas that are characterized by the maintenance of most original ecological processes and by communities with most of their original suite of native species."[14] The northern reaches of the continent contain relatively high proportions of intact habitat, according to maps prepared by the World Wildlife Fund. The patterns across southern Canada and the contiguous portions of the United States show a much more complex pattern, however. In general, the eastern half of the United States and the Pacific coastal regions show much greater habitat loss than do the Intermountain West and the west-ernmost portions of the prairies. Several areas in the prairie states and provinces also show very heavy loss of habitat, although pockets of intact habitat remain scattered across the continent.

Appendix B: Data Sources

Conservation Directories and Libraries

Conservation Directory from the National Wildlife Federation. This directory allows one to look up conservation groups around Canada and the United States. One can search by location, type of organization (federal, state/local, nongovernmental, and so on), and topics of interest. The directory includes contact information, including telephone numbers and Web links. http://www.nwf.org/conservationdirectory.

Conserve Online. An online library from The Nature Conservancy (TNC), Conserve Online is a rapidly growing collection of documents, including several about TNC's ecoregional planning efforts and some excellent maps. If TNC has completed and published an ecoregional plan for your study area, this can be an excellent source of information about local biodiversity. http://www.conserveonline.org/.

Maps and Aerial Photos

Atlas of the Biosphere. The University of Wisconsin's Institute for Environmental Studies' Center for Sustainability and the Global Environment (SAGE) has assembled some great maps on many topics concerning human land use, soil and plant characteristics, elevation, and so on. Best viewed using Internet Explorer. http://www.sage.wisc.edu/atlas/. Also see the maps section at http://www.sage.wisc.edu/atlas/maps.php.

Gap Analysis Program (GAP). The Biological Resources Division of the United States Geological Survey created the Gap Analysis Program to determine where gaps exist in protected area networks (i.e., regions where certain native species are not adequately protected). This site has links to state gap analysis programs, many of which have free land cover data that can be useful for planners working at the scale of cities, counties, or watersheds. http://www.gap.uidaho.edu/.

Geographic information system (GIS) data. Most states and provinces. and many towns, cities, and counties, have a GIS department that can provide much useful information. Contact your local department to find out what kinds of data it has.

National Geographic Map Machine. This site has good maps, including some excellent information about individual ecoregions throughout the world and especially in North America. http://www.nationalgeographic.com/wildworld/terrestrial. html. The following Web address offers additional maps: http://plasma.nationalgeographic.com/mapmachine/.

Terraserver. This site offers free color or black-and-white satellite images down to one-meter resolution for much of the United States. http://terraserver.microsoft.com/.

The Nature Conservancy. TNC offers good maps showing different ecoregions of the United States and Canada, managed areas in the contiguous United States, and other useful features. Best viewed using Internet Explorer. Select "TNC General Items" at the following URL. http://gis.tnc.org/data/IMS/.

U.S. Federal Emergency Management Agency (FEMA). FEMA supplies maps designating flood hazard zones throughout the United States. http://www.fema.gov.

U.S. Geological Survey (USGS). The USGS offers satellite images, aerial photographs, and maps, which are available for purchase and download. http://earthexplorer.usgs.gov.

U.S. National Wetlands Inventory (NWI). The NWI provides an interactive map of wetlands as well as GIS data. http://www.nwi.fws.gov/.

U.S. Natural Resources Conservation Service (NRCS). The NRCS provides numerous maps, including soil maps, as well as access to a database of North American plants. http://www.nrcs.usda.gov/technical/dataresources/.

Species and Ecological Community Information

Natural Heritage programs. Every state and eleven of Canada's provinces and territories have a natural heritage program. These programs provide in-depth information on the biodiversity located within a region. NatureServe (see the following entry) is the clearinghouse for these programs: http://www.natureserve.org/visitLocal/index.jsp.

NatureServe (an offshoot of The Nature Conservancy). The "NatureServe Explorer" is a huge database of information about species and ecosystems of the United States and Canada: http://www. natureserveexplorer.org/. It can be a bit cumbersome to use (you more or less have to know what you are looking for), but once you get the hang of it, you can retrieve large amounts of information. For NatureServe's home page, see http://www.natureserve.org/.

U.S. Animal and Plant Health Inspection Service (APHIS). APHIS provides in-depth information on invasive species. This branch of the U.S. Department of Agriculture is continually updated and provides very timely information on new outbreaks of pests and diseases. http://www.aphis.usda.gov/.

U.S. Forest Service (USFS). The USFS has a great database of information on native tree species. This database, which has few or no graphics as of this writing, is a treasure house of information on individual tree species—including excellent material on the fire ecology of different tree species. http://www.fs.fed.us/database/feis/plants/tree/.

Glossary

biodiversity: The entire diversity of life, usually defined to include all of the species, genes, and ecosystems on earth or within a given area.

biological disturbance: A discrete or ongoing event in which the proliferation of a plant, animal, or disease organism profoundly alters the functioning of a natural community. See also *disturbance.*

biome: A broad region characterized by similar vegetation growth forms such as forest, grassland, or tundra.

biota: All of the living organisms in a particular area.

biotic: Pertaining to living organisms.

community: All of the organisms living and interacting within an area; in other words, the living components of an *ecosystem.*

conservation easement: A legally binding agreement between a landowner and an easement holder that restricts the types of land uses or activities that can occur on the landowner's property. Conservation easements are often used to prohibit or restrict development on a piece of property to protect conservation values or maintain such land uses as forestry, agriculture, and natural habitat.

conservation subdivision: A subdivision that sets aside a significant portion of the development site as protected open space. This is usually accomplished by clustering houses on smaller lots, ideally on the least environmentally sensitive lands.

conservation target: An element of biodiversity (such as a population of organisms or a natural community) considered to be of particular importance for conservation. Conservation plans generally focus on specific conservation targets.

core habitat: The areas on the *landscape conservation and development plan* designated for nature reserves.

corridor: A landscape feature that is long and relatively narrow that either connects two or more patches or interrupts or dissects the matrix. Roads, streambanks, hedgerows, and ribbons of natural habitat are all examples of corridors. See also *matrix* and *patch*.

disturbance: Any event that significantly changes the environmental conditions or resources available to the biota. Disturbances can be natural physical events, such as hurricanes, landslides, and fires; natural biological events, such as pest or disease outbreaks; or human-induced events, such as plowing, logging, and mining. Disturbances can occur at any scale.

disturbance regime: The pattern, scale, frequency, and effects of disturbance in a given area through time. Different ecosystems have different types of disturbance regimes—for example, some are subject to frequent small fires, while others experience only rare windstorms.

dominant species: Species that are important in their ecological communities because of the large number of individuals or total biomass they represent.

ecological community: See *community*.

ecological due diligence: The process of learning about the ecological form, functioning, and context of one's study area before formulating plans. A key aspect of ecological due diligence is understanding natural processes of disturbance and succession that could affect human communities in the study area.

ecological health: A criterion for land use that requires that human activities on a site (1) avoid irreversible or long-lasting degradation to the land (such as soil loss or toxic contamination) and (2) prevent negative off-site impacts, such as pollution or habitat fragmentation.

ecological integrity: The condition in which ecosystems retain their natural structure and function and are able to sustain themselves indefinitely with minimal human intervention. An ecosystem's integrity is based on such factors as its biota (genes, species, and communities), physical environment (soil and water), and ecosystem processes (biotic interactions, nutrient flows, and energy dynamics).

ecology: A wide-ranging scientific discipline that seeks to examine, explain, and predict how species interact with one another and with the nonliving world.

ecoregion: An area of land—typically on the order of hundreds of miles or kilometers across—consisting of several different landscapes but united by common environmental conditions, species, and disturbance processes.

ecosystem: A group of living organisms plus their nonliving environment, including soil, water, nutrients, and climate. Forests, grasslands, deserts, and lakes are all examples of ecosystems.

ecosystem services: Ecosystem functions that provide economic utility to humans, such as flood control, water purification, and nutrient cycling.

edge effect: The different physical and biological processes that occur at the edge of a patch compared to its interior. Components of edge effect may include altered microclimate, increased predation, or a greater proportion of exotic species.

edge habitat: Habitat situated at the boundary between two land cover types (e.g., farmland and forest) and extending a few tens to hundreds of feet from this boundary. Also, the area of habitat where *edge effects* are present. Edge habitat is often abundant in human-influenced landscapes where natural habitats abut urban, suburban, or agricultural land uses.

edge species: Species that occupy *edge habitat*.

endemic species: Species that are found only in a restricted geographic area. A species (or genus or family) may be endemic to a very small region, such as an island, or to an entire continent or hemisphere.

eutrophication: Nutrient enrichment. Often refers to the artificial enrichment of freshwater bodies by human pollution from farm runoff, sewage treatment systems, and other sources, which can result in weed growth, fish kills, and other ecological changes.

exotic species: A species that is not native to the place it inhabits. Also known as an *introduced species* or a *non-native species*.

flagship species: Large charismatic species, such as whooping cranes and pandas, that are especially useful in gaining public support for a conservation project.

food web: The feeding interactions among the species of a *community*.

fragmentation: The process that occurs when human land uses such as agriculture and urban areas divide native habitats into discontinuous patches.

gap analysis: A methodology for prioritizing land protection needs by identifying biologically valuable lands that are threatened by development or degradation.

generalists: Animals that can feed on many different species and survive in many different habitats, as opposed to *specialists*.

genetic diversity: Genetic variation among the individuals of a population or species.

genetic drift: The change in the proportions of different genetic traits in a population as a result of random processes. Genetic drift can be especially powerful in small populations.

greenprint: A map created at the sub-landscape scale (the scale of cities or towns) that identifies lands important for conservation, such as wetlands, steep slopes, rare species habitat, and rare ecological communities. The greenprint can be used to direct new growth away from these sensitive lands so that an interconnected conservation network takes shape within the matrix of developed lands.

guild: A group of species that performs similar roles within an ecological community.

home range: The area of land used by an animal (or by a pair, family, or allied group of animals) for day-to-day feeding and shelter.

intensive production areas: The areas on the *landscape conservation and development plan* designated for agriculture or heavily managed forestry plantations.

interior habitat: Natural habitat that is situated away from human land uses such as urban development or agriculture, and not influenced by *edge effect*.

interior species: Species that require *interior habitat* for feeding, nesting, mating, or other activities, as opposed to *edge species*.

introduced species: See *exotic species*.

invasive species: Exotic (non-native) species that spread rapidly, outcompeting native species and sometimes altering entire ecosystems.

keystone species: Species that play especially large roles in their ecological communities even though their populations and biomass may be relatively small. Keystone species can exert powerful effects either by changing the physical environment or by playing a critical role in the functioning of the food web.

landscape: An area of land—usually tens of miles or kilometers across—in which a given combination of local ecosystems or land uses is repeated in similar form. This is roughly the area of land that one can see from a mountaintop or an airplane.

landscape conservation and development plan (LCDP): An ecologically based land use plan created at the landscape scale that identifies where and how intensively humans should use land. The LCDP zones the landscape into four categories: *core habitat, secondary habitat, intensive production areas,* and *urban areas*. It is a large-scale, long-term plan that should be complemented by more detailed plans at smaller scales. (See Figure 10-2.)

landscape ecology: The branch of ecology that studies the form and function of features on the landscape.

land suitability analysis: The process of collecting, analyzing, and overlaying data on different land characteristics, such as vegetation, soils, slope, and floodplains, to identify the best locations for conservation, agriculture, and other land uses.

large-lot zoning: Zoning laws that require a large minimum lot size for new development. What is considered "large" varies from place to place across North America; in the East, it may be one to five acres (0.4 to 2 ha), while in the Midwest and the West it may be twenty to forty acres (8 to 16 ha).

late successional species: Species that germinate and grow well in shady conditions, unlike *pioneer species*.

matrix: The dominant land use type or ecosystem in any given landscape.

metapopulation: A group of linked populations living in distinct habitat patches. Although each population is at risk of dying out, the metapopulation as a whole may survive as individuals recolonize the habitat patches from other populations.

migration: Seasonal movement from one habitat to another, usually along a latitudinal or altitudinal gradient.

minimum dynamic area: The minimum area of land needed to be reasonably confident that natural processes of succession and disturbance will not eliminate any species or habitat type native to a particular ecosystem.

minimum viable population: The minimum number of individuals needed for a given population to survive in the long term.

mosaic: The variegated pattern of different land uses and habitat types across a landscape, which can be represented as *patches, corridors,* and *matrix.*

multihabitat species: Species that depend on resources from two or more habitat types.

mutualism: An interaction between two species in which both species benefit. For example, a pollinator and the plant it pollinates both receive benefits from their relationship.

native biodiversity: Individuals, populations, species, and ecosystems that are indigenous to a given area (i.e., that were not transported there by humans).

natural selection: The process of populations adapting to their physical and biological environments over time.

niche: The role that a species plays in its ecological community. Alternatively, the ecological and habitat requirement of a species.

non-native species: See *exotic species.*

nonpoint source pollution: Pollution that originates from diffuse sources across the landscape rather than from a specific point source. Examples of nonpoint source pollution include sediment, petroleum, excess nutrients, and chemical pollutants from farms, roads, lawns, and septic systems.

patch: A discrete land use, vegetation type, or other landscape element that is distinct from the surrounding matrix.

pioneer species: Species that first colonize an area following disturbance. Pioneer species are usually fast-growing and shade intolerant.

population: A group of individuals of a single species that all live in the same place and that are somewhat isolated or distinct from other populations. Members of a population interact with one another much more than they do with members of other populations.

primary production: The process of plants converting sunlight to stored chemical energy in plant tissue. Also, the total amount of plant growth (or energy captured) in a given organism, community, or ecosystem.

purchase of development rights: A land conservation technique in which a government body or private conservation organization pays a landowner not to develop his or her property.

receiving area: An area designated to receive higher-density development as part of a *transfer of development rights (TDR)* program.

reclamation: The process of remediating a heavily damaged site so that it can serve some useful purpose, even if it is not returned to its original condition. See also *restoration.*

rescue effect: The process by which individuals from populations in a region recolonize and bolster failing populations at nearby sites.

restoration: The process of returning an ecosystem to its original condition or state.

secondary habitat: The area on the *landscape conservation and development plan* intended to buffer *core habitat* lands, sustain ecosystem services, and provide habitat for species that can tolerate low to moderate levels of human activity. Secondary habitat areas could include very low-density development, low-intensity forestry, or other low-impact human activities.

sending area: An area designated to retain its rural land uses (such as habitat or agriculture) as part of a *transfer of development rights (TDR)* program.

shifting mosaic: A landscape or ecosystem within which individual patches change from early successional to late successional vegetation and vice versa but the system as a whole remains in general equilibrium.

sink populations: Populations that do not produce enough young to maintain themselves; instead, they depend on immigration from nearby *source populations.*

source populations: Populations that produce more young than can be accommodated within their area; these populations export individuals to *sink populations.*

specialists: Animals that have very specific habitat requirements or that feed on only one or a very few species, as opposed to *generalists.*

speciation: The evolution of a new species from an existing one.

species: A group of similar individuals that can or actually do interbreed with one another in nature and do not interbreed with individuals of other species. This definition, typical of many introductory textbooks, frequently fails in practice, and biologists have created dozens of other definitions of the term. In practice, most biologists distinguish individuals of different species based on their physical characteristics and genetic traits.

species richness: A simple measure of biodiversity; the count of the number of species found in an area.

stepping stone: A disconnected patch or island of suitable habitat in a matrix of less suitable habitat. Stepping stones can aid in the migration and dispersal of many birds, insects, and other species.

subspecies: Subgroups within a species that are physically distinct and geographically separated but can still interbreed. Not all biologists use the subspecies as a taxonomic category.

succession: The changing patterns of species found in an area over time, especially following a disturbance.

sustainability: The combination of *ecological integrity* with the human objectives of long-term economic prosperity and social equality.

transfer of development rights (TDR): A planning tool that is used to protect rural lands from development while encouraging higher-density development in designated suitable locations. TDR programs allow landowners in areas where development is discouraged (often called *sending areas*) to sell the rights to develop their land to developers in areas where development is encouraged (often called *receiving areas*), thus transferring those rights from one site to the other. As a result of the transfer, the land in the sending area is permanently protected from development while additional development is allowed to be built in the receiving area. (See Figure 10-3.)

umbrella species: Species with large home ranges that require several distinct habitats. If a large population of an umbrella species receives good protection, many other species will likely be protected as well.

urban areas: The areas on the *landscape conservation and development plan* designated for residential, commercial, and industrial development at urban or suburban densities.

urban growth boundary (UGB): A designated area within which urban development is encouraged and outside of which development is prohibited or strongly discouraged. Urban growth boundaries can help curb sprawl by targeting growth into preexisting cities and immediately adjacent areas.

watershed: The area of land that drains to a given water body, such as a lake or stream.

Notes

Introduction

1. United Nations Environment Programme, "GEO: Global Environment Outlook 3," http://www.unep.org/GEO/geo3/english/448.htm#fig272 (accessed December 14, 2003).

Chapter 1. Humans Plan

1. National Research Council, *Watershed Management for Potable Water Supply: Assessing the New York City Strategy* (Washington, DC: National Academy Press, 2000), p. 45, http://www.nap.edu/catalog/9677.html.

2. "New York City 2000 Drinking Water Supply and Quality Report," http://www.ci.nyc.ny.us/html/dep/html/wsstate.html (accessed June 11, 2001).

3. National Research Council, *Watershed Management for Potable Water Supply,* p. 47.

4. Executive Summary to National Research Council, *Watershed Management for Potable Water Supply,* http://search.nap.edu/html/watershed_mgmt/ (accessed June 13, 2001).

5. New York City Department of Environmental Protection, "Mayor Michael R. Bloomberg and EPA Administrator Michael Leavitt Announce $25 Million for Land Acquisition to Protect Croton Watershed," press release, http://www.nyc.gov (accessed June 6, 2004).

6. David Tobias, personal communication, December 28, 2003.

7. "Hi Meadow Fire Contained," *Denver Post,* June 21, 2000.

8. Randall Arendt, *Growing Greener: Putting Conservation into Local Plans and Ordinances* (Washington, DC: Island Press, 1999).

9. Richard T. T. Forman, *Land Mosaics: The Ecology of Landscapes and Regions* (Cambridge, UK: Cambridge University Press, 1995), p. xviii.

10. Quoted in "An Oasis of Fire Safety Planning Stands Out," *New York Times*, November 2, 2003.

11. Frederick Steiner, *The Living Landscape: An Ecological Approach to Landscape Planning*, 2nd ed. (New York: McGraw-Hill, 2000).

Chapter 2. An Introduction to Ecology and Biodiversity

1. American Rivers, "#4 Upper San Pedro River (1999)," http://www.amrivers.org/index.php?module=HyperContent&func=display&cid=1198 (accessed April 11, 2004).

2. Bruce A. Stein, Lynn S. Kutner, and Jonathan S. Adams, *Precious Heritage: The Status of Biodiversity in the United States* (Oxford: Oxford University Press, 2000), p. 67.

3. For an in-depth discussion on biodiversity, see Dan L. Perlman and Glenn Adelson, *Biodiversity: Exploring Values and Priorities in Conservation* (Malden, MA: Blackwell Scientific, 1997).

4. H. G. Andrewartha and L. C. Birch, *The Distribution and Abundance of Animals* (Chicago: University of Chicago Press, 1954).

5. American Forests, *Urban Ecosystem Analysis Phase 2: Data for Decision Making, San Antonio, TX*, http://www.americanforests.org/downloads/rea/AF_SanAntonio2.pdf (accessed November 23, 2003).

6. R. Costanza et al., "The Value of the World's Ecosystem Services and Natural Capital," *Nature* 387 (1997): 253–59.

7. Chicago Wilderness Coalition, "Why Biodiversity Matters," http://www.chiwild.org/biodiversity/why/index.cfm (accessed November 22, 2003).

8. U.S. National Park Service, *Economic Impacts of Protecting Rivers, Trails, and Greenway Corridors*, 4th ed. (1995), http://www.nps.gov/pwro/rtca/econ_all.pdf.

9. David A. King, Jody L. White, and William W. Shaw, "Influence of Urban Wildlife Habitats on the Value of Residential Properties," in Lowell W. Adams and Daniel L. Leedy, eds., *Wildlife Conservation in Metropolitan Environments* (Columbia, MD: National Institute for Urban Wildlife, 1991), pp. 165–69.

10. F. F. Gilbert, "Public Attitudes toward Urban Wildlife: A Pilot Study in Guelph, Ontario," *Wildlife Society Bulletin* 10 (1982): 245–53, cited in Lowell W. Adams and Louise E. Dove, *Wildlife Reserves and Corridors in the Urban Environment* (Columbia, MD: National Institute for Urban Wildlife, 1989).

11. M. S. Loreau et al., "Biodiversity and Ecosystem Functioning: Current Knowledge and Future Challenges," *Science* 294 (2001): 804–8.

12. "Desert on Fire: A New Kind of Grass Turns the Arid Southwest into a Fire Trap," *Boston Globe*, June 26, 2001.

13. Adam R. Sears and Stanley H. Anderson, "Correlations between Birds and Vegetation in Cheyenne, Wyoming," in Lowell W. Adams and Daniel L. Leedy, eds., *Wildlife Conservation in Metropolitan Environments* (Columbia, MD: National Institute for Urban Wildlife, 1991), pp. 75–80.

14. William K. Stevens, *Miracle under the Oaks: The Revival of Nature in America* (New York: Pocket Books, 1995).

15. The Nature Conservancy, "Coronado National Forest," http://www.lastgreatplaces.org/SanPedro/coronado.html (accessed July 7, 2003).

16. Most of the historical account in this section comes from Barbara Tellman, Richard Yarde, and Mary G. Wallace, *Arizona's Changing Rivers: How People Have Affected the Rivers* (Tucson: Water Resources Research Center, College of Agriculture, University of Arizona, 1997).

17. City of Sierra Vista, Arizona, "Facts and Figures," http://www.ci.sierra-vista.az.us/Community%20Profile/facts.htm (accessed December 11, 2003); Southwest Center for Environmental Research and Policy, *A Watershed at a Watershed: Strategies for Sustainability in the Upper San Pedro River Drainage Basin* (Tempe: School of Planning and Landscape Architecture, Arizona State University, 2000), p. 22.

18. American Rivers, "San Pedro River Named One of Nations Most Endangered Rivers," April 12, 1999. http://www.americanrivers.org/index.php?module=HyperContent&func=display&cid=416 (accessed June 6, 2004).

19. See Barbara Kingsolver, "San Pedro River," *National Geographic*, April, 2000.

Chapter 3. When Humans and Nature Collide

1. F. B. Samson and F. L. Knopf, "Prairie Conservation in North America," *Bioscience* 44, no. 6 (1994): 418–21.

2. Natural Resources Conservation Service, *America's Private Land: A Geography of Hope* (Washington, DC: U.S. Department of Agriculture, 1996), p. 33.

3. A. P. Dobson, A. D. Bradshaw, and A. J. M. Baker, "Hope for the Future: Restoration Ecology and Conservation Biology," *Science* 277 (1997): 515–22.

4. Michael J. Mac et al., *Status and Trends of the Nation's Biological Resources,* 2 vols. (Reston, VA: U.S. Department of the Interior, U.S. Geological Survey, 1998).

5. Aldo Leopold, "What Is a Weed?" in J. Baird Callicott and Eric T. Freyfogle, eds., *For the Health of the Land* (Washington, DC: Island Press, 1999), p. 212.

6. Direct quote from Leslie J. Mehrhoff, "The Biology of Plant Invasiveness," *New England Wild Flower* 2 (1998): 8–10.

7. Madhoolika Agrawal and S. B. Agrawal, "Effects of Air Pollution on Plant Diversity," in Madhoolika Agrawal and S. B. Agrawal, eds., *Environmental Pollution and Plant Responses* (Boca Raton, FL: Lewis, 2000).

8. U.S. Environmental Protection Agency, *Inventory of U.S. Greenhouse Gas Emissions and Sinks, 1990–2001* (Washington, DC: U.S. Environmental Protection Agency, 2003), http://yosemite.epa.gov/oar/globalwarming.nsf/content/ResourceCenterPublicationsGHGEmissionsUSEmissionsInventory2003.html (accessed October 14, 2003).

9. "Two Gigantic Icebergs Break Free from the Antarctic Ice Cap," *New York Times*, April 11, 2000.

10. National Assessment Synthesis Team, U.S. Global Change Research Program, "Climate Change Impacts on the United States: The Potential Consequences of Climate Variability and Change" (2001), p. 20 of the overview report, http://www.gcrio.org/NationalAssessment/ (accessed January 16, 2001).

11. Environment Canada, "Climate Change: Overview," http://www.ec.gc.ca/climate/

overview_science-e.html (accessed October 14, 2003); Intergovernmental Panel on Climate Change (IPCC), "Climate Change 2001: Impacts, Adaptation and Vulnerability," IPCC Third Assessment Report (2003), http://www.grida.no/climate/ipcc_tar/wg2/index.htm (accessed October 14, 2003).

12. Intergovernmental Panel on Climate Change (IPCC). "Climate Change 2001: Synthesis Report," IPCC Third Assessment Report (2003), http://www.grida.no/climate/ipcc_tar/vol4/english/index.htm (accessed October 14, 2003).

13. Intergovernmental Panel on Climate Change, "Climate Change 2001: Impacts, Adaptation and Vulnerability."

14. Janine Bloomfield and Steven Hamburg, *Global Warming and New England's White Mountains* (Washington, DC: Environmental Defense Fund, 1997).

15. Intergovernmental Panel on Climate Change, "Climate Change 2001: Synthesis Report."

16. "Like the U.S., China Favors Fuel Standards, Not Taxes," *New York Times*, November 23, 2003.

17. U.S. Department of Agriculture, Natural Resources Conservation Service, *Conquest of the Land through 7,000 Years*, Agriculture Information Bulletin No. 99 (1953), http://www.nrcs.usda.gov/technical/ecs/agecol/conquest.html.

18. Scott Faber, *On Borrowed Land: Public Policies for Floodplains* (Cambridge, MA: Lincoln Institute for Land Policy, 1996).

19. T. N. Chase et al., "Potential Impacts on Colorado Rocky Mountain Weather Due to Land Use Changes on the Adjacent Great Plains," *Journal of Geophysical Research—Atmospheres* 104, no. D14 (1999): 16673–90.

20. Curtis H. Marshall, Roger A. Pielke Sr., and Louis T. Steyaert, "Crop Freezes and Land-Use Change in Florida," *Nature* 426 (2003): 29–30.

21. Lowell W. Adams, *Urban Wildlife Habitats: A Landscape Perspective* (Minneapolis: University of Minnesota Press, 1994); "Scientists Watch Cities Make Their Own Weather," *New York Times*, August 15, 2000.

22. Quoted in Richard T. T. Forman, *Land Mosaics: The Ecology of Landscapes and Regions* (Cambridge, UK: Cambridge University Press, 1995), p. 482.

Part Two. The Science of Ecology

1. Jared Diamond, "Must We Shoot Deer to Save Nature?" *Natural History* 8 (1992): 2–4.

Chapter 4. Change through Time

1. The description of the ecological history of central Massachusetts draws heavily on the work of John F. O'Keefe and David R. Foster at Harvard Forest and particularly on John F. O'Keefe and David R. Foster, "An Ecological History of Massachusetts Forests," in Charles H. W. Foster, ed., *Stepping Back to Look Forward: A History of the Massachusetts Forest* (Petersham, MA: Harvard Forest, 1998), pp. 19–66.

2. John D. Black and Ayers Brinser, *Planning One Town: Petersham—A Hill Town in Massachusetts* (Cambridge, MA: Harvard University Press, 1952).

3. Jeffrey C. Milder, Jeong-Ah Choi, and Imge Ceranoglu, *Petersham Town Master Plan* (Petersham, MA: Petersham Ad-Hoc Planning Committee, 2003).

4. National Assessment Synthesis Team, U.S. Global Change Research Program, "Climate Change Impacts on the United States: The Potential Consequences of Climate Variability and Change" (2000), http://www.usgcrp.gov/usgcrp/Library/nationalassessment/5NE.pdf (accessed July 9, 2003).

5. William Holland Drury Jr., *Chance and Change: Ecology for Conservationists* (Berkeley: University of California Press, 1998), ch. 1.

6. "As Mt. St. Helens Recovers, Old Wisdom Crumbles," *New York Times,* May 16, 2000.

7. Michael J. Mac et al., *Status and Trends of the Nation's Biological Resources,* 2 vols. (Reston, VA: U.S. Department of the Interior, U.S. Geological Survey, 1998), p. 551.

8. T. D. Allison, R. E. Moeller, and M. B. Davis, "Pollen in Laminated Sediments Provides Evidence for a Mid-Holocene Forest Pathogen Outbreak," *Ecology* 67 (1986): 1101–5.

9. "Experts Learn from 2 Colo. Sites, "*Denver Post,* August 19, 2000.

10. "Experts Learn from 2 Colo. Sites."

11. U.S. Forest Service, "Fire Ecology—Species: Sequoia Sempervirens," http://www.fs.fed.us/database/feis/plants/tree/seqsem/fire_ecology.html (accessed December 28, 2003).

12. Stephen J. Pyne, *Fire in America: A Cultural History of Wildland and Rural Fire* (Seattle: University of Washington Press, 1997), chs. 2 and 3.

13. Neil Jorgensen, *Sierra Club Naturalist's Guide to Southern New England* (San Francisco: Sierra Club, 1978), p. 104.

14. National Park Service, "Yosemite National Park: Giant Sequoias," http://www.nps.gov/yose/nature/sequoias.htm (accessed October 1, 2003).

15. U.S. Forest Service, "Species: Pinus Contorta var. Latifolia," http://www.fs.fed.us/database/feis/plants/tree/pinconl/botanical_and_ecological_characteristics.html, and "Species: Pinus Rigida," http://www.fs.fed.us/database/feis/plants/tree/pinrig/botanical_and_ecological_characteristics.html (accessed October 2, 2003).

16. U.S. Forest Service, "Species: Tsuga Canadensis," http://www.fs.fed.us/database/feis/plants/tree/tsucan/botanical_and_ecological_characteristics.html (accessed October 1, 2003).

Chapter 5. Populations and Communities

1. Robert C. Stebbins, *A Field Guide to Western Reptiles and Amphibians,* 3rd ed. (Boston: Houghton Mifflin, 2003), pp. 225, 479.

2. Glossary entry on "species" in Teresa Audesirk and Gerald Audesirk, *Biology: Life on Earth* (Upper Saddle River, NJ: Prentice Hall, 1996).

3. U.S. Department of the Interior, U.S. Fish and Wildlife Service, "Endangered and Threatened Wildlife and Plants; Determination of Threatened Status for the California Red-Legged Frog," 50 CFR Part 17, RIN 1018-AC 34, in *Federal Register* 61, no. 101 (May 23, 1996).

4. Curt D. Meine and George W. Archibald, eds., 1996. *The Cranes: Status Survey and Conservation Action Plan.* Gland, Switzerland, and Cambridge, UK: World Conservation Union (IUCN), 1996, http://www.npwrc.usgs.gov/resource/distr/birds/cranes/cranes.htm and http://www.npwrc.usgs.gov/resource/distr/birds/cranes/gruscana.htm#country (accessed October 10, 2003).

5. U.S. Department of the Interior, U.S. Fish and Wildlife Service, "Endangered and Threat- ened Wildlife and Plants."

6. Stebbins, *A Field Guide to Western Reptiles and Amphibians,* p. 225.

7. NatureServe, "NatureServe Explorer: An Online Encyclopedia of Life" (version 1.8), http:// www.natureserve.org/explorer (accessed January 8, 2004).

8. Seneca White Deer Inc., http://www.senecawhitedeer.org (accessed August 30, 2003).

9. For example, see Dale R. McCullough, ed., *Metapopulations and Wildlife Conservation* (Washington, DC: Island Press, 1996).

10. Meine and Archibald, eds., *The Cranes.*

11. University of Manitoba, Experimental Lakes Area Project, "Eutrophication (Nutrient Pol- lution)," http://www.umanitoba.ca/institutes/fisheries/eutro.html (accessed October 10, 2003).

12. U.S. Forest Service, "Species: Tsuga Canadensis," http://www.fs.fed.us/database/feis/ plants/tree/tsucan/botanical_and_ecological_characteristics.html (accessed October 1, 2003).

13. Michael J. Mac et al., *Status and Trends of the Nation's Biological Resources,* 2 vols. (Res- ton, VA: U.S. Department of the Interior, U.S. Geological Survey, 1998), p. 200.

14. Ronald M. Nowak, *Walker's Mammals of the World,* 5th ed. (Baltimore, MD: Johns Hop- kins University Press, 1991), p. 637.

15. Center for Watershed Protection, "The Return of the Beaver," *Watershed Protection Tech- niques* 401–10. http://www.stormwatercenter.net/Library/Practice/44.pdf.

16. David R. Klein, "The Introduction, Increase, and Demise of Wolves on Coronation Island, Alaska," in Ludwig N. Carbyn, Steven H. Fritts, and Dale R. Seip, eds., *Ecology and Conservation of Wolves in a Changing World* (Edmonton, Alberta: Canadian Circumpolar Institute, 1995), pp. 275–80; Steve W. Chadde and Charles E. Kay, "Tall-Willow Communities on Yellowstone's North- ern Range: A Test of the 'Natural-Regulation' Paradigm," in Robert B. Keiter and Mark S. Boyce, eds., *The Greater Yellowstone Ecosystem: Redefining America's Wilderness Heritage* (New Haven, CT: Yale University Press, 1991), pp. 231–62.

17. "Wolves Bring a Surprising Ecological Recovery to Yellowstone," *Boston Globe,* Septem- ber 30, 2003.

Chapter 6. The Ecology of Landscapes

1. Richard T. T. Forman and Michel Godron, *Landscape Ecology* (New York: Wiley, 1986); Zev Navah and Arthur Lieberman, *Landscape Ecology: Theory and Application,* 2nd ed. (New York: Springer-Verlag, 1994).

2. Richard T. T. Forman, *Land Mosaics: The Ecology of Landscapes and Regions* (Cambridge, UK: Cambridge University Press, 1995).

3. Forman, *Land Mosaics,* p. 3.

4. Taylor H. Ricketts et al., *Terrestrial Ecoregions of North America: A Conservation Assess- ment* (Washington, DC: Island Press, 1999), p. 7.

5. Forman, *Land Mosaics,* p. 435.

6. Reed F. Noss, "Context Matters: Considerations for Large-Scale Conservation," *Conserva- tion in Practice* 3 (2002): 10–19.

7. Robert H. MacArthur and Edward O. Wilson, *The Theory of Island Biogeography* (Prince- ton, NJ: Princeton University Press, 1967).

8. W. J. Boecklen and N. J. Gotelli, "Island Biogeographic Theory and Conservation Practice: Species-Area or Specious-Area Relationships?" *Biological Conservation* 29 (1984): 63–80.

9. Gary K. Meffe, C. Ronald Carroll, and contributors, *Principles of Conservation Biology* (Sunderland, MA: Sinauer Associates, 1994), and references therein; Forman, *Land Mosaics,* and references therein; M. L. Cadenasso, M. M. Traynor, and S.T.A. Pickett, "Functional Location of Forest Edges: Gradients of Multiple Physical Factors," *Canadian Journal of Forest Research* 27, no. 5 (1997): 774–82; R. J. Davies-Colley, G. W. Payne, and M. van Elswijk, "Microclimate Gradients across a Forest Edge," *New Zealand Journal of Ecology* 24, no. 2 (2000): 111–21; Jiquan Chen, Jerry F. Franklin, and Thomas A. Spies, "Contrasting Microclimates along a Clear-cut, Edge, and Interior of Old-growth Douglas-fir Forest," *Agricultural and Forest Meteorology* 63, no. 3/4 (1993): 219–37.

10. Dan Cooper, personal communication, September 26, 2003.

11. Anna D. Chalfoun, Frank R. Thompson III, and Mary J. Ratnaswamy, "Nest Predators and Fragmentation: A Review and Meta-Analysis," *Conservation Biology* 16, no. 2 (2002): 306–18.

12. Meffe, Carroll, and contributors, *Principles of Conservation Biology.*

13. Forman, *Land Mosaics.*

14. A. F. Bennett, "Roads, Roadsides and Wildlife Conservation: A Review," in Denis A. Saunders and Richard J. Hobbs, eds., *Nature Conservation 2: The Role of Corridors* (Chipping Norton, Australia: Surrey Beatty, 1991), pp. 99–117.

15. S. J. Hannon et al., "Abundance and Species Composition of Amphibians, Small Mammals, and Songbirds in Riparian Forest Buffer Strips of Varying Widths in the Boreal Mixedwood of Alberta," *Canadian Journal of Forest Research* 32, no. 10 (2002): 1784–1800.

16. J. Baudry and H. G. Merriam, "Connectivity and Connectedness: Functional Versus Structural Patterns in Landscapes," in K-F. Schreiber, ed., *Connectivity in Landscape Ecology* (1988), Proceedings of the 2nd International Seminar of the International Association for Landscape Ecology, Paderborn, Germany: Ferdinand Schoningh.

17. Forman, *Land Mosaics.*

18. ConservationEconomy.net, "The Patterns of a Conservation Economy: Wildlife Corridors," http://www.conservationeconomy.net/content.cfm?PatternID=21 (accessed September 7, 2003).

19. Paul Beier and Reed F. Noss, "Do Habitat Corridors Provide Connectivity?" *Conservation Biology* 12, no. 6 (1998): 1241–52; Diane M. Debinski and Robert D. Holt, "A Survey and Overview of Habitat Fragmentation Experiments," *Conservation Biology* 14, no. 2 (2000): 342–55; John Lyle and Ronald D. Quinn, "Ecological Corridors in Urban Southern California," in Lowell W. Adams and Daniel L. Leedy, eds., *Wildlife Conservation in Metropolitan Environments* (Columbia, MD: National Institute for Urban Wildlife, 1991), pp. 105–16.

20. Daniel Simberloff et al., "Movement Corridors: Conservation Bargains or Poor Investments?" *Conservation Biology* 6 (1992): 493–504.

21. Andy Dobson et al., "Corridors: Reconnecting Fragmented Landscapes," in Michael E. Soulé and John Terborgh, eds., *Continental Conservation: Scientific Foundations of Regional Reserve Networks* (Washington, DC: Island Press, 1999), p. 148.

22. Patricia A. White and Michelle Ernst, *Second Nature: Improving Transportation without Putting Nature Second* (Washington, DC: Defenders of Wildlife, 2003), http://www.defenders.org/ habitat/highways/secondnature.html (accessed November 13, 2003).

23. Richard T. T. Forman et al., *Road Ecology: Science and Solutions* (Washington, DC: Island Press, 2003), p. 145.

24. Bonnie L. Harper-Lore and Maggie Wilson, eds., *Roadside Use of Native Plants* (Washington, DC: Island Press, 2000); Iowa's Living Roadway Trust Fund, http://www. iowalivingroadway. com (accessed November 14, 2003).

25. L. Ries, D. M. Debinski, and M. L. Wieland, "Conservation Value of Roadside Prairie Restoration to Butterfly Communities," *Conservation Biology* 15, no. 2 (2001): 401–11.

26. Everose Schluter, personal communication, September 15, 2003.

27. Forman, *Land Mosaics*, p. 407.

28. Assumes that each house has a 30- by 50-foot footprint with 50 feet of lawn, garden, driveway, or other disturbed area on each side.

29. Sharon K. Collinge and Richard T. T. Forman, "A Conceptual Model of Land Conversion Processes: Predictions and Evidence from a Microlandscape Experiment with Grassland Insects," *Oikos* 82, no. 1 (1998): 66–84.

30. Forman, *Land Mosaics*, p. 452.

31. Richard T. T. Forman and Sharon K. Collinge, "The 'Spatial Solution' to Conserving Biodiversity in Landscapes and Regions," in R. M. DeGraaf and R. I. Miller, eds., *Conservation of Faunal Diversity in Forested Landscapes* (London: Chapman and Hall, 1996), pp. 537–68.

32. Jeremy D. Maestas, Richard L. Knight, and Wendell C. Gilgert, "Biodiversity across a Rural Land-Use Gradient," *Conservation Biology* 17, no. 5 (2003): 1425–34.

33. David M. Theobald, James R. Miller, and N. Thompson Hobbs, "Estimating the Cumulative Effects of Development on Wildlife Habitat," *Landscape and Urban Planning* 39 (1997): 25–36.

34. A. G. Tansley, "The Use and Abuse of Vegetational Terms and Concepts," *Ecology* 16 (1935): 284–307. For accounts of the early history of ecology, see Kristin S. Shrader-Frechette and Earl D. McCoy, *Method in Ecology: Strategies for Conservation* (Cambridge, UK: Cambridge University Press, 1994). See also Robert P. McIntosh, *Background of Ecology: Concept and Theory* (Cambridge: Cambridge University Press, 1985).

35. S. B. Weiss, "Cars, Cows, and Checkerspot Butterflies: Nitrogen Deposition and Management of Nutrient-poor Grasslands for a Threatened Species," *Conservation Biology* 13, no. 6 (1999): 1476–86; E. K. Green and S. M. Galatowitsch, "Effects of Phalaris Arundinacea and Nitrate-N Addition on the Establishment of Wetland Plant Communities," *Journal of Applied Ecology* 39, no. 1 (2002): 134–44; R. Ostertag and J. H. Verville, "Fertilization with Nitrogen and Phosphorus Increases Abundance of Non-Native Species in Hawaiian Montane Forests," *Plant Ecology* 162, no. 1 (2002): 77–90; M. L. Brooks, "Effects of Increased Soil Nitrogen on the Dominance of Alien Annual Plants in the Mojave Desert," *Journal of Applied Ecology* 40, no. 2 (2003): 344–53.

36. Arthur J. Bulger Jr., "Blood, Poison and Death: Effects of Acid Deposition on Fish," in James C. White, ed., *Acid Rain: Are the Problems Solved?* (Bethesda, MD: American Fisheries Society, 2003).

37. Van Bowersox, "Sources and Receptors: Monitoring the Data," in James C. White, ed., *Acid Rain: Are the Problems Solved?* (Bethesda, MD: American Fisheries Society, 2003).

38. James J. MacKenzie and Mohamed T. El-Ashry, *Ill Winds: Airborne Pollution's Toll on Trees and Crops* (Washington, DC: World Resources Institute, 1988).

39. MacKenzie and El-Ashry, *Ill Winds*.

40. Lawrence L. Master, Stephanie R. Flack, and Bruce A. Stein, eds., *Rivers of Life* (Arlington, VA: The Nature Conservancy, 1998).

41. D. R. Barton, W. D. Taylor, and R. M. Biette, "Dimensions of Riparian Buffer Strips Required to Maintain Trout Habitat in Southern Ontario Streams," *North American Journal of Fisheries Management* 5 (1985): 364–78.

42. For further information on using indicator species to assess freshwater habitats, see M. T. Barbour et al., *Rapid Bioassessment Protocols for Use in Streams and Wadeable Rivers: Periphyton, Benthic Macroinvertebrates and Fish,* 2nd ed., EPA 841-B-99-002 (Washington, DC: U.S. Environmental Protection Agency, Office of Water, 1999), http://www.epa.gov/owow/monitoring/rbp/.

43. James R. Karr, "Ecological Integrity and Ecological Health Are Not the Same," in Peter C. Schulze, ed., *Engineering within Ecological Constraints* (Washington, DC: National Academy Press, 1996), pp. 97–109.

44. Forman, *Land Mosaics,* p. 499.

45. Karr, "Ecological Integrity and Ecological Health."

46. W. E. Rees, 2000. "Patch Disturbance, Ecofootprints, and Biological Integrity," in David Pimentel, Laura Westra, and Reed F. Noss, eds., *Ecological Integrity* (Washington, DC: Island Press, 2000).

Part Three. Applications

1. D. A. Falk, "From Conservation Biology to Conservation Practice: Strategies for Protecting Plant Diversity," in P. L. Fielder and S. K. Jain, eds., *Conservation Biology: The Theory and Practice of Nature Conservation, Preservation and Management* (London: Chapman and Hall, 1992), pp. 397–431. Quoted in Craig L. Shafer, "Terrestrial Nature Reserve Design at the Urban/Rural Interface," in Mark W. Schwartz, ed., *Conservation in Highly Fragmented Landscapes* (London: Chapman and Hall, 1997), pp. 345–78 .

Chapter 7. Conservation Planning

1. Yellowstone to Yukon Conservation Initiative, *A Sense of Place: Issues, Attitudes and Resources in the Yellowstone to Yukon Ecoregion* (1998), http://www.y2y.net/science/conservation/y2yatlas.pdf (accessed November 20, 2003).

2. U.S. Bureau of Land Management, http://www.blm.gov:80/nhp/efoia/ca/Public/IMs/1997/CAIM97-031—P.html (accessed October 21, 2003).

3. Jae C. Choe, personal communication, September 1, 2000.

4. Terraserver, http://terraserver.microsoft.com/ (accessed November 20, 2003).

5. George R. Hess and Terri J. King, "Planning Open Spaces for Wildlife I: Selecting Focal Species Using a Delphi Survey Approach," *Landscape and Urban Planning* 58 (2002): 25–40.

6. Bill Fleming and David Henkel, "Community-Based Ecological Monitoring: A Rapid Appraisal Approach," *Journal of the American Planning Association* 67, no. 4 (2001): 456–65.

7. Michael E. Soulé and Dan Simberloff, "What Do Genetics and Ecology Tell Us about the Design of Nature Reserves?" *Biological Conservation* 35 (1986): 19–40.

8. R. L. Pressey et al., "Beyond Opportunism: Key Principles for Systematic Reserve Selection," *Trends in Ecology and Evolution* 8 (1993): 124–28.

9. Gap Analysis Program, http://www.gap.uidaho.edu/ (accessed November 20, 2003).

10. Gary K. Meffe, C. Ronald Carroll, and contributors, *Principles of Conservation Biology* (Sunderland, MA: Sinauer Associates, 1994), p. 266.

11. National Park Service, "Wildland Fire," http://www.nps.gov/yell/nature/fire/wildfire.htm (accessed April 11, 2004).

12. World Resources Institute, *World Resources 1998–1999: A Guide to the Global Environment* (New York: Oxford University Press, 1998), p. 321.

13. S.T.A. Pickett and J. N. Thompson, "Patch Dynamics and the Design of Nature Reserves," *Biological Conservation* 13 (1978): 27–37.

14. Richard T. T. Forman, *Land Mosaics: The Ecology of Landscapes and Regions* (Cambridge, UK: Cambridge University Press, 1995), pp. 70–71.

Chapter 8. Nature in the Neighborhood

1. E. O. Wilson, "The Little Things That Run the World," *Conservation Biology* 1 (1987): 344–46.

2. Joe Schaefer et al., "A Natural Resources Management and Protection Plan for the Econlockhatchee River Basin," in Lowell W. Adams and Daniel L. Leedy, eds., *Wildlife Conservation in Metropolitan Environments* (Columbia, MD: National Institute for Urban Wildlife, 1991), pp. 145–50.

3. Lowell W. Adams and Louise E. Dove, *Wildlife Reserves and Corridors in the Urban Environment* (Columbia, MD: National Institute for Urban Wildlife, 1989).

4. C. A. Gavareski, "Relation of Park Size and Vegetation to Urban Bird Populations in Seattle, Washington," *Condor* 78 (1976): 375–82. Cited in Adams and Dove, *Wildlife Reserves and Corridors in the Urban Environment.*

5. J. Howard, "The Garden of Earthly Remains," *Horticulture* 65 (1987): 46–56. Cited in Adams and Dove, *Wildlife Reserves and Corridors in the Urban Environment.*

6. New York City Parks and Recreation Department, Natural Resources Group, "The Rare Plant Propagation Project," http://www.nycgovparks.org/sub_about/parks_divisions/nrg/nrg_rareplant.html (accessed November 22, 2003).

7. "From Nests above the City, Baby Peregrines Test Their Wings," *New York Times,* June 25, 2002.

8. American Farmland Trust, http://www.farmland.org (accessed January 9, 2004).

9. Brian Donahue, *Reclaiming the Commons: Community Farming and Forestry in a New England Town* (New Haven, CT: Yale University Press, 1999).

10. U.S. Department of Agriculture, Natural Resources Conservation Service, *National Resources Inventory* (2001).

11. Elizabeth M. McKinnon, letter to Newton, Massachusetts, officials John B. Penney, commissioner of recreation; Aaron Fink, superintendent of schools; and Edward C. Uehlein, alderman for Ward 5, regarding the use of the Cold Spring area, January 17, 1970.

12. Frances E. Putz, "A Breeding Ground for Conservation Biologists," *Conservation Biology* 11 (1997): 813–14.

13. Madhav Gadgil, personal communication, April 1998, at the Biodiversity Conservation Prioritisation Program conference in New Delhi, India.

14. Peter H. Kahn Jr., "Children's Affiliation with Nature: Structure, Development, and the Problem of Environmental Generational Amnesia," in Peter H. Kahn Jr. and Stephen R. Kellert, eds., *Children and Nature: Psychological, Sociocultural, and Evolutionary Investigations* (Cambridge, MA: MIT Press, 2002), p. 104.

15. J. G. Blake, "Species-area Relationship of Migrants in Isolated Woodlots in East-central Illinois," *Wilson Bulletin* 98 (1986): 291–96, cited in Adams and Dove, *Wildlife Reserves and Corridors in the Urban Environment.*

16. Kansas City Power & Light, "Blue River Glade Connects Cultural, Biological Diversity," http://www. kcplkids.com/tr_blueriver.html (accessed November 25, 2003).

17. N. G. Tilghman, "Characteristics of Urban Woodlands Affecting Breeding Bird Diversity and Abundance," *Landscape and Urban Planning* 14 (1987): 481–95.

18. Washington School, http://www.berkeley.k12.ca.us/OS/schools/elementary/wash.html (accessed January 4, 2004); Lowell W. Adams, *Urban Wildlife Habitats* (Minneapolis: University of Minnesota Press, 1994).

19. Ruth Eckdish Knack, "The Plotting o' the Green," *Planning* 67, no. 5 (2001): 14–19.

20. Christopher Uhl, "Conservation Biology in Your Own Front Yard," *Conservation Biology* 12, no. 6 (1998): 1175–77.

21. Beyond Pesticides, http://www.beyondpesticides.org/main.html (accessed June 4, 2004).

22. Margaret Livingston, William W. Shaw, and Lisa K. Harris, "A Model for Assessing Wildlife Habitats in Urban Landscapes of Eastern Pima County, Arizona (USA)," *Landscape and Urban Planning* 64 (2003): 131–44.

23. Kenneth F. Lane, "Landscape Planning and Wildlife: Methods and Motives," in Lowell W. Adams and Daniel L. Leedy, eds., *Wildlife Conservation in Metropolitan Environments* (Columbia, MD: National Institute for Urban Wildlife, 1991), pp. 139–42.

24. Adams, *Urban Wildlife Habitats,* pp. 84–85.

25. A. Jorgensen, J. Hitchmough, and T. Calvert, "Woodland Spaces and Edges: Their Impact on Perception of Safety and Preference," *Landscape and Urban Planning* 60, no. 3 (2002): 135–50.

26. Adams and Dove, *Wildlife Reserves and Corridors in the Urban Environment.*

27. Adams and Dove, *Wildlife Reserves and Corridors in the Urban Environment.*

28. American Lyme Disease Foundation, "Deer Tick Ecology," http://www.aldf.com/DeerTick Ecology.asp (accessed November 20, 2003).

29. B. F. Allan, F. Keesing, and R. S. Ostfeld, "Effect of Forest Fragmentation on Lyme Disease Risk," *Conservation Biology* 17, no. 1 (2003): 267–72.

30. "Lyme Disease Rises as More Build in Woods," *New York Times,* March 16, 2001.

Chapter 9. Restoration and Management

1. The discussion of the Butte mining situation comes largely from personal communications with Jon Sesso, director of the Butte–Silver Bow Planning Department; Edwin Dobb, historian and author; and John Driscoll, director of the Storyteller Project, which is intended to record the lives of Butte's miners and their families.

2. Michael P. Malone, *The Battle for Butte: Mining and Politics on the Northern Frontier 1864–1906* (Helena: Montana Historical Society Press, 1981); Berkeley Pit Public Education Committee, Butte–Silver Bow Planning Department, http://www.pitwatch.org (accessed March 13, 2001).

3. Edwin Dobb, "Pennies from Hell," *Harper's,* October 1996, pp. 40–54.

4. Berkeley Pit Public Education Committee, Butte–Silver Bow Planning Department.

5. Prairie Crossing, http://www.prairiecrossing.com/pc/site/about-us.html (accessed November 14, 2003).

6. Richard J. Hobbs and David A. Norton, "Towards a Conceptual Framework for Restoration Ecology," *Restoration Ecology* 4 (1996): 93–110.

7. Montana Department of Justice, "Remediation and Restoration of Silver Bow Creek: A Superfund Success Story," http://www.doj.state.mt.us/lands/nrdpdocuments/SBCfactsheet.pdf (accessed November 9, 2003).

8. Material in this paragraph is based on personal communication with Steven Apfelbaum, president of Applied Ecological Services, Brodhead, Wisconsin, November 2003.

9. Following is a sampling of restoration titles published between 1997 and 2004 by Island Press and CRC Press. Island Press: *The Tallgrass Restoration Handbook* (1997); *Restoring Diversity* (1996); *The Once and Future Forest* (1998); *Restoring Streams in Cities* (1998); *The Historical Ecology Handbook* (2001); *Restoring Life in Running Waters* (1999); *Ecological Restoration of Southwestern Ponderosa Pine Forests* (2003); *Large Mammal Restoration: Ecological and Sociological Challenges in the Twenty-First Century* (2001); *Wildlife Restoration* (2002). CRC Press: *Estuary Restoration and Maintenance* (2000); *Handbook for Restoring Tidal Wetlands* (2001); *Landscape Restoration Handbook* (1999); *Restoration of Contaminated Aquifers* (2000); *Remediation and Management of Degraded Lands* (1999); *Restoration of Boreal and Temperate Forests* (in press); *In-Situ Restoration of Metals-Contaminated Sites* (in press); *Subsurface Restoration* (1997).

10. Tifft Nature Preserve, http://www.buffalomuseumofscience.org/tifft.html (accessed January 4, 2004); Lowell W. Adams and Louise E. Dove, *Wildlife Reserves and Corridors in the Urban Environment* (Columbia, MD: National Institute for Urban Wildlife, 1989).

11. Gary K. Meffe, C. Ronald Carroll, and contributors, *Principles of Conservation Biology* (Sunderland, MA: Sinauer Associates, 1994), p. 277.

12. Lloyd Raleigh, Joseph Capece, and Alison Berry, *Sand Barrens Habitat Management: A Toolbox for Managers* (Vineyard Haven, MA: The Trustees of Reservations, Islands Regional Office, 2003), http://www.thetrustees.org/documents.cfm?documentID=206 (accessed December 29, 2003).

13. Raleigh, Capece, and Berry, *Sand Barrens Habitat Management.*

14. Lowell W. Adams, *Urban Wildlife Habitats* (Minneapolis: University of Minnesota Press, 1994), pp. 95–96.

15. Daniel Simberloff, "Impacts of Introduced Species in the United States," *Consequences* 2, no. 2 (1996), http://www.gcrio.org/CONSEQUENCES/vol2no2/article2.html (accessed November 26, 2003).

Chapter 10. Ecologically Based Planning and Design Techniques

1. Regarding per capita land consumption, see Leon Kolankiewicz and Roy Beck, *Analysis of U.S. Bureau of the Census Data on the 100 Largest Urbanized Areas of the United States* (2001), http://www.sprawlcity.org/studyUSA/USAsprawlz.pdf (accessed December 15, 2003). Regarding vehicle miles traveled, see U.S. Bureau of Transportation Statistics, http://www.bts.gov/publications/transportation_indicators/december_2002/Mobility/html/US_Highway_Vehicle_Miles_Traveled.html (accessed December 15, 2003).

2. Ian McHarg, *Design with Nature* (New York: Wiley, 1969).

3. Maryland Department of Planning, "Smart Growth Priority Funding Areas Act of 1997," http://www.mdp.state.md.us/fundingact.htm (accessed December 15, 2003).

4. For an overview of several of TDR's variations and a profile of four established TDR programs, see Robert A. Johnston and Mary E. Madison, "From Landmarks to Landscapes: A Review of Current Practices in the Transfer of Development Rights," *Journal of the American Planning Association* 63, no. 3 (1997): 365–78. More detailed coverage is available in Richard Roddewig and Cheryl A. Inghram, *Transferable Development Rights Programs,* Planning Advisory Service Report 401 (Chicago: American Planning Association, 1987).

5. A landmark U.S. Supreme Court case in this regard is the 1992 ruling in *Lucas v. South Carolina Coastal Council.* The court found that a state regulation prohibiting all permanent structures on a portion of South Carolina oceanfront prone to hurricanes denied all economic value of the property and thus amounted to an unconstitutional "regulatory taking." The question of regulatory takings becomes less clear-cut when a regulation greatly reduces the property's economic value but does not completely eliminate it.

6. James G. MacBroom, *The River Book* (Hartford: Connecticut Department of Environmental Protection, 1998); W. W. Budd et al., "Stream Corridor Management in the Pacific Northwest: I. Determination of Stream-corridor Widths," *Environmental Management* 11 (1987): 587–97; M. W. Binford and M. Buchenau, "Riparian Greenways and Water Resources," in D. S. Smith and P. C. Hellmund, eds., *Ecology of Greenways: Design and Function of Linear Conservation Areas* (Minneapolis: University of Minnesota Press, 1993); J. R. Cooper, J. W. Gilliam, and T. C. Jacobs, "Riparian Areas as a Control of Nonpoint Pollutants," in David L. Correll, ed., *Watershed Research Perspectives* (Washington, DC: Smithsonian Institution Press, 1986).

7. R. S. Palone and A. H. Todd, eds., *Chesapeake Bay Riparian Handbook: A Guide for Establishing and Maintaining Riparian Forest Buffers,* NA-TP-02-97 (Radnor, PA: USDA Forest Service, 1997), http://www.chesapeakebay.net/pubs/subcommittee/nsc/forest/handbook.htm (accessed November 18, 2003).

8. Massachusetts Department of Environmental Protection, "An Act Providing Protection for the Rivers of the Commonwealth," http://www.state.ma.us/dep/brp/ww/files/riveract.htm (accessed February 11, 2004); Clark County, Washington, Department of Community Development, http://www.clark.wa.gov/commdev/documents/devservices/handouts/31b-habfaq.pdf (accessed February 11, 2004); MacBroom, *The River Book.*

9. Alex Wilson et al., *Green Development: Integrating Ecology and Real Estate* (New York: Wiley, 1998).

10. Randall Arendt, *Conservation Design for Subdivisions: A Practical Guide to Creating Open Space Networks* (Washington, DC: Island Press, 1996). See also Randall Arendt, *Growing Greener: Putting Conservation into Local Plans and Ordinances* (Washington, DC: Island Press, 1999).

11. Robert L. Ryan, "Preserving Rural Character in New England: Local Residents' Perceptions of Alternative Residential Development," *Landscape and Urban Planning* 61 (2002): 19–35.

12. "A Flood of Development," *St. Louis Post-Dispatch,* July 27, 2003.

13. "A Flood of Development."

14. David R. Godschalk, Edward J. Kaiser, and Philip R. Berke, "Integrating Hazard Mitigation and Local Land Use Planning," in Raymond J. Burby, ed., *Cooperating with Nature: Confronting Natural Hazards with Land-Use Planning for Sustainable Communities* (Washington, DC: Joseph Henry Press, 1998).

15. Raymond J. Burby, "Natural Hazards and Land Use: An Introduction," in Raymond J. Burby, ed., *Cooperating with Nature: Confronting Natural Hazards with Land-Use Planning for Sustainable Communities* (Washington, DC: Joseph Henry Press, 1998).

16. Burby, "Natural Hazards and Land Use."

17. Robert B. Olshansky, "Land Use Planning for Seismic Safety," *Journal of the American Planning Association* 67, no. 2 (2001): 173–85.

18. Robert Lawton, personal communication, January 8, 2004.

19. Raymond J. Burby, ed., *Cooperating with Nature: Confronting Natural Hazards with Land-Use Planning for Sustainable Communities* (Washington, DC: Joseph Henry Press, 1998).

20. Boulder County, Colorado, Wildfire Mitigation Program, "Creating Wildfire-Defensible Zones," http://www.co.boulder.co.us/lu/pdf/defensespace.pdf (accessed April 11, 2004).

21. Boulder County, Colorado, Wildfire Mitigation Program, "Construction Design and Materials," http://www.co.boulder.co.us/lu/wildfire/construction. htm (accessed December 15, 2003).

22. Burby, ed., *Cooperating with Nature.*

Chapter 11. Principles in Practice

1. *The Random House College Dictionary,* rev. ed. (New York: Random House, 1984).

2. Lewis D. Hopkins, "Methods for Generating Land Suitability Maps: A Comparative Evaluation," *Journal of the American Institute of Planners* 43 (1977): 386–400.

3. Eric R. Britzke, Michael J. Harvey, and Susan C. Loeb, "Indiana Bat, *Myotis Sodalis,* Maternity Roosts in the Southern United States," *Southeastern Naturalist* 2, no. 2 (2003): 235–42.

4. National Assessment Synthesis Team, *Climate Change Impacts on the United States: The Potential Consequences of Climate Variability and Change* (Washington, DC: U.S. Global Change Research Program, 2000).

5. For example, the American Institute of Certified Planners (AICP) Code of Ethics and Professional Conduct states: "A planner must strive to protect the integrity of the natural environment."

6. David J. Zaber, *Southern Lessons: Saving Species through the National Forest Management Act* (1998), Defenders of Wildlife, http://www.defenders.org/pubs/sfor01.html (accessed August 4, 2003).

Afterword

1. Peter H. Kahn Jr., "Children's Affiliation with Nature: Structure, Development, and the Problem of Environmental Generational Amnesia," in Peter H. Kahn Jr. and Stephen R. Kellert, eds., *Children and Nature: Psychological, Sociocultural, and Evolutionary Investigations* (Cambridge, MA: MIT Press, 2002).

Appendix A. Current Status of Biodiversity across North America

1. Robert G. Bailey, *Ecoregions: The Ecosystem Geography of the Oceans and Continents* (New York: Springer-Verlag, 1998), p. 44.

2. Bailey, *Ecoregions,* p. 44.

3. Bruce A. Stein, Lynn S. Kutner, and Jonathan S. Adams, *Precious Heritage: The Status of Biodiversity in the United States* (Oxford: Oxford University Press, 2000), pp. 126–27.

4. This definition is based on the one developed by the Conservation Science Department of the World Wildlife Fund–United States and Canada, as quoted in Taylor H. Ricketts et al., *Terrestrial Ecoregions of North America: A Conservation Assessment* (Washington, DC: Island Press, 1999), p. 7.

5. Stein, Kutner, and Adams, *Precious Heritage;* Ricketts et al., *Terrestrial Ecoregions of North America,* p. 7; Michael J. Mac et al., *Status and Trends of the Nation's Biological Resources,* 2 vols. (Reston, VA: U.S. Department of the Interior, U.S. Geological Survey, 1998).

6. Robin A. Abell et al., *Freshwater Ecoregions of North America: A Conservation Assessment* (Washington, DC: Island Press, 2000); Ricketts et al., *Terrestrial Ecoregions of North America;* Stein, Kutner, and Adams, *Precious Heritage.*

7. Ricketts et al., *Terrestrial Ecoregions of North America.*

8. Ricketts et al., *Terrestrial Ecoregions of North America,* p. 34; Stein, Kutner, and Adams, *Precious Heritage;* Mac et al., *Status and Trends of the Nation's Biological Resources.*

9. Mac et al., *Status and Trends of the Nation's Biological Resources,* p. 439.

10. T. E. Dahl, *Wetlands Losses in the United States 1780s to 1980s* (Washington, DC: U.S. Department of the Interior, Fish and Wildlife Service, 1990).

11. Reed F. Noss, Edward T. LaRoe III, and J. Michael Scott, *Endangered Ecosystems of the United States: A Preliminary Assessment of Loss and Degradation,* Biological Report 28 (Washington, DC: U.S. Department of the Interior, National Biological Service, 1995), p. 37.

12. Mary Byrd Davis, ed., *Eastern Old-Growth Forests: Prospects for Rediscovery and Recovery* (Washington, DC: Island Press, 1996).

13. Noss, LaRoe, and Scott, *Endangered Ecosystems of the United States,* p. 48.

14. Ricketts et al., *Terrestrial Ecoregions of North America,* p. 120.

Bibliography

Abell, Robin A., et al. 2000. *Freshwater ecoregions of North America: A conservation assessment.* Washington, DC: Island Press.

Adams, Lowell W. 1994. *Urban wildlife habitats: A landscape perspective.* Minneapolis: University of Minnesota Press.

Adams, Lowell W., and Louise E. Dove. 1989. *Wildlife reserves and corridors in the urban environment.* Columbia, MD: National Institute for Urban Wildlife.

Adams, Lowell W., and Daniel L. Leedy, eds. 1991. *Wildlife conservation in metropolitan environments.* Columbia, MD: National Institute for Urban Wildlife.

Agrawal, Madhoolika, and S. B. Agrawal. 2000. Effects of air pollution on plant diversity. In Madhoolika Agrawal and S. B. Agrawal, eds., *Environmental pollution and plant responses.* Boca Raton, FL: Lewis.

Allan, B. F., F. Keesing, and R. S. Ostfeld. 2003. Effect of forest fragmentation on Lyme disease risk. *Conservation Biology* 17(1): 26772.

American Farmland Trust. http://www.farmland.org.

American Forests. *Urban ecosystem analysis phase 2: Data for decision making, San Antonio, TX.* http://www.americanforests.org/downloads/rea/AF_SanAntonio2.pdf.

American Lyme Disease Foundation. Deer tick ecology. http://www.aldf.com/DeerTickEcology.asp.

American Rivers. http://www.americanrivers.org/.

Andrewartha, H. G., and L. C. Birch. 1954. *The distribution and abundance of animals.* Chicago: University of Chicago Press.

Arendt, Randall. 1996. *Conservation design for subdivisions: A practical guide to creating open space networks.* Washington, DC: Island Press.

Arendt, Randall. 1999. *Growing greener: Putting conservation into local plans and ordinances.* Washington, DC: Island Press.

Arnold, C. L., and C. J. Gibbons. 1996. Impervious surface: The emergence of a key urban environmental indicator. *Journal of the American Planning Association* 62: 243–58.

Bailey, Robert G. 1998. *Ecoregions: The ecosystem geography of the oceans and continents.* New York: Springer-Verlag.

Barbour, M.T., et al. 1999. *Rapid bioassessment protocols for use in streams and wadeable rivers: Periphyton, benthic macroinvertebrates and fish.* 2nd ed. EPA 841-B-99-002. Washington, DC: U.S. Environmental Protection Agency, Office of Water. http://www.epa.gov/owow/monitoring/rbp/.

Barton, D. R., W. D. Taylor, and R. M. Biette. 1985. Dimensions of riparian buffer strips required to maintain trout habitat in southern Ontario streams. *North American Journal of Fisheries Management* 5: 364–78.

Baudry, J., and H. G. Merriam. 1988. Connectivity and connectedness: Functional versus structural patterns in landscapes. In K-F. Schreiber, ed., *Connectivity in landscape ecology.* Proceedings of the 2nd International Seminar of the International Association for Landscape Ecology. Paderborn, Germany: Ferdinand Schoningh.

Bean, Michael J., and Melanie J. Rowland. 1997. *The evolution of national wildlife law.* 3rd ed. Westport, CT: Praeger.

Beier, Paul, and Reed F. Noss. 1998. Do habitat corridors provide connectivity? *Conservation Biology* 12(6): 124–52.

Bennett, A. F. 1991. Roads, roadsides and wildlife conservation: A review. In Denis A. Saunders and Richard J. Hobbs, eds., *Nature conservation 2: The role of corridors,* pp. 99–117. Chipping Norton, Australia: Surrey Beatty.

Berkeley Pit Public Education Committee. http://www.pitwatch.org/.

Binford, M. W., and M. Buchenau. 1993. Riparian greenways and water resources. In D. S. Smith and P. C. Hellmund, eds., *Ecology of greenways: Design and function of linear conservation areas.* Minneapolis: University of Minnesota Press.

Bloomfield, Janine, and Steven Hamburg. 1997. *Global warming and New England's White Mountains.* Washington, DC: Environmental Defense Fund.

Boecklen, W. J., and N. J. Gotelli. 1984. Island biogeographic theory and conservation practice: Species-area or specious-area relationships? *Biological Conservation* 29: 63–80.

Boulder County, Colorado, Wildfire Mitigation Program. Construction design and materials. http://www.co.boulder.co.us/lu/wildfire/construction.htm.

Boulder County, Colorado, Wildfire Mitigation Program. Defensible space. http://www.co.boulder.co.us/lu/wildfire/dpsace.htm.

Bowersox, Van. 2003. Sources and receptors: Monitoring the data. In James C. White, ed., *Acid rain: Are the problems solved?* Bethesda, MD: American Fisheries Society.

Britzke, Eric R., Michael J. Harvey, and Susan C. Loeb. 2003. Indiana bat, *Myotis sodalis,* maternity roosts in the southern United States. *Southeastern Naturalist* 2(2): 235–42.

Brooks, M. L. 2003. Effects of increased soil nitrogen on the dominance of alien annual plants in the Mojave Desert. *Journal of Applied Ecology* 40(2): 344–53.

Budd, W. W., et al. 1987. Stream corridor management in the Pacific Northwest: I. Determination of stream-corridor widths. *Environmental Management* 11:587–97.

Bulger, Arthur J., Jr. 2003. Blood, poison and death: Effects of acid deposition on fish. In James C. White, ed., *Acid rain: Are the problems solved?* Bethesda, MD: American Fisheries Society.

Burby, Raymond J., ed. 1998. *Cooperating with nature: Confronting natural hazards with land-use planning for sustainable communities.* Washington, DC: Joseph Henry Press.

Burby, Raymond J. 1998. Natural hazards and land use: An introduction. In Raymond J. Burby, ed., *Cooperating with nature: Confronting natural hazards with land-use planning for sustainable communities.* Washington, DC: Joseph Henry Press.

Cadenasso, M. L., M. M. Traynor, and S.T.A. Pickett. 1997. Functional location of forest edges: Gradients of multiple physical factors. *Canadian Journal of Forest Research* 27(5): 774–82.

Carpenter, S. R., et al. 1998. Nonpoint pollution of surface waters with phosphorus and nitrogen. *Ecological Applications* 8(3): 559–68.

Chalfoun, Anna D., Frank R. Thompson III, and Mary J. Ratnaswamy. 2002. Nest predators and fragmentation: A review and meta-analysis. *Conservation Biology* 16(2): 306–18.

Chambers, Patricia A., et al. 2001. *Nutrients and their impact on the Canadian environment.* Hull, Quebec: Environment Canada.

Chase, T.N., et al. 1999. Potential impacts on Colorado Rocky Mountain weather due to land use changes on the adjacent Great Plains. *Journal of Geophysical Research—Atmospheres* 104(D14): 16673–90.

Chen, Jiquan, Jerry F. Franklin, and Thomas A. Spies. 1993. Contrasting microclimates along a clear-cut, edge, and interior of old-growth Douglas-fir forest. *Agricultural and Forest Meteorology* 63(3/4): 219–37.

Chicago Wilderness Coalition. http://www.chiwild.org/.

Collinge, S. K., and Richard T. T. Forman. 1998. A conceptual model of land conversion processes: Predictions and evidence from a microlandscape experiment with grassland insects. *Oikos* 82(1): 66–84.

Cooper, J. R., J. W. Gilliam, and T. C. Jacobs. 1986. Riparian areas as a control of nonpoint pollutants. In David L. Correll, ed., *Watershed research perspectives.* Washington, DC: Smithsonian Institution Press.

Costanza, R., et al. 1997. The value of the world's ecosystem services and natural capital. *Nature* 387: 253–59.

Dahl, T. E. 1990. *Wetlands losses in the United States 1780s to 1980s.* Washington, DC: U.S. Department of the Interior, Fish and Wildlife Service.

Davies-Colley, R. J., G. W. Payne, and M. van Elswijk. 2000. Microclimate gradients across a forest edge. *New Zealand Journal of Ecology* 24(2): 111–21.

Davis, Mary Byrd, ed. 1996. *Eastern old-growth forests: Prospects for rediscovery and recovery.* Washington, DC: Island Press.

Debinski, Diane M., and Robert D. Holt. 2000. A survey and overview of habitat fragmentation experiments. *Conservation Biology* 14(2): 342–55.

DeGraff. 1987. Urban wildlife habitat research—application to landscape design. In Lowell W. Adams and Daniel L. Leedy, eds., *Integrating man and nature in the metropolitan environment.* Columbia, MD: National Institute for Urban Wildlife.

Diamond, Jared. 1992. Must we shoot deer to save nature? *Natural History* 8: 2–4.

Dobson, Andy P., A. D. Bradshaw, and A.J.M. Baker. 1997. Hope for the future: Restoration ecology and conservation biology. *Science* 277: 515–22.

Dobson, Andy, et al. 1999. Corridors: Reconnecting fragmented landscapes. In Michael E. Soulé and John Terborgh, eds., *Continental conservation: Scientific foundations of regional reserve networks.* Washington, DC: Island Press.

Donahue, Brian. 1999. *Reclaiming the commons: Community farming and forestry in a New England town.* New Haven, CT: Yale University Press.

Drury, William Holland, Jr. 1998. *Chance and change: Ecology for conservationists.* Berkeley: University of California Press.

Ecotrust. Conservation economy Web site. http://www.conservationeconomy.net/.

Environment Canada. Climate change Web site. http://www.ec.gc.ca/climate.

Faber, Scott. 1996. *On borrowed land: Public policies for floodplains.* Cambridge, MA: Lincoln Institute for Land Policy.

Fleming, Bill, and David Henkel. 2001. Community-based ecological monitoring: A rapid appraisal approach. *Journal of the American Planning Association* 67(4): 456–65.

Forman, Richard T. T. 1995. *Land mosaics: The ecology of landscapes and regions.* Cambridge: Cambridge University Press.

Forman, Richard T. T. 2000. Estimate of the area affected ecologically by the road system in the United States. *Conservation Biology* 14(1): 31–35.

Forman, Richard T. T., and Lauren E. Alexander. 1998. Roads and their major ecological effects. *Annual Review of Ecology and Systematics* 29: 207–31.

Forman, Richard T. T., and Sharon K. Collinge. 1996. The "spatial solution" to conserving biodiversity in landscapes and regions. In R. M. DeGraaf and R. I Miller, eds., *Conservation of faunal diversity in forested landscapes,* pp. 537–68. London: Chapman and Hall.

Forman, Richard T. T., and Michel Godron. 1986. *Landscape ecology.* New York: Wiley.

Forman, Richard T. T., et al. 2003. *Road ecology: Science and solutions.* Washington, DC: Island Press.

Gavareski, C. A. 1976. Relation of park size and vegetation to urban bird populations in Seattle, Washington. *Condor* 78: 375–82.

Gilbert, F. F. 1982. Public attitudes toward urban wildlife: A pilot study in Guelph, Ontario. *Wildlife Society Bulletin* 10: 245–53.

Godschalk, David R., Edward J. Kaiser, and Philip R. Berke. 1998. Integrating hazard mitigation and local land use planning. In Raymond J. Burby, ed., *Cooperating with nature: Confronting natural hazards with land-use planning for sustainable communities.* Washington, DC: Joseph Henry Press.

Green, E. K., and S. M. Galatowitsch. 2002. Effects of *Phalaris arundinacea* and nitrate-N addition on the establishment of wetland plant communities. *Journal of Applied Ecology* 39(1): 134–44.

Grove, Noel. 1992. *Preserving Eden: The Nature Conservancy.* New York: Harry N. Abrams.

Hannon, S. J., et al. 2002. Abundance and species composition of amphibians, small mammals, and songbirds in riparian forest buffer strips of varying widths in the boreal mixedwood of Alberta. *Canadian Journal of Forest Research* 32(10): 1784–1800.

Harper-Lore, Bonnie L., and Maggie Wilson, eds. 2000. *Roadside use of native plants.* Washington, DC: Island Press.

Hess, George R., and Terri J. King. 2002. Planning open spaces for wildlife I: Selecting focal species using a Delphi survey approach. *Landscape and Urban Planning* 58: 25–40.

Hobbs, Richard J., and David A. Norton. 1996. Towards a conceptual framework for restoration ecology. *Restoration Ecology* 4: 93–110.

Hopkins, Lewis D. 1977. Methods for generating land suitability maps: A comparative evaluation. *Journal of the American Institute of Planners* 43: 386–400.

Howard, J. 1987. The garden of earthly remains. *Horticulture* 65: 46–56.

Intergovernmental Panel on Climate Change. 2003. Climate change 2001: Impacts, adaptation and vulnerability. IPPC Third Assessment Report. http://www.grida.no/climate/ipcc_tar/wg2/index.htm.

Intergovernmental Panel on Climate Change. 2003. Climate change 2001: Synthesis report. IPCC Third Assessment Report. http://www.grida.no/climate/ipcc_tar/vol4/english/index.htm.

Iowa Living Roadway Trust Fund. http://www.iowalivingroadway.com/.

Johnston, Robert A., and Mary E. Madison. 1997. From landmarks to landscapes: A review of current practices in the transfer of development rights. *Journal of the American Planning Association* 63(3): 365–78.

Jorgensen, A., J. Hitchmough, and T. Calvert. 2002. Woodland spaces and edges: Their impact on perception of safety and preference. *Landscape and Urban Planning* 60(3): 135–50.

Jorgensen, Neil. 1978. *Sierra Club naturalist's guide to southern New England.* San Francisco: Sierra Club.

Kahn, Peter H., Jr., 2002. Children's affiliation with nature: Structure, development, and the problem of environmental generational amnesia. In Peter H. Kahn Jr. and Stephen R. Kellert, eds., *Children and nature: Psychological, sociocultural, and evolutionary investigations.* Cambridge, MA: MIT Press.

Karr, James R. 1996. Ecological integrity and ecological health are not the same. In Peter C. Schulze, ed., *Engineering within ecological constraints,* pp. 97–109. Washington, DC: National Academy Press.

Keiter, Robert B., and Mark S. Boyce, eds. 1991. *The greater Yellowstone ecosystem: Redefining America's wilderness heritage.* New Haven, CT: Yale University Press.

King, David A., Jody L. White, and William W. Shaw. 1991. Influence of urban wildlife habitats on the value of residential properties. In Lowell W. Adams and Daniel L. Leedy, eds., *Wildlife conservation in metropolitan environments,* pp. 165–69. Columbia, MD: National Institute for Urban Wildlife.

Knack, Ruth Eckdish. 2001. The plotting o' the green. *Planning* 67(5): 14–19.

Kolankiewicz, Leon, and Roy Beck. 2001. *Analysis of U.S. Bureau of the Census data on the 100 largest urbanized areas of the United States.* http://www.sprawlcity.org/studyUSA/USAsprawlz.pdf.

Lane, Kenneth F. 1991. Landscape planning and wildlife: Methods and motives. In Lowell W. Adams and Daniel L. Leedy, eds., *Wildlife conservation in metropolitan environments.* Columbia, MD: National Institute for Urban Wildlife.

Leopold, Aldo. 1999. What is a weed? In J. Baird Callicott and Eric T. Freyfogle, eds., *For the health of the land.* Washington, DC: Island Press.

Livingston, Margaret, William W. Shaw, and Lisa K. Harris. 2003. A model for assessing wildlife habitats in urban landscapes of eastern Pima County, Arizona (USA). *Landscape and Urban Planning* 64: 131–44.

Loreau, M. S., et al. 2001. Biodiversity and ecosystem functioning: Current knowledge and future challenges. *Science* 294: 804–8.

Low Impact Development Center. http://www.lowimpactdevelopment.org/.

Lyle, John, and Ronald D. Quinn. 1991. Ecological corridors in urban southern California. In Lowell W. Adams and Daniel L. Leedy, eds., *Wildlife conservation in metropolitan environments.* Columbia, MD: National Institute for Urban Wildlife.

Mac, Michael J., et al. 1998. *Status and trends of the nation's biological resources.* 2 vols. Reston, VA: U.S. Department of the Interior, U.S. Geological Survey.

MacArthur, Robert H., and Edward O. Wilson. 1967. *The theory of island biogeography.* Princeton, NJ: Princeton University Press.

MacBroom, James G. 1998. *The river book.* Hartford: Connecticut Department of Environmental Protection.

MacKenzie, James J., and Mohamed T. El-Ashry. 1988. *Ill winds: Airborne pollution's toll on trees and crops.* Washington, DC: World Resources Institute.

Mackintosh, Barry. 2000. *The National Parks: Shaping the system.* 3rd ed. http://www.cr.nps.gov/history/online_books/mackintosh1/sts2.htm.

Mader, H.-J. 1984. Animal habitat isolation by roads and agricultural fields. *Biological Conservation* 29: 81–96.

Maestas, Jeremy D., Richard L. Knight, and Wendell C. Gilgert. 2003. Biodiversity across a rural land-use gradient. *Conservation Biology* 17(5): 1425–34.

Malone, Michael P. 1981. *The battle for Butte: Mining and politics on the northern frontier 1864–1906.* Helena: Montana Historical Society Press.

Marshall, Curtis H., Roger A. Pielke Sr., and Louis T. Steyaert. 2003. Crop freezes and land-use change in Florida. *Nature* 426:29–30.

Master, Lawrence L., Stephanie R. Flack, and Bruce A. Stein, eds. 1998. *Rivers of life.* Arlington, VA: The Nature Conservancy.

McCullough, Dale R., ed. 1996. *Metapopulations and wildlife conservation.* Washington, DC: Island Press.

McHarg, Ian. 1969. *Design with nature.* New York: Wiley.

McIntosh, Robert P. 1985. *Background of ecology: Concept and theory.* Cambridge: Cambridge University Press.

Meffe, Gary K., C. Ronald Carroll, and contributors. 1997. *Principles of conservation biology.* 2nd ed. Sunderland, MA: Sinauer Associates.

Mehrhoff, Leslie J. 1998. The biology of plant invasiveness. *New England Wild Flower* 2: 8–10.

Meine, Curt D., and George W. Archibald, eds. 1996. *The cranes: Status survey and conservation action plan.* Gland, Switzerland, and Cambridge, UK: World Conservation Union (IUCN); Northern Prairie Wildlife Research Center. http://www.npwrc.usgs.gov/.

Minnesota Environmental Quality Board and Biko Associates. 2000. *From policy to reality: Model ordinances for sustainable development.* http://www.mnplan.state.mn.us/pdf/2000/eqb/modelordwhole.pdf.

National Agricultural Pest Information System (NAPIS). http://www.ceris.purdue.edu/napis/pests/egm/facts.txt.

National Assessment Synthesis Team. 2000. *Climate change impacts on the United States: The potential consequences of climate variability and change.* Washington, DC: U.S. Global Change Research Program. http://www.gcrio.org/NationalAssessment/.

National Research Council. 2000. *Watershed management for potable water supply: Assessing the New York City strategy.* Washington, DC: National Academy Press. http://www.nap.edu/catalog/9677.html.

Natural Resources Conservation Service. 1996. *America's private land: A geography of hope.* Washington, DC: U.S. Department of Agriculture. http://www.nhq.nrcs.usda.gov/CCS/GHopeHit.html.

NatureServe. 2003. NatureServe Explorer: An online encyclopedia of life. Version 1.8. http://www.natureserve.org/explorer.

Navah, Zev, and Arthur Lieberman. 1994. *Landscape ecology: Theory and application*. 2nd ed. New York: Springer-Verlag.

New York City Department of Parks and Recreation, Natural Resources Group. The rare plant propagation project. http://www.nycgovparks.org/sub_about/parks_divisions/nrg/nrg_rareplant.html.

Noss, Reed F. 1993. Wildlife corridors. In Daniel S. Smith and Paul C. Hellmund, eds., *Ecology of greenways*. Minneapolis: University of Minnesota Press.

Noss, Reed F. 2002. Context matters: Considerations for large-scale conservation. *Conservation in practice* 3:10–19.

Noss, Reed F., Edward T. LaRoe III, and J. Michael Scott. 1995. *Endangered ecosystems of the United States: A preliminary assessment of loss and degradation*. Biological Report 28. Washington, DC: U.S. Department of the Interior, National Biological Service.

Nowak, Ronald M. 1991. *Walker's mammals of the world*. 5th ed. Baltimore, MD: Johns Hopkins University Press.

Obrecht, H. H., III, W. J. Fleming, and J. H. Parsons. 1991. Management of powerline rights-of-way for botanical and wildlife value in metropolitan areas. In Lowell W. Adams and Daniel L. Leedy, eds., *Wildlife conservation in metropolitan environments*. Columbia, MD: National Institute for Urban Wildlife.

Odell, Eric A., David M. Theobald, and Richard L. Knight. 2003. Incorporating ecology into land use planning: The songbirds' case for clustered development. *Journal of the American Planning Association* 69(1): 72–82.

O'Keefe, John F., and David R. Foster. 1998. An ecological history of Massachusetts forests. In Charles H. W. Foster, ed., *Stepping back to look forward: A history of the Massachusetts forest*, pp. 19–66. Petersham, MA: Harvard Forest.

Olshansky, Robert B. 2001. Land use planning for seismic safety. *Journal of the American Planning Association* 67(2): 173–85.

Ostertag, R., and J. H. Verville. 2002. Fertilization with nitrogen and phosphorus increases abundance of non-native species in Hawaiian montane forests. *Plant Ecology* 162(1): 77–90.

Palone, R. S., and A. H. Todd, eds. 1997. *Chesapeake Bay riparian handbook: A guide for establishing and maintaining riparian forest buffers*. NA-TP-02-97. Radnor, PA: USDA Forest Service. http://www.chesapeakebay.net/pubs/subcommittee/nsc/forest/handbook.htm.

Perlman, Dan L., and Glenn Adelson. 1997. *Biodiversity: Exploring values and priorities in conservation*. Malden, MA: Blackwell Scientific.

Pickett, S.T.A, and J. N. Thompson. 1978. Patch dynamics and the design of nature reserves. *Biological Conservation* 13: 27–37.

Pimm, Stuart L., et al. 1995. The future of biodiversity. *Science* 269: 347–50.

Prairie Crossing. http://www.prairiecrossing.com/.

Pressey, R. L., et al. 1993. Beyond opportunism: Key principles for systematic reserve selection. *Trends in Ecology and Evolution* 8: 124–28.

Putz, Frances E. 1997. A breeding ground for conservation biologists. *Conservation Biology* 11: 813–14.

Pyne, Stephen J. 1997. *Fire in America: A cultural history of wildland and rural fire*. Seattle: University of Washington Press.

Raleigh, Lloyd, Joseph Capece, and Alison Berry. 2003. *Sand barrens habitat management: A toolbox for managers.* Vineyard Haven, MA: Trustees of Reservations, Islands Regional Office. http://www.thetrustees.org/documents.cfm?documentID=206.

Rees, W. E. 2000. Patch disturbance, ecofootprints, and biological integrity. In David Pimentel, Laura Westra, and Reed F. Noss, eds., *Ecological integrity.* Washington, DC: Island Press.

Ricketts, Taylor H., et al. 1999. *Terrestrial ecoregions of North America: A conservation assessment.* Washington, DC: Island Press.

Ries, L., D. M. Debinski, and M. L. Wieland. 2001. Conservation value of roadside prairie restoration to butterfly communities. *Conservation Biology* 15(2): 401–11.

Roddewig, Richard, and Cheryl A. Inghram. 1987. *Transferable development rights programs.* Planning Advisory Service Report 401. Chicago: American Planning Association.

Ryan, Robert L. 2002. Preserving rural character in New England: Local residents' perceptions of alternative residential development. *Landscape and Urban Planning* 61: 19–35.

Samson, F. B., and F. L. Knopf. 1994. Prairie conservation in North America. *Bioscience* 44(6): 418–21.

Sears, Adam R., and Stanley H. Anderson. 1991. Correlations between birds and vegetation in Cheyenne, Wyoming. In Lowell W. Adams and Daniel L. Leedy, eds., *Wildlife conservation in metropolitan environments,* pp. 75–80. Columbia, MD: National Institute for Urban Wildlife.

Shrader-Frechette, Kristin S., and Earl D. McCoy. 1994. *Method in ecology: Strategies for conservation.* Cambridge: Cambridge University Press.

Simberloff, Daniel. 1996. Impacts of introduced species in the United States. *Consequences* 2(2). http://www.gcrio.org/CONSEQUENCES/vol2no2/article2.html.

Simberloff, Daniel, et al. 1992. Movement corridors: Conservation bargains or poor investments? *Conservation Biology* 6: 493–504.

Soulé, Michael E., and Dan Simberloff. 1986. What do genetics and ecology tell us about the design of nature reserves? *Biological Conservation* 35: 19–40.

Southwest Center for Environmental Research and Policy. 2000. *A watershed at a watershed: Strategies for sustainability in the Upper San Pedro River drainage basin.* Tempe: School of Planning and Landscape Architecture, Arizona State University.

Stebbins, Robert C. 2003. *A field guide to western reptiles and amphibians.* 3rd ed. Boston: Houghton Mifflin.

Stein, Bruce A., Lynn S. Kutner, and Jonathan S. Adams. 2000. *Precious heritage: The status of biodiversity in the United States.* Oxford: Oxford University Press.

Steiner, Frederick. 2000. *The living landscape: An ecological approach to landscape planning.* 2nd ed. New York: McGraw-Hill.

Stevens, William K. 1995. *Miracle under the oaks: The revival of nature in America.* New York: Pocket Books.

Tellman, Barbara, Richard Yarde, and Mary G. Wallace. 1997. *Arizona's changing rivers: How people have affected the rivers.* Tucson: Water Resources Research Center, College of Agriculture, University of Arizona.

Theobald, David M., James R. Miller, and N. Thompson Hobbs. 1997. Estimating the cumulative effects of development on wildlife habitat. *Landscape and Urban Planning* 39: 25–36.

Tilghman, N. G. 1987. Characteristics of urban woodlands affecting breeding bird diversity and abundance. *Landscape and Urban Planning* 14: 481–95.

Uhl, Christopher. 1998. Conservation biology in your own front yard. *Conservation Biology* 12(6): 1175–77.

University of Manitoba. Experimental Lakes Area Project. http://www.umanitoba.ca/institutes/fisheries/eutro.html.

U.S. Department of Agriculture, Natural Resources Conservation Service. 1953. *Conquest of the land through 7,000 years.* Agriculture Information Bulletin No. 99. http://www.nrcs.usda.gov/technical/ecs/agecol/conquest.html.

U.S. Department of Agriculture, Natural Resources Conservation Service. 2001. *National resources inventory.* http://www.nrcs.usda.gov/technical/NRI/.

U.S. Environmental Protection Agency. 2003. *Inventory of U.S. greenhouse gas emissions and sinks, 1990–2001.* Washington, DC: U.S. Environmental Protection Agency.

U.S. Fish and Wildlife Service. *History of the National Wildlife Refuge system.* http://refuges.fws.gov/history/index.html.

U.S. Forest Service. *Information on U.S. tree species.* http://www.fs.fed.us/database/feis/plants/tree/.

U.S. Geological Survey. *National Gap Analysis Program.* http://www.gap.uidaho.edu/.

U.S. National Park Service. 1995. *Economic impacts of protecting rivers, trails, and greenway corridors.* 4th ed. http://www.nps.gov/pwro/rtca/econ_all.pdf.

Weiss, S. B. 1999. *Cars, cows, and checkerspot butterflies: Nitrogen deposition and management of nutrient-poor grasslands for a threatened species. Conservation Biology* 13(6): 1476–86.

Westbrooks, R. 1998. *Invasive plants: Changing the landscape of America.* Washington, DC: Federal Interagency Committee for the Management of Noxious and Exotic Weeds. http://www.denix.osd.mil/denix/Public/ES-Programs/Conservation/Invasive/intro.html.

White, Patricia A., and Michelle Ernst. 2003. *Second nature: Improving transportation without putting nature second.* Washington, DC: Defenders of Wildlife. http://www.defenders.org/habitat/highways/secondnature.html.

Wilcox, B. A., and D. D. Murphy. 1989. *Migration and control of purple loosestrife* (Lythrium salicaria L.) *along highway corridors. Environmental Management* 13: 365–70.

Wilson, Alex, et al. 1998. *Green development: Integrating ecology and real estate.* New York: Wiley.

Wilson, Edward O. 1987. *The little things that run the world. Conservation Biology* 1: 344–46.

Wilson, Edward O. 1992. *The diversity of life.* Cambridge, MA: Harvard University Press.

World Resources Institute. 1998. *World resources 1998–1999: A guide to the global environment.* New York: Oxford University Press.

Yellowstone to Yukon Conservation Initiative. 1998. *A sense of place: Issues, attitudes and resources in the Yellowstone to Yukon ecoregion.* http://www.y2y.net/science/conservation/y2yatlas.pdf.

About the Authors

Dan L. Perlman received his PhD training in ecology and has since become an expert in the field of conservation biology. For nine years, he taught a multidisciplinary field-based course on conservation biology and biodiversity at Harvard University. He is a coauthor, with Glenn Adelson, of *Biodiversity: Exploring Values and Priorities in Conservation* (Blackwell Scientific, 1997). He has also developed an interactive CD-ROM with Harvard biologist E. O. Wilson that is used on college campuses around the United States to teach conservation biology and environmental studies. He teaches ecology and conservation biology at Brandeis University in Waltham, Massachusetts.

Jeffrey C. Milder is a planner and conservationist who has worked extensively on land use planning and design projects for governments, developers, and landowners. He founded and managed the community and regional planning group at Daylor Consulting Group, Inc., a multidisciplinary planning, engineering, and environmental sciences firm located in Massachusetts. He is a graduate of Harvard University and a member of the American Institute of Certified Planners. Currently, he is working toward a PhD in Natural Resources at Cornell University in Ithaca, New York.

Index